T0295964

# Construction Workforce Management in the Fourth Industrial Revolution Era

# Construction Workforce Management in the Fourth Industrial Revolution Era

BY

## LERATO AGHIMIEN

*University of Johannesburg, South Africa*

## CLINTON OHIS AIGBAVBOA

*University of Johannesburg, South Africa*

AND

## DOUGLAS AGHIMIEN

*De Montfort University, United Kingdom/University of
Johannesburg, South Africa*

United Kingdom – North America – Japan – India – Malaysia – China

Emerald Publishing Limited
Emerald Publishing, Floor 5, Northspring, 21-23 Wellington Street, Leeds LS1 4DL.

First edition 2024

**Reprints and permissions service**
Contact: www.copyright.com

**British Library Cataloguing in Publication Data**
A catalogue record for this book is available from the British Library

ISBN: 978-1-83797-019-3 (Print)
ISBN: 978-1-83797-018-6 (Online)
ISBN: 978-1-83797-020-9 (Epub)

Printed and bound by CPI Group (UK) Ltd, Croydon, CR0 4YY

INVESTOR IN PEOPLE

# Contents

# List of Figures and Tables

## Figures

## Tables

# About the Authors

**Lerato Aghimien** is a Senior Lecturer in the Construction Management and Quantity Surveying Department at the University of Johannesburg, South Africa. She draws from her years of experience working in the construction industry in teaching students in price analysis and estimating, construction management, and human resource management in construction. She holds a PhD in Construction Management from the University of Johannesburg, South Africa. She has published many peer-reviewed journal and conference papers on diverse built environment-related issues, including human resource management, sustainable construction, and digitalisation.

**Clinton Ohis Aigbavboa** is a Professor in the Department of Construction Management and Quantity Surveying and Director of Cidb Centre of Excellence & Sustainable Human Settlement and Construction Research Centre, University of Johannesburg, South Africa. Currently, he is the Chair of SARChI in Sustainable Construction Management and Leadership in the Built Environment at the University of Johannesburg, South Africa. Before delving into academics, he was a Quantity Surveyor on several infrastructural projects in Nigeria and South Africa. He completed his PhD in Engineering Management and has published several research papers in housing, construction and engineering management, and research methodology for construction students. Also, he has published over seventeen research books. He has extensive knowledge in practice, research, training, and teaching.

**Douglas Aghimien** is a Senior Lecturer in Built Environment and the Programme Leader for BSc Quantity Surveying and Construction at the School of Arts, Design and Architecture, De Montfort University, Leicester, United Kingdom. He has a PhD in Engineering Management from the University of Johannesburg (UJ), South Africa. In 2021, he received the UJ PDRF Excellence Award for the best-performing postdoctoral fellow from the Faculty of Engineering and the Built Environment. His contributions to built environment-related research earned him a Y2-rated researcher status by the National Research Foundation of South Africa. He has a keen interest in construction digitalisation, sustainable construction, as well as construction and value management.

# Preface

The construction industry worldwide is a massive employer of labour. The industry depends on these workers to carry out its activities of contributing to economic growth and societal development. However, the relationship between the construction industry and its workforce is best described as paradoxical. This is because, despite being heavily dependent on workers, the industry has been notorious for its poor workforce management and lack of attention to workforce management issues. Because most construction organisations operate on project bases, whereby some workers are employed for a particular project, the relationship between employers and employees becomes transient and fluid. This lack of attention to workforce management issues has contributed to the overall poor performance noticed in the construction industry of most countries worldwide. To address this problem, it is necessary to understand the practices needed for construction organisations to manage their workforce effectively.

The review of extant literature shows a wide range of studies on workforce management. Some of these studies have proposed several practices needed for organisations to improve the management of employees. However, the current fourth industrial revolution era, which is revolutionising every industry in countries worldwide, offers the construction industry an opportunity to solve its age-long problems through digital technologies. When adopted correctly, these technologies will also impact how workers are managed and the management practices adopted by construction organisations. However, the construction industry has been lagging in adopting these digital technologies compared to other sectors. This lag is not unconnected to the constant fear of job losses among construction workers, which has led to resistance to the use of technologies on the part of the construction workforce, as noticed within the industry. To alienate this fear and resistance to change among construction workers, adopting the right practices that will lead to effective management becomes crucial.

Therefore, this book explores construction workforce management in the fourth industrial revolution era. The book, through a critical review of existing related theories, models, and practices, unearths the gaps in existing construction workforce management studies and proposes a conceptual model designed to improve the management of workers in the construction industry. The conceptualised model was further examined through experts' opinions to determine the suitability and applicability of the proposed workforce management practices and their attributed measurement variables. Furthermore, the book explored the impact of emerging digital technologies on construction workforce management while giving insight into the envisioned challenges of deploying digital tools for effective workforce management in construction.

This book is timely as it is designed to give direction for effectively managing the construction workforce. It promises value to readers as it presents a roadmap designed to ensure the effective management of workers within the construction industry. Owners of construction organisations can benefit from the conceptualised construction workforce management model proposed in the book in their quest for improved workers' productivity. Also, the book will support construction regulatory bodies in ensuring organisations within the industry uphold proper workforce management practices. The book's content will also benefit researchers seeking to expand the frontiers of knowledge on workforce management in construction. To this end, the authors confirm that the text utilised in this work reflects original work and, where necessary, the material has benefited from relevant context-setting / referencing.

Lerato Aghimien
Clinton Ohis Aigbavboa
Douglas Aghimien

# Chapter 1

# General Introduction

## Abstract

This first chapter provides a general overview of the book. The chapter describes workforce management and the lack of adequate attention to this concept within construction organisations. In the fourth industrial revolution era, where emerging technologies have continued to change how business functions, the need for an effective approach towards managing the construction workforce becomes crucial. Having a construction workforce management practice model was deemed vital at this point, where technological advancement is rapidly changing the construction environment, and skill shortage is evident in the construction industry of most countries around the world. As such, this chapter establishes that the development of a construction workforce management model that will help improve the management of construction workers serves a critical value of the book.

*Keywords*: Construction; construction workers; employee management; human resources; personnel management; workforce management

## Introduction

The significance of the construction industry and its importance in enhancing socio-economic development in countries worldwide has been reiterated within the body of literature. Also, the industry's direct and indirect effects on other sectors and, ultimately, on any country's wealth have been noted (Aigbavboa et al., 2022; Dandan et al., 2020; Ofori, 2012). As such, the construction industry has been adjudged as a vital contributor to economic growth (World Economic Forum, 2016). The industry contributes to socio-economic development through its contribution to gross domestic product, infrastructure delivery and provision of employment. To this end, the construction industry has been described as a huge employer of labour, with significant employment of workers recorded in developed and developing countries worldwide (Durdyev & Ismail, 2012;

**Construction Workforce Management in the Fourth Industrial Revolution Era, 1–10**
Copyright © 2024 by Lerato Aghimien, Clinton Ohis Aigbavboa and Douglas Aghimien
Published under exclusive licence by Emerald Publishing Limited
doi:10.1108/978-1-83797-018-620241001

Mitchell, 2020; Vitharana et al., 2015). Before the Coronavirus (COVID-19) pandemic, the industry had a 7.7% contribution to global employment, with an envisaged growth of up to 13.4% in 2020 (International Labour Organisation (ILO), 2021). Despite the devastating impact of the pandemic on the industry, which saw a momentous loss of jobs and revenues for construction organisations (Aigbavboa et al., 2022), the construction industry globally has been taunted as the global engine for economic growth and recovery from COVID-19 (Robinson et al., 2021).

The construction industry has many stakeholders and depends on resources such as labour, plant, material, capital, and energy to deliver its services (Hillebrandt & Cannon, 1990). From the perspective of labour, Ofori (2012) noted that the construction industry requires human effort to deliver its products successfully. Despite the numerous emerging digital, physical, and biological technologies offered by the fourth industrial revolution (Aghimien et al., 2021; Schwab, 2017), the construction industry still relies heavily on people. These people are referred to as human resources or the organisation's workforce, and they are an organisation's most valuable asset, especially in a labour-intensive industry such as construction (Malkani and Kambekar, 2013). This workforce can be skilled, semi-skilled or unskilled, and effectively managing them is germane to successfully delivering construction projects (Ngwenya & Aigbavboa, 2017; Oke et al., 2019; Vitharana et al., 2015). The management of these workforces is known as human resource management or workforce management. Since the most common term for labour in the construction industry is 'construction workers', this book adopts the phrase workforce and workforce management in place of the popular 'human resources' and 'human resource management'.

## Workforce Management

Workforce management plays a significant role in the success of any organisation (Werner, 2017). According to Dessler (2015), workforce management refers to how people are managed within organisations. Traditionally, workforce management involves the strategic management of workers (Spooner & Kaine, 2010), knowledge management amongst workers and within the organisation (Prusak, 2001), organisation development, resourcing, and performance management (DeNisi & Smith, 2014), reward management (Armstrong & Murlis, 2007), employee relations (Farnham, 2000) and occupational health and safety (ILO, 2001). Invariably, workforce management is centred around people and their relation to their organisation. With the constant changes in the social, economic, and technological climate, organisations are saddled with the responsibility of coming up with unique ways of developing and retaining their most valuable asset (i.e. their workers). This is crucial as Marchington and Wilkinson (2005) have earlier noted that the way workers are managed impacts the organisation's performance. Therefore, workforce management is responsible for improving organisational performance and capability by effectively managing employees. To this end, Kinnie and Swart (2016) submitted that employees and organisational performance depend largely on the workforce management practices adopted within the organisation. Aside from performance improvement, Nzuve (2007) noted that adopting effective workforce management practices enhances employee productivity, and by extension, leads to attaining organisational goals. Ivancevich et al. (2008) also noted that good workforce management practices help organisations retain existing employees while attracting new ones.

There is no gainsaying that the construction industry relies heavily on its workforce to survive. Although capital, materials, and plant are equally significant for successful project delivery, workers serve as the 'engine room' that brings these other resources into good use. Since the construction industry is project-based, many workers are required to deliver successful projects at several stages. As such, it is necessary to manage these workers carefully to attain successful project delivery within the industry. More so, workforce management can assist in nurturing and improving employee performance and creativity (Chang & Teng, 2017; Zhai et al., 2014). Through this improvement, employees who are creative and innovative in their ideas are groomed. In the long run, construction organisations tend to benefit more, as ingenious thinkers can create a remarkable competitive advantage for their organisations by providing quick and positive responses to challenges (Jafri et al., 2016).

### *Workforce Management in Construction*

Albeit the importance of effectively managing workers for the successful delivery of projects and improved performance of organisations and workers, the concept of workforce management has continued to be on the back foot for many construction organisations (Aghimien et al., 2023). This situation is not ideal for an industry that is labour intensive (Loosemore et al., 2003) and characterised by project-based work for a defined period (Druker et al., 1996). This is coupled with the fact that getting the skills the industry needs are not always easy (Aghimien et al., 2023; Oke et al., 2019); one would expect proper management of the few available skills. Dainty et al. (2007) noted earlier that because construction activities may differ from project to project, there may be substantial changes in the knowledge and skills required from one project to another. Likewise, high levels of labour turnover are evident in the construction industry, ultimately leading to skills shortages (Erlick & Grabelsky, 2005; McGrath-Champ et al., 2011; Oke et al., 2019). According to Olsen et al. (2012), the skills shortage is not necessarily the number of workers unavailable but the unavailability of adequately trained skilled and productive workers within the industry. To battle the skills shortage issue, some construction organisations rely on outsourced labour, collaboration, joint ventures, and subcontracting (ILO, 2001; Rubery et al., 2004). While these approaches have helped cushion the effect of labour shortage in many construction organisations, the resultant effect is the lack of attention given to workforce management within these organisations, as the responsibility of managing the outsourced workforce is left to the company from whence, they were outsourced (Dainty et al., 2004; Loosemore et al., 2003).

Othman et al. (2012) submitted that the effectiveness of workforce management in construction as a technique for performance improvement is still unclear. It was noted that if managing workers through project-based work was considered the strategy of project-oriented organisations, it would imply that the workforce management policies, processes, and practices in such organisations support project-oriented work. Consequently, the management of workers can move from project to project with the experience gained from one project being transferred to the next. Loosemore et al. (2003) believe workforce management focus has been centralised as a head-office function, yet most problems and operational issues arise on construction sites. Hence, Othman et al. (2012) concluded that workforce management in construction might differ from traditional workforce management functions and practices designed for typically managed organisations. It was suggested that workforce management changes in construction organisations should be tailored to workers' needs and the working environment. Likewise, Keegan and Turner (2003) highlighted that management should implement their policies and strategies based on their employees' needs to ensure they can contribute positively to the organisation.

Armstrong and Stephens (2006) confirmed that workforce management practices aid in attracting and retaining talents in an organisation. Garavan (2007) noted that there is now a recognised trend in well-chosen workforce management practices that directly affect individual and organisational performance. As such, there is the need to embrace workforce management practices such as planning, recruitment, selection, training, and development, which are imperative for the survival of any organisation (Ngwenya et al., 2019; Walker, 2001). Similarly, other studies have noted the need to adopt practices such as compensation, benefits, occupational health and safety, and labour relations, among others (Chukwuma & Obiefuna, 2014; Ernawati & Ambarini, 2010; Warnich et al., 2014). Understanding these necessary workforce management practices is important for construction organisations which have been lagging in giving attention to their workforce management. Aside from these practices mentioned above, other factors need to be considered. For example, there is a deficiency in the literature on workforce management in construction regarding considering issues surrounding the emotional intelligence of both employees and management. Although emotional intelligence plays a crucial role in attaining improved performance (Love et al., 2011), studies on emotional intelligence assessment in workforce management within organisations (construction in particular) are few. The handful of available studies emphasises peripheral and broad issues such as the role of the emotional intelligence of people (Cao & Fu, 2011; Darvishmotevali et al., 2018; Lindebaum & Cassell, 2012; Love et al., 2011; Mo & Andrew, 2007; Oke et al., 2017). Integrating this critical aspect of human psychology into existing workforce management practices will improve the management of workers within construction organisations.

Similarly, as noted earlier by Othman et al. (2012), when selecting the right management practices based on workers' needs, it is essential to consider the working environment. The current fourth industrial revolution era, which is revolutionising every industry in diverse countries worldwide, offers the construction industry an opportunity to solve its age-long problems through digital technologies. Evidently, when adopted correctly, these technologies will also impact how workers are managed and the practices adopted by construction organisations. Furthermore, it is necessary to note that construction organisations do not function in silos. They operate within a defined environment; the norms and mode of operation might influence how these organisations function and manage their workforce. Past studies have noted the importance of assessing the external environment. However, most developed models have embedded external environmental factors within other workforce management practices. More so, none have assessed this external environment from the perspective of handling the environment's pressure as a crucial workforce management practice that could shape organisations' overall performance. Those above necessitated this book on construction workforce management in the fourth industrial revolution era.

## Objectives of the Book

This book was conceptualised based on the understanding that workforce management is not given adequate consideration within construction organisations and the need for a well-defined workforce management practice model that considers factors peculiar to the construction industry. Having a workforce management practice model was deemed crucial at this point, where technological advancement is rapidly changing the construction environment, and skill shortage is evident in the construction industry of most countries around the world. To this end, the objective of this book was to provide a conceptualised construction workforce management model that will serve as a catalyst for reducing employee turnover, enhancing employee skills, and ultimately increasing employee and organisational performance. To achieve this objective, the book explores the concept of workforce management, related theories, models, and practices to unearth the gaps in existing workforce management in construction, and the impact of the pervasive digital technologies offered by the fourth industrial revolution on the effective management of the construction workforce.

## The Value of the Book

Past studies have emphasised that construction organisations have placed less focus on workforce management and its practices (Dainty et al., 2004; Loosemore et al., 2003; Shafeek, 2016). This situation is worsened with the advent of ubiquitous digital technologies of the fourth industrial revolution, which offers better delivery of construction projects. While these technologies provide better project delivery, their adoption has been trailed by the fear of job losses (Aghimien et al., 2021). It is, therefore, crucial to determine how workers can be effectively managed to ensure their continuous development and alienate their fear of losing their jobs to technology.

This book becomes valuable as its submissions are important to owners and those in top management within construction organisations, the workers, and construction industry regulatory bodies. For construction organisations, the proposed conceptual model for construction workforce management will guide them to better manage their workforce by adopting the right practices. The conceptualised model showcases seven crucial practices that management in construction organisations needs to consider to manage their workforce successfully.

For instance, the model emphasises the need for top management's commitment to employees' training and development, empowerment, and involvement in crucial organisational activities. By promoting training and skills development, ensuring newly acquired skills are shared with other workers, and also applied on the job, construction organisations will be able to identify the strength of their workers and ensure that the right individual with the right training driven by digital technology is given the right project to handle. Also, organisational learning and knowledge management can be attained by sharing knowledge gained from training within the organisations. Construction organisations can also channel the pressure from their environment to promote and improve the management of their employees. With proper attention to the coercive and normative pressure coming from the external environment, construction organisations can redefine their workforce management activities and gain more legitimacy in the process.

For construction workers, if construction organisations adopt the submissions of this book, improvement in skills and more job satisfaction can be derived from working in the construction industry. This is because the proposed conceptual model advocates the 'soft' workforce management concept, where practices that promote proactiveness, participation, and improved skills are adopted to give better quality and flexibility within construction organisations. Furthermore, issues revolving around how employees are recruited and selected, how they are remunerated, the evaluation of their performance, and the management of their EI can be carefully managed for optimum positive outcomes. For construction industry regulatory bodies, the book's submissions can be used to assess members' compliance regarding improving their respective workforce. Regulatory bodies can assist construction organisations in improving their workforce management by ensuring that favourable regulations (including regulations that support emerging digital technologies) are developed. Also, many countries around the world are faced with the problem of unemployment. As such, several initiatives are being implemented to address this excruciating problem. Should construction organisations adopt the submissions of this book, there will be a better-trained and developed skilled construction workforce, which will lead to less employee turnover and, by extension, a reduction in the number of unemployed individuals.

Aside from these practical values of the book, it also offers some theoretical value. The study theorised that a construction organisation that will attain its strategic objectives in the current fourth industrial revolution era must be willing to promote the EI of its workers and external environment factors along with other traditional practices such as recruitment and selection, compensation and benefits, performance management and appraisal, employee involvement and empowerment, training and development. This submission can serve as an excellent platform for future researchers who seek to explore further the concept of worker management within the construction industry.

## Structure of the Book

This book is divided into eight chapters, with Chapter 1 presenting a general introduction of the book. Chapter 2 is designed to illuminate the concept of construction workforce management. This chapter gives an overview of the construction industry and its inherent challenges while expanding on workforce management, particularly in the construction industry. The challenges facing effective workforce management, as well as the measures for improving this management of workers, were explored. Chapter 3 centred around construction workforce management in the fourth industrial revolution era. This chapter explored the fourth industrial revolution and its relationship to the construction industry. Also, the relationship between the emerging technologies of this industrial revolution with workforce management was explored. The chapter also gave insight into the key opportunities for workforce management in deploying digital technologies within construction organisations. Chapter 4 explored related workforce management theories, models, and practices. This chapter set the base for the proposed conceptual construction workforce management model. Based on the reviewed theories, models, and practices, Chapter 5 was developed to showcase the gaps in construction workforce management studies. This chapter emphasised the need for two major practices (i.e. emotional intelligence and external environment). Chapter 6 provided the conceptualised construction workforce management model, while Chapter 7 showcased the exploration of the conceptualised model through experts' opinions. Chapter 8 gave the conclusion, contribution to knowledge and the book's recommendations.

## Summary

This chapter provides the readers with the idea behind the conception of this book. The high dependence on labour and the lack of adequate attention given to the management of these workforces necessitated the development of a conceptual model that can help construction organisations effectively manage their workers. This is coupled with the fact that the current fourth industrial revolution era offers organisations digital tools that can help them better manage their workers effectively. The chapter gave an overview of the construction industry, and workforce management in construction. It also revealed the need for a construction workforce management model in the current fourth industrial revolution era, the objectives and the value of conducting the study. The next chapter describes the concept of construction workforce management in the construction industry.

## References

Aghimien, D. O., Aigbavboa, C. O., Oke, A. E., & Thwala, W. D. (2021). *Construction digitalisation – A capability maturity model for construction organisations*. Routledge, UK.

Aghimien, L. M., Aigbavboa, C. O., Anumba, C. J., & Thwala, W. D. (2023). A confirmatory factor analysis of the challenges of effective management of construction workforce in South Africa. *Journal of Engineering, Design and Technology, 21*(4), 1134–1152.

Aigbavboa, C. O., Aghimien, D. O., Thwala, W. D., & Ngozwana, N. (2022). Unprepared industry meet pandemic: COVID-19 and the South Africa construction industry. *Journal of Engineering Design and Technology, 20*(1), 183–200.

Armstrong, M., & Stephens, T. (2006). *Employee reward management practice*. Kogan Page.
Armstrong, M., & Murlis, H. (2007). *Reward management: A handbook of remuneration strategy and practice* (5th ed.). Kogan Page.
Cao, J., & Fu, Y. (2011). A survey on the role of emotional intelligence in construction project. *Advances in Information Sciences and Service Sciences, 3*(9), 107–113.
Chang, J., & Teng, C. (2017). Intrinsic or extrinsic motivations for hospitality employees' creativity: The moderating role of organisation-level regulatory focus. *International Journal of Hospitality Management, 60*, 133–141.
Chukwuma, E. M., & Obiefuna, O. (2014). Effect of motivation on employee productivity: A study of manufacturing companies in Nnewi. *Journal of Managerial Studies and Research, 2*(7), 137–147.
Dainty, A., Ison, S. G., & Root, D. (2004). Bridging the skills gap: a regionally driven strategy for resolving the construction labour market crisis. *Engineering, Construction and Architectural Management, 11*(4), 275–283.
Dainty, A., Green, S., & Bagilhole, B. (2007). *People and culture in construction*. Taylor and Francis.
Dandan, T. H., Sweis, G., Sukkari, L. S., & Sweis, R. J. (2020). Factors affecting the accuracy of cost estimate during various design stages. *Journal of Engineering, Design and Technology, 18*(4), 787–819.
Darvishmotevali, M., Altinay, L., & De Vita, G. (2018). Emotional intelligence and creative performance: Looking through the lens of environmental uncertainty and cultural intelligence. *International Journal of Hospitality Management, 73*, 44–54.
DeNisi, A. S., & Smith, C. E. (2014). Performance appraisal, performance management, and firm-level performance: A review, a proposed model, and new directions for future research. *The Academy of Management Annals, 8*(1), 127–179.
Dessler, G. (2015). *Human resource management* (14th ed.). Pearson Education.
Druker, J., White, G., Hegewisch, A., & Mayne, L. (1996). Between hard and soft HRM: Human resource management in the construction industry. *Construction Management and Economics, 14*(5), 405–416.
Durdyev, S., & Ismail, S. (2012). Pareto analysis of on-site productivity constraints and improvement techniques in construction industry. *Scientific Research and Essays, 7*(4), 824–833.
Erlick, M., & Grabelsky, J. (2005). Standing at the crossroads: The building trade in the twenty-first century. *Labor History, 46*(4), 421–445.
Ernawati, N., & Ambarini. (2010). Influence employment relations and working environment on employee performance with work motivation as moderating variables. *Journal of Economics and Entrepreneurship, 10*(2), 109–118.
Farnham, D. (2000). *Employee relations in context* (2nd ed.). CIPD.
Garavan, T. N. (2007). A strategic perspective on human resource development. *Advances in Developing Human Resources, 9*(1), 11–30.
Hillebrandt, P., & Cannon, J. (1990). *Growth and diversification in the modern construction firm*. Palgrave Macmillan.
International Labor Organization (ILO). (2001). *The construction industry in the twenty-first century: Its image, employment prospects and skill requirements*. ILO, www.ilo.org/public/english/standards/relm/gb/docs/gb283/pdf/tmcitr.pdf
International Labour Organisation (ILO). (2021). *Impact of COVID-19 on the construction sector, ILO Sectorial Brief*. https://www.ilo.org/wcmsp5/groups/public/-ed_dialogue/-sector/documents/briefingnote/wcms_767303.pdf
Ivancevich, J., Konopaske, R., & Matteson, M. T. (2008). *Organizational behaviour and management* (8th ed.). McGraw-Hill Higher Education.
Jafri, M. H., Dem, C., & Choden, S. (2016). Emotional intelligence and employee creativity: Moderating role of proactive personality and organisational climate. *Business Perspectives and Research, 4*(1), 54–66.
Keegan, A. E., & Turner, J. R. (2003). Managing human resources in the project-based organization. In J. R. Turner (Ed.), *People in project management*. Gower.

Kinnie, N., & Swart, J. (2016). Human resource management and organisational performance: In search of the HR advantage. In T. Redman, A. Wilkinson, & T. Dundon (Eds.), *Contemporary human resource management: Text and cases* (5th ed.). Pearson Publishing.

Lindebaum, D., & Cassell, C. (2012). A contradiction in terms? Making sense of emotional intelligence in a construction management environment. *British Journal of Management, 23*, 65–79.

Loosemore, M., Dainty, A. R. J., & Lingard, H. (2003). *Human resource management in construction projects – Strategic and operational approaches*. Taylor and Francis.

Love, P., Edwards, D., & Wood, E. (2011). Loosening the Gordian knot: The role of emotional intelligence in construction. *Engineering, Construction and Architectural Management, 18*(1), 50–65.

Malkani, Z. A. K., & Kambekar, A. R. (2013). Management of human resource in construction industry introduction. *International Journal of Engineering Research and Technology, 6*(3), 353–362.

Marchington, M., & Wilkinson, A. (2005). *Human resource management at work: People management and development* (3rd ed.). Chartered Institute of Personnel and Development.

McGrath-Champ, S., Rosewarne, S., & Rittau, Y. (2011). From one skill shortage to the next: The Australian construction industry and geographies of a global labour market. *Journal of Industrial Relations, 53*(4), 467–485.

Mitchell, A. (2020). *CLC Statement on payment and contracts*. https://www.construction-leadershipcouncil.co.uk/news/clc-statement-on-payment-and-contracts

Mo, Y. Y., & Andrew, R. J. (2007). Measuring and enhancing the emotional intelligence of construction management students: An empirical investigation. *Journal for Education in the Built Environment, 2*(1), 110–129.

Ngwenya, L. M., & Aigbavboa, C. (2017). Improvement of productivity and employee performance through an efficient human resource management practice. *Advances in Intelligent Systems and Computing, 498*, 727–737.

Ngwenya, L. M., Aigbavboa, C., & Thwala, W. (2019). *Effects of training and development on employee performance in a South African construction company*. 14th International Organization, Technology and Management in Construction Conference, Zagreb, Croatia, 4–7 September, pp. 845–852.

Nzuve, S. N. M. (2007). *Management of human resources, a Kenyan perspective* (4th ed.). Basic Modern Management Consultants Publisher.

Ofori, G. (2012). *Contemporary issues in construction in developing countries*. Spon Press.

Oke, A., Aigbavboa, C., & Sepuru, M. (2017). *Benefits of emotional intelligence to construction industry: A case of Gauteng region, South Africa*. Proceedings of Environmental Design and Management International Conference (EDMIC) held between 22th – 24th of May, at the Obafemi Awolowo University, Ile-Ife, Nigeria, pp. 523–531.

Oke, A., Ngwenya, L. M., Aigbavboa, C., & Khangale, T. (2019). *Mitigating skills shortage in the South African construction industry*. Construction in the 21st Century, London, UK, 9–11 September, pp. 421–429.

Olsen, D., Tatun, M., & Defnall, C. (2012). *How industrial contractors are handling skilled labor shortages in the United States*. 48th ASC Annual International Conference Proceeding, Birmingham City University, UK, April 11–14.

Othman, I., Idrus, A., & Napiah, M. (2012). Human resource management in the construction of a sustainable development project: Towards successful completion. *WIT Transactions on Ecology and the Environment, 162*, 169–180.

Prusak, L. (2001). Where did knowledge management come from? *IBM Systems Journal, 40*(4), 1002–1007.

Robinson, G., Leonard, J., & Whittington, T. (2021). *Future of construction: A global forecast for construction to 2030*. https://resources.oxfordeconomics.com/hubfs/Africa/Future-of-Construction-Full-Report.pdf

Rubery, J., Carroll, M., Cooke, F., Grugulis, I., & Earnshaw, J. (2004). Human resource management and the permeable organisation: The case of the multiclient call Centre. *Journal of Management Studies, 41*(7), 1199–1222.

Schwab, K. (2017). *The fourth industrial revolution* (1st ed.). Crown Business.

Shafeek, H. (2016). The impact of human resources management practices in SMES. *ANNALS of Faculty Engineering Hunedoara – International Journal of Engineering, 16*(4), 91–102.

Spooner, K., & Kaine, S. (2010). Defining sustainability and human resource management. *International Employment Relations Review, 16*(2), 70–81.

Vitharana, V. H. P., De Silva, G. H. M. J., & De Silva, S. (2015). Health hazards, risk and safety practices in construction sites – A review study. *Engineer: Journal of the Institution of Engineers, Sri Lanka, 48*(3), 35–44.

Walker, J. W. (2001). Perspectives – Zero Defections? *Human Resource Planning, 24*, 6–10.

Warnich, S., Carrell, M. R., Elbert, N. F., & Hatfield, R. D. (2014). *Human resource management in South Africa* (5th ed.). RR Donnelley Publishing.

Werner, A. (2017). Introduction to human resource management. In Nel & Werner (Eds.), *Human resource management* (10th ed.). Oxford University Press.

World Economic Forum. (2016). *Shaping the future of construction: A breakthrough in mindset and technology.* www3.weforum.org/docs/WEF_Shaping_the_Future_of_Construction_full_report__.pdf

Zhai, X., Liu, A. M. M., & Fellows, R. (2014). Role of human resource practices in enhancing organisational learning in Chinese construction organisation. *Journal of Management in Engineering, 30*(2), 194–220.

# Chapter 2

# Construction Workforce Management

## Abstract

In the quest for better construction workforce management, this chapter explored the background of workforce management and related theories, models, and practices. Through a review, the chapter provided meaning to the concept of construction and workforce management. The chapter concluded that while the construction industry worldwide is important to the economic growth of the countries where it operates, the industry's management of its workforce is challenged by several problems. These problems include the nature of the industry, skill shortage, unhealthy working environment, and poor image of the industry, among others. Also, while the construction industry is rich in diversity, this has been a major source of problems for workforce management. The chapter further revealed that to improve workforce management and attain better-performing construction organisations, careful recruitment, effective training, providing a safe working environment, putting policies to promote diversity, and ensuring innovativeness, among others, are essential.

*Keywords*: Construction workers; human resource management; personnel management; motivation; workforce; workforce management

## Introduction

The construction industry worldwide employs a large number of workers in its quest to deliver projects successfully. The industry relies on these workers to carry out its activities of contributing to economic growth and societal development. However, the relationship between the construction industry and its workforce can be described as a paradox. This is because, despite being heavily dependent on workers, the industry has been notorious for its lack of its poor workforce management and lack of attention to workforce management issues. Since most construction organisations operate on a project basis, whereby some workers are employed for a particular project, the relationship between employers and

*Construction Workforce Management in the Fourth Industrial Revolution Era*, 11–39
Copyright © 2024 by Lerato Aghimien, Clinton Ohis Aigbavboa and Douglas Aghimien
Published under exclusive licence by Emerald Publishing Limited
doi:10.1108/978-1-83797-018-620241002

employees becomes momentary and fluid. This lack of attention to workforce management issues has contributed to the overall poor performance noticed in the construction industry of most countries worldwide. To address this problem through well-defined construction workforce management practices, it is necessary to understand the background of workforce management and the existing practices. Therefore, this chapter reviews the theoretical background of workforce management and practices vis-à-vis its relation to the construction industry. Issues surrounding the adoption of workforce management in the construction industry, the different practices, challenges, as well as measures for improving workforce management adoption within the industry were discussed.

## The Construction Industry

The term 'construction' is as old as humankind itself. The quest for shelter has been described as the second most important requirement of man after food. This construction involves the erection of suitable structures that can serve as shelters and supporting facilities (Vatan, 2017; Wells, 1985). Vatan (2017) noted that early constructions involved delivering simple structures constructed from stone, wood, and adobe blocks, among other naturally available materials. However, advancement in the human standard of living and taste has changed the demand for shelter. This has seen the development of more sophisticated construction systems, and a more organised construction industry saddled with the responsibility of delivering better construction. Lange and Mills (1979) described this construction industry as businesses dealing with similar related activities in providing real estate, buildings, and public infrastructures. Ibrahim et al. (2010) noted that this industry is essential in transforming the needs and aspirations of people into reality. The industry does this through the physical implementation of varied construction projects.

According to Pearce's report (2003), the construction industry can be described from two dissimilar angles. These are known as the narrow and broad views of the industry. On the one hand, the industry conducts on-site assembly of buildings and infrastructure. This is the most common view of the industry, and it is termed 'the narrow view'. On the other hand, the industry is seen beyond its ability to deliver on-site construction projects. This broad view of the industry encompasses the supply chain (including materials manufacturing) required for project delivery and the diverse professional services required. Anaman and Osei-Amponsah (2007) described the construction industry as one that constructs, renovates, repairs, or extends fixed assets such as buildings and other infrastructure. It was also noted that fundamental physical structures such as roads, dams, schools, irrigation work, houses, hospitals, stadiums, factories, and others are the vital economic contributions the construction industry brings to most countries. Through these contributions, growth and living standards are established. Therefore, the construction industry positively impacts economic growth in any country (Kazaz & Ulubeyli, 2009; Olatunji et al., 2016). In fact, according to Ayodele and Alabi (2011), the wellness of a country's economy is determined by the growth of its construction industry. Ogunsemi (2015) submitted that other industries, such as manufacturing, agriculture, entertainment, transportation, education, health, and sports, which significantly contribute to a country's economy, depend on the construction industry through the industry's ability to provide infrastructure. This dependence on the construction industry is a pointer to the industry's important role in every nation's socio-economic development (Anaman & Osei-Amponsah, 2007).

The World Economic Forum (2016) noted that the worldwide construction industry is an important industry needed for national development. According to Saka and Lowe (2010), the industry's importance to economic growth and development is obvious from its significant contribution to the gross domestic product (GDP), capital formation, and employment of every nation worldwide. The World Economic Forum (2016) submitted that the industry contributes about 6% to the world's GDP, which is about 3.6 trillion dollars. In the same vein, Chitkara (2004) observed that the industry accounts for 6% to 10% of most countries' GDP. Dixit et al. (2017) noted an 8% contribution to the GDP of India by the construction industry, while Statista Research Department (2019) submitted a 6.8% contribution to the GDP of China. The story is similar in other countries like Malaysia, Nigeria, and South Africa, where the industry makes a 4.2%, 3.21%, and 3.0% contribution to the country's GDP (Department of Statistics Malaysia, 2020; National Bureau of Statistics, 2020; Zingoni, 2020). In the United Kingdom (UK), Mitchell (2020) noted an 8% contribution to the country's GDP by the construction industry and a 10% contribution to employment growth. The European Commission (2020) observed a 9% contribution made by the construction industry to the GDP of European countries and the provision of 18 million jobs to these countries. Earlier, Durdyev and Ismail (2012) noted that about 111 million workers globally could be found in the construction industry alone. This shows the immense importance of the construction sector to economic growth and job creation. Vitharana et al. (2015) noted that diverse job opportunities are available within the construction industry, and this can be in the form of management, specialised teams, skilled, partly skilled, and under-skilled workforce. Albeit the setback to economic development and job availability caused by the global pandemic (COVID-19), the construction industry globally has been taunted as the worldwide engine of economic growth and recovery from COVID. A growth rate of almost 42% is expected within the construction industry from 2020 to 2030, which will significantly drive the world's economic growth (Robinson et al., 2021).

## Constraints of the Construction Industry

By nature, the construction industry worldwide is complex and non-static. Rezgui and Zarli (2006) describe the industry as diversified, highly fragmented and multifaceted. The industry depends on many different entities to meet the ever-growing pressures from clients seeking sophisticated facilities on time and within budget. As a result, Bertelsen and Koskela (2004) described construction as a complex production of a unique product through the cooperation of multi-skilled ad-hoc teams. This means that the construction industry's unique and complex product is delivered through the cooperation of temporary organisations (Ibrahim et al., 2010). Based on this notion, Navon (2005) asserted that the construction industry is complex because it requires large numbers of parties to deliver its services.

Despite the importance of the construction industry, it has been noted that the industry has been suffering from a poor image (Aghimien et al., 2021). According to Haupt and Harinarain (2016), the physically demanding, dirty and dangerous nature of the industry makes the sector unattractive and less prestigious compared to other industries. Siew (2014) also described the industry as an industry known for its '3D' image (dirty, difficult, and dangerous). There are numerous perceptions about the image of the construction sector, such as blue-collar workers being synonymous with low-status jobs requiring little or no education or skill. They are also perceived as disadvantaged (ILO, 2001). Furthermore, a career in manual labour is regarded as a low-status career without a clear career path (Tucker et al., 1999). In addition, the sector is commonly associated with the practice of fraud and corruption, political influence in the awarding of public sector projects, unprincipled and unethical practices by key construction companies, and the dominance of male workers (Ameyaw et al., 2017; Maseko, 2017; Paul et al., 2021).

The constraints of the construction industry worldwide have been explored significantly by researchers. For instance, Fox (2003) noted several constraints and categorised them into traditional and cultural constraints. This includes constraints relating to institutional infrastructure, financial and human resources, technical know-how for complex production, policy for long-term growth, and learning culture. The inadequacy of these identified factors has constrained the construction industry in most countries and has truncated the industry's growth. Elkhalifa (2012) also grouped the constraints of construction into four major factors. These are:

(1) the socio-economic and political environment where the industry operates;
(2) the availability of financial, physical, and human resources;
(3) the nature of the construction environment, including structure, capacity, and behaviour; and
(4) available supporting systems such as regulations and research and development.

Further study by Windapo and Cattell (2013) noted several factors, including the rising cost of materials, high-interest rates, a mismatch between skills required and skills available, unfavourable government legislation, poverty, and lack of technology adoption. Ogunmakinde et al. (2019) noted that issues relating to the nature of the construction industry, the type of clients, professionals and projects all create some constraints that deter the success of the construction industry. In a similar study, Mengistu and Mahesh (2020) submitted that the government's role, the available resources, the nature of the industry and the industry's vision of its development all play a crucial part in truncating the construction industry's development. Furthermore, Aghimien et al. (2021) noted issues such as the poor image of the industry, poor health and safety, lack of collaboration between stakeholders, unethical practices, resistance to change, lack of innovation, skill shortage, lack of adequate financial resources, lack of government support, and economic conditions.

Aside from the above constraints observed in the studies mentioned above, the global pandemic (COVID-19) has also dealt a significant blow to the development of the construction industry worldwide. For instance, the UK experienced a significant shrink in the construction industry, with an almost 40% reduction in the early period of the nationwide lockdown in 2020 (The Office of National Statistics, ONS, 2020). This was followed by the significant loss of jobs that characterised the construction industry during the COVID-19 pandemic (Sierra, 2022). The pandemic brought about issues relating to labour and material shortages as well as problems relating to the construction procurement system in the UK. The situation is the same in other countries around the world. In the United States of America (USA), Heimgartner (2020) noted a discontinuation of construction activities which led to supply chain disruption and loss of jobs for construction workers who rely heavily on construction works for their survival. In the early periods of the pandemic, Arndt et al. (2020) noted a severe decline of 60% in the construction industry in South Africa. A similar study by Aigbavboa et al. (2022) revealed disruption in construction activities, severe job losses for individuals and organisations, loss of revenue and potential bankruptcy as some of the impacts of the pandemic on the country's construction industry. Gamil and Alhagar (2020) noted the issues of discounted projects, job losses, and delay in project delivery in Malaysia, while in Oman, delay in project delivery, staff shortage, lack of supplies, and economic decline were the resultant effect of the pandemic on the construction industry (Amri & Marey-Pérez, 2020). A similar observation was made in Ghana, where Agyekum et al. (2022) observed a decline in the rate of work, delays in payment for jobs done and a rise in the cost of construction materials.

The constraints of the construction industry globally have evolved since the COVID-19 pandemic. Fusing the emerging challenges with the previously identified issues, below is the list of constraints facing the construction industry globally that require significant attention for the growth of the industry:

(1)  A mismatch between skills required and skills available.
(2)  High interest rates.
(3)  Inadequacy in policies for long-term growth.
(4)  Ineffective procurement systems.
(5)  Insatiable clients.
(6)  Lack of adequate financial resources.
(7)  Lack of government support and unfavourable government policies.
(8)  Lack of innovativeness and technology adoption.
(9)  Lack of investment in research and development.
(10)  Lack of synergy between stakeholders.
(11)  Lack of technical know-how for complex production.
(12)  Nature and the poor image of the industry.
(13)  Poor health and safety.
(14)  Poor learning culture.
(15)  Poor management of construction activities and resources.
(16)  Poor socio-economic conditions.
(17)  Poor sustainability consideration.

(18)   Resistance to change.
(19)   Skill shortage.
(20)   The rising cost of materials.
(21)   Unethical practices.

While the constraints mentioned above of the construction industry cut across diverse areas, there is a noteworthy pointer to the role of construction workers and how they impact the industry. This includes a shortage of specialised skills, a mismatch between available and required skills and poor management of the available workforce. The unappealing nature of the construction industry has become part of the reason for the skill shortage in the construction industries of most countries globally (Aghimien et al., 2021). Tucker et al. (1999) noted that young people prefer obtaining university degrees to secure white-collar jobs, with less desire to take up blue-collar jobs. Bilau et al. (2015) also submitted that on the one hand, the construction industry is believed to be the highest employer of labour after agriculture, while on the other, it is faced with challenges in a shortage of technically skilled workers, which affects organisations' productivity, quality of work, duration of projects as well as firms' profits. This situation therefore calls for the proper management of the available human resources (workforce) within the construction industry to strategically retain the existing workforce and, at the same time, attract more talent to the industry.

## Understanding Workforce Management

The concept of workforce management, popularly known as human resource management, stems from several theories relating to behavioural science, strategic management, human capital, and industrial relations. According to Dessler (2015), workforce management cuts across the employment and management of people. Studies have shown that workforce management encompasses strategic human resource management (Spooner & Kaine, 2010), human capital management (Schultz, 1961), corporate social responsibility (Bowen, 1953), knowledge management (Prusak, 2001), organisation development, resourcing, performance management (DeNisi & Smith, 2014), reward management (Armstrong & Murlis, 2007), employee relations (Farnham, 2000), and occupational health and safety (ILO, 2001). Furthermore, proper workforce management is crucial to the recent quest to attain vital social sustainability issues within organisations (Harmon et al., 2010; Siew, 2014; Wirtenberg et al., 2007).

According to Beer et al. (1984), workforce management comprises all managerial decisions and actions that impact the employer and employees' relationship. Guest (1987) opined that workforce management involves a set of policies intended to maximise organisational integration, employee commitment, flexibility, and work quality. Storey (1995) described workforce management as a distinctive employment management approach designed to achieve competitive advantage through highly committed and capable employees by integrating cultural, structural, and personnel techniques. Grimshaw and Rubery (2007) maintained that workforce management is about how organisations manage their employees. Based on the different descriptions, it can be concluded that workforce management is a strategically integrated and articulated method concerned with the employment, development and well-being of workers within an organisation.

In the current fourth industrial revolution era, shaped by pervasive digital technologies, organisations face several challenges in developing and retaining their most valuable asset (people). Marchington and Wilkinson (2005) observed that the way workers are managed has a substantial impact on the performance of organisations. Thus, workforce management aims to improve organisational performance through its employees. As such, Kinnie and Swart (2016) submitted that both organisational and employee performance depend largely on the workforce management practices adopted within the organisation. Earlier, Huselid (1995) showed that organisations' increased productivity and financial performance are closely linked to the workforce management practices such organisations adopt. Some of these practices are training, motivating, and compensating.

### *Overview of Workforce Management Practices*

Workforce management practices mediate the employee–organisation relationship and are essential for activating and managing employee engagement (Imperatori, 2017). Previous studies support the significance of workforce management practices in enhancing the connection between employees and organisations. It has been observed that through workforce management practices, organisational values are communicated and enhanced, thus making these practices strategic instruments for aligning organisational strategy with worker's behaviours (Huselid & Becker, 2011). Boxall and Macky (2009) state that workforce management systems comprise work and employment practices. Work practices denote the way work and processes are organised. In contrast, employment practices include procedures for recruiting individuals into the company, managing, motivating, and enabling them to carry out their jobs while in the company, as well as processes for retaining them but, if necessary, for terminating their employment contracts.

Aktar and Pangil (2018) submitted that workforce management practices are policies or systems that play a major role in employees' attitudes and behaviour. Similarly, Snell and Bohlander (2012) outlined how organisational goals and objectives can be achieved through employee encouragement in a typical workforce management practice. Workforce management practices, both separately and as a bundle, contribute to people-to-people relationships, significant organisational abilities, and workers' involvement. This was evident when Saks and Gruman's (2010) study revealed a positive relationship between workers' engagement and newcomer induction on the one hand and socialisation practices and performance management practices on the other hand. Furthermore, the development and performance of workers are closely related to workforce management practices such as selection, training, rewards systems, career management, development opportunities, and feedback mechanisms (Alfes et al., 2013; Shuck et al., 2011).

One persistent issue in workforce management studies is whether a single set of practices represents a universally superior attitude to people management (Chandler & McEvoy, 2000). While the goal of implementing these practices is mostly to improve how people are managed, best practice theories indicate that universally, certain workforce management practices, when adopted individually or collectively, can help attain organisational efficiency. Pfeffer (1994) initially recognised sixteen best-practice methods. These 16 initial practices are:

 (1) employment security;
 (2) selectivity in recruiting;
 (3) high wages;
 (4) incentive pay;
 (5) employee ownership;
 (6) information sharing;
 (7) participation and empowerment;
 (8) teams and job-redesign;
 (9) training and skills development;
(10) cross-utilisation and cross-training;
(11) symbolic egalitarianism;
(12) wage compression;
(13) promotion from within;
(14) long-term perspective;
(15) measurement of practices; and
(16) overarching philosophy.

Pfeffer (1998) further reduced these 16 practices to 7 major practices in assessing organisation success. These new practices advocated are:

(1) employment security;
(2) selective hiring;
(3) decentralised decision-making;
(4) compensation based on organisational performance;
(5) extensive training;
(6) minimal status distinction and barriers; and
(7) sharing financial and performance information.

Mondy and Noe (1996) observed some best practices connected with efficient workforce management. These practices include:

(1) planning, recruitment, and selection;
(2) training and development;
(3) compensation and benefits;
(4) health and safety;
(5) employee and labour relations; and
(6) human resource information systems.

Redman and Mathews (1998) also noted some workforce management vital practices that promote quality organisational strategies, and they include:

(1)  recruitment and selection;
(2)  remuneration systems;
(3)  job design;
(4)  training and learning;
(5)  employee involvement; and
(6)  performance appraisals.

Similarly, Har et al. (2010) assessed the impact of selected practices on managing knowledge within an organisation. The practices assessed include:

(1)  selective hiring;
(2)  reward and recognition;
(3)  appraising performance;
(4)  self-management of teams; and
(5)  extensive training.

Dessler (2015) noted important practices such as recruitment, training, rewards, and employee participation.

Several studies have continued to explore diverse workforce management practices and how they influence or relate to certain organisational outcomes. In New Zealand, Edgar and Geare (2005) surveyed management and employees in 37 selected organisations to determine the relationship between the adopted workforce management practices and the employees' attitudes. Four major practices were observed to impact employees' attitudes significantly. These practices are safe working conditions, training and development, equal employment opportunities, and recruitment selection. It was concluded that a significant relationship exists between employees' attitudes and workforce management practices. In Belgium, Marescaux et al. (2013) studied the role of basic need satisfaction in workforce management and noted that five practices are generally referred to as soft workforce management practices designed to develop and empower employees. These five practices are career development, training, employee participation, development appraisal, and mentoring. In India, Chand (2010) explored the impact of some selected workforce management practices on the quality of service and performance of organisations. These practices are recruitment and selection, planning, job analysis and job design, training and development, employee consultation and cooperation, and employee compensation. Naidu and Chand (2014) adopted this same set of practices to analyse the best workforce management practices in Samoa and Tonga. The study concluded that best practices differ in both study areas due to certain internal and external environmental influences.

In Jordan, Aladwan et al. (2015) assessed the effects of workforce management practices on employees' organisational commitment. The major practices assessed were recruitment and selection, training and development, performance appraisal, rewards, and benefits. Similarly, Aboramadan et al. (2019) assessed the impact of workforce management practices on organisational commitment in Palestine. The practices assessed include selection and recruitment, training and development, performance appraisal, reward and compensation, and job security. It was found that the workforce management practices adopted significantly influence workers' organisational commitment. From the dimension of 'green' workforce management, which is geared towards aligning the workforce management practices of organisations with the management of environmental systems, Ojo and Raman (2019) posit that workforce management practices such as recruitment and selection, training and development, compensation and reward, performance management, and empowerment and participation are major practices that can lead to pro-environmental information technology practices by employees in Malaysia.

From the numerous existing literature sources on workforce management, it is evident that most of the studies draw from Pfeffer's (1994) 16 practices. Although these studies assessed the practices that best suit the domain in which they were investigated and accompanied by the theory backing such studies, some workforce management practices remain reoccurring factors. Drawing from the diverse studies existing on workforce management practices, below are some of the most common practices that have been explored:

(1)  Decentralised decision-making.
(2)  Employee and labour relations.
(3)  Employee participation.
(4)  Employment security.
(5)  Health and safety/safe working conditions.
(6)  Human resource information systems.
(7)  Job analysis and design.
(8)  Management and appraisal of performance.
(9)  Mentoring.
(10)  Planning.
(11)  Recruitment and selection.
(12)  Reward/compensation system.
(13)  Self-management of teams.
(14)  Training and development.

## Workforce Management in the Construction Industry

Managing modern-day construction projects has proven to be increasingly challenging owing to many complex factors. To meet these challenges, it is necessary to employ efficient management throughout project delivery. Moreover, given the dynamic environment and multifaceted project-based operations, construction organisations must develop well-structured workforce management practices to manage their employees (Zhai & Liu, 2009). More so, there is a consensus that workforce management practices should be encouraged since they have a desirable effect on employee and organisational performance (Wright et al., 2003).

The construction industry is labour-intensive, characterised by project-based work for a determined period (Druker et al., 1996). This is because most construction projects are unique. Ordinarily, they are delivered by labour outsourcing, joint ventures, subcontracting, or creating a new organisation specifically set up for project delivery (Rubery et al., 2004). Loosemore et al. (2003) also noted that the construction industry's nature is 'low tech' and requires considerable human input. However, there is a shortage of required skills within the industry (Werner, 2017), leading to the industry relying heavily on outsourced labour (ILO, 2001; Rubery et al., 2004). Unfortunately, despite the industry's over-dependence on human input, little attention has been given to properly managing its workers (Loosemore et al., 2003; Othman et al., 2012). It has been observed that the use of procurement options which allow organisations to get labour from outside has affected the commitment of most organisations to invest in the training and management of their in-house workforce (Dainty et al., 2004).

There is no gainsaying that as construction works differ from project to project, changes in the knowledge and skills required from one project to another abound (Dainty et al., 2007). Only through appropriate management of the available skills can the proper transfer of knowledge from project to project be obtained. Also, high labour turnover is a common occurrence in the construction industry, leading to skills shortages (Chan et al., 2011; Erlick & Grabelsky, 2005; McGrath-Champ et al., 2011). Olsen et al. (2012) reckoned that skills shortage is not necessarily the number of workers unavailable but the unavailability of adequately trained skilled and productive workers within the industry. This is a pointer to the fact that effectively managing the available skills within the industry will go a long way in attaining construction organisations' goals.

Egan (1998) acknowledged the need to commit to people as a pertinent driver to foster change and progress within the construction industry. Hence, construction professionals need careful management and development to contribute to the organisation's performance and be retained in the long run (Dainty et al., 2000). According to Guest (1989), workforce management should be considered in the framework of organisational theory and policies to maximise organisational inclusion, worker engagement, flexibility, and quality of work. However, the construction sector has maintained methods that represent a workforce management framework of 'hard' systems, where workers are treated like any other factor of production (Druker et al., 1996). In the United States, Yankov and Kleiner (2001) noted that while several experts in the construction industry are coming up with theories that could help improve the management of workers, the key to achieving successful implementation of these theories is motivation. This motivation of employees can be attained through encouraging workers' participation, worker recognition, giving workers a sense of belonging in teams, management commitment, and effective training of the employees. Huemann et al. (2007) also explored workforce management in project-oriented organisations and developed a model centred on the well-being and ethical treatment of an employee at the completion of individual projects. Just as in the mainstream workforce management literature that holds recruitment strongly as a key practice, Huemann et al. (2007) developed model also recognises the significance of recruitment. However, it further proposes that recruited employees should be allocated to projects based on the needs of such a project and the employees' expertise and experience to work on such a project and with particular clients. Apart from recruitment, the need for on-the-job training and quality feedback while on a specific project to help improve employees' career development was also noted. At the end of the project, three possible ways of treating employees ethically were proposed. This includes:

(1) assigning employees to the new project immediately after the completion of one;
(2) assigning employees to future projects that require experience and expertise; and
(3) suspending the employees' services until a new project emerges.

In China, Zhai et al. (2014) investigated the role of workforce management practices in improving organisational learning. Using Structural Equation Modelling (a second-generation multivariate analysis), the study concluded that the practices of workforce management in China's construction industry are multidimensional. This includes creating a job description, participation, training, staffing, and rewards. Zhai et al. (2014) study further concluded that the practices adopted within the industry positively influence the organisation's performance.

### Research Focus in Construction Workforce Management

The labour-intensive nature of the construction industry has attracted research from diverse aspects to protect the industry's human resources while delivering successful projects in the process. Assessing recent trends in workforce management research within the construction industry has become significant for properly understanding this book's contribution to the existing body of knowledge. A bibliometric review that allows for identifying and mapping scientific knowledge areas using evidential research patterns and boundaries (Olawumi & Chan, 2018) was adopted to review recent studies on workforce management in construction. In doing this, relevant literature was extracted from the Scopus database since Scopus is one of the major scientific research databases that has gained prominence among researchers in recent times (Guz & Rushchitsky, 2009). This database substantially overlaps with other scientific databases, such as the Web of Science (Aghimien et al., 2020). The search for related literature was conducted using keywords such as 'human resource management', OR 'HRM', strategic human resource management', OR 'talent management', OR 'workforce management', AND 'construction', OR 'construction industry'. These keywords were searched in both journal articles and conference proceedings published between 2010 and 2023. The choice of extracting information from both journals and conference proceedings was premised on the fact that both sources have been adjudged as reliable means of academic information owing to their peer-review nature (Aghimien et al., 2020; Ramos-Rodríguez & Ruíz-Navarro, 2004; Zheng et al., 2016). Also, the selected time frame (2010–2023) was chosen because of the need for recency in the information gathered. The Scopus initial extraction gave 3,489 documents from different fields of study. By refining the search using 'engineering' alone as the field of study (since that is where construction is located) and the English language as the preferred publication language, a total of 686 documents were retained for further evaluation. Using the extracted bibliographic data, a co-occurrence network visualisation was developed using Visualisation of Similarities Viewer (VOSviewer). According to Van Eck and Waltman (2014), the VOSviewer is software that displays only the nodes in a bibliometric network and its visualisation through distance-based visualisations. This network visualisation was used to understand the area of research focus on workforce management in construction-related studies. This software has been favoured in recent bibliometric studies due to its ease of use and ready availability (Aghimien et al., 2020; Nazir et al., 2020).

Analysis of the extracted documents revealed that 470 were from conference proceedings, while 216 were from journals. In line with Aghimien et al. (2020), the high number of publications from conference proceedings can be attributed to the rigour, long review period and publication in journals which slows down the publication rate in this medium. Fig. 2.1 shows the number of publications on workforce management in construction from 2013 to 2023. More documents emanated in 2014 and 2016, with a continuous rise and fall in the number of documents from 2016 to 2023. Only eight documents emanated from 2023 because the bibliographic data search was conducted in the early half of the year (April 2023). There is the possibility of increased publications as the year evolves.

All the documents originated from 74 different countries. Some of these countries overlap due to collaborations between authors and some authors having more than one affiliation and country. As such, Fig. 2.2 shows only countries with at least 10 documents. The figure shows that the USA ($f = 241$) and China ($f = 106$) have the highest number of publications. These two countries also have the highest number of cited documents, with the USA having 2,181 and China having 1,211 citations. Next is the UK ($f = 49$), Australia ($f = 41$), Canada ($f = 41$), South Africa ($f = 35$), Hong Kong ($f = 26$), and South Korea ($f = 20$).

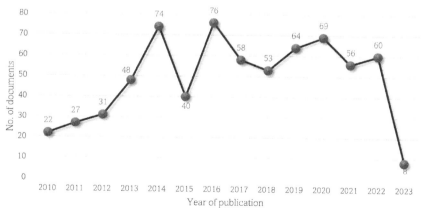

Fig. 2.1.    Publication Per Year. *Source*: Author's compilation (2023)

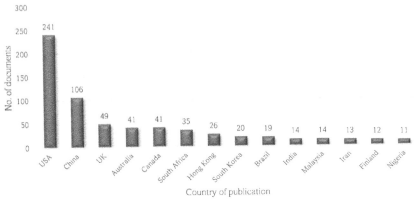

Fig. 2.2. Countries with at Least 10 Publications. *Source*: Author's compilation (2023)

These countries have invested significantly in workforce management research to improve construction projects through effective management of construction human resources.

Based on the bibliographic data gathered, to understand the area of concentration of workforce management research in construction-related fields, a co-occurring network analysis was created using VOSviewer. For keyword extraction, the predefined minimum number in VOSviewer is 5. However, to avoid extracting an overly large number of keywords that are not significant to the study's context, the minimum extraction was set at 15. This is owing to the large number of initial keywords of 5,267 observed for all 686 documents under examination. Based on the set minimum threshold, 69 keywords grouped into four distinct clusters became evident. Table 2.1 shows the clusters of the co-occurring keywords.

Cluster 1 – arbitrarily named 'Occupational health and safety', has the highest number of keywords (23 items) grouped as one. These keywords include the construction industry, construction managers, construction sites, construction activities, occupational risks, risk management, risk assessment, risk perception, safety, safety engineering, safety performance, construction safety, safety management, hazards, and health & safety, among others. These keywords relate to the occupational health and safety of construction workers.

Cluster 2 – arbitrarily named 'human resource and project management', has 21 keywords extracted. These keywords include human resource management, information management, decision-making, building information management, information theory, project management, quality management, management science, and construction equipment, among others. These keywords all relate to studies on human resource and project management.

Cluster 3 – arbitrarily named 'workforce management and sustainable construction process' – has 13 keywords. These keywords are construction projects, construction process, productivity, lean construction, lean production, decision-making, sustainable development, waste management, intelligent buildings,

Table 2.1   Co-occurring keywords

| Keyword | f | TLS | Keyword | f | TLS |
|---|---|---|---|---|---|
| **Cluster 1 (*occupational health and safety*)** | | | **Cluster 2 (*human resource and Project management*)** | | |
| Construction industry | 290 | 1545 | Human resource management | 664 | 2829 |
| Occupational risks | 103 | 634 | Project management | 289 | 1473 |
| Construction workers | 73 | 405 | Construction | 94 | 529 |
| Accident prevention | 71 | 504 | Contractors | 52 | 287 |
| Managers | 68 | 415 | Information management | 45 | 203 |
| Construction safety | 58 | 378 | Construction companies | 39 | 246 |
| Safety engineering | 58 | 351 | Structural design | 39 | 212 |
| Construction sites | 51 | 296 | Building information model - BIM | 30 | 148 |
| Risk assessment | 47 | 267 | Design and construction | 30 | 115 |
| Risk management | 47 | 283 | Construction equipment | 27 | 155 |
| Personnel training | 46 | 253 | Costs | 26 | 131 |
| Safety management | 40 | 255 | Design | 26 | 114 |
| Accidents | 39 | 228 | Life cycle | 24 | 126 |
| Construction manager | 28 | 174 | Quality control | 18 | 85 |
| Hazards | 22 | 148 | Quality management | 18 | 84 |
| Safety performance | 21 | 145 | Building information modelling | 17 | 87 |
| Health | 20 | 115 | Construction project management | 17 | 82 |

| | | |
|---|---|---|
| Workers' | 20 | 122 |
| Safety | 19 | 147 |
| Disasters | 18 | 97 |
| Health and safety | 16 | 101 |
| Risk perception | 16 | 129 |
| Construction activities | 15 | 100 |
| **Cluster 3 (workforce management and sustainable construction process)** | | |
| Construction projects | 134 | 725 |
| Sustainable development | 50 | 231 |
| Lean production | 46 | 239 |
| Lean construction | 40 | 220 |
| Productivity | 40 | 213 |
| Knowledge management | 29 | 130 |
| Project managers | 21 | 131 |
| Construction process | 20 | 100 |
| Planning | 17 | 71 |
| Production control | 17 | 81 |
| Behavioural research | 16 | 87 |
| Intelligent buildings | 15 | 78 |
| Waste management | 15 | 82 |

| | | |
|---|---|---|
| Information theory | 17 | 102 |
| Buildings | 15 | 73 |
| Management science | 15 | 79 |
| **Cluster 4 (construction workforce education and development)** | | |
| Construction management | 70 | 401 |
| Decision making | 49 | 254 |
| Students | 49 | 272 |
| Engineering education | 35 | 192 |
| Budget control | 33 | 174 |
| Education | 24 | 152 |
| Curricula | 21 | 120 |
| Construction professionals | 20 | 134 |
| Personnel | 18 | 90 |
| Commerce | 17 | 92 |
| Bridges | 15 | 70 |
| Construction organizations | 15 | 76 |
| Teaching | 15 | 97 |

product control, behavioural research, knowledge management, and planning. These keywords relate to workforce management and the sustainable construction process.

Cluster 4 – arbitrarily named 'construction workforce education and development' has 12 keywords. These keywords include construction management, construction organisations, construction profession, personnel, students, engineering education, education, teaching, and curricula, among others. These keywords can be regarded as construction workforce education and development.

Based on the bibliometric analysis conducted and careful examination of the extracted documents, it is evident that studies related to construction workforce management since 2010 have been directed more towards the safety of the construction workforce. This is depicted in the top cited articles extracted as they were published on issues relating to the safety of construction workers. Park and Kim (2013) developed a framework to manage construction safety, and the study has gained traction among researchers, with 237 citations recorded. Cheng et al. (2011) also evaluated the performance of ultra-wideband technology for tracking construction resources in harsh environments and has garnered 201 citations. The study by Yan et al. (2017), which has garnered over 180 citations, focused on using smart wearables to prevent musculoskeletal disorders among construction workers. The studies and others highlight the rising need for careful attention to occupational health and safety within the construction industry. Also, from the bibliometric assessments, it was noticed that research focussed on using information technology to better manage project information and resources for better service delivery in construction. More so, the focus has been placed on workforce management, sustainable construction processes, as well as education and development of construction workers. These identified focus areas further bolster the need for this book, as not much concentration has been placed on workforce management in the current era of pervasive technologies.

## Challenges Facing Effective Workforce Management in the Construction Industry

Over the years, construction workforce management has faced several challenges preventing most organisations' human resource management departments from performing effectively. Implementing and monitoring changes in workforce management strategies pose a challenge in the construction sector due to the mobile nature of construction workers (Zhai & Liu, 2009). This mobile nature of construction workers means that human resource practitioners often need to hire skilled and experienced construction workers on a project-specific basis. Finding the correct talent requires both time and effort, with each project being unique. Moreover, the industry, by its very nature, operates on very tight timelines for project delivery. Therefore, attracting and maintaining critical skills is an important component for any organisation. To this end, Hillebrandt and Cannon (1990) noted that a major problem facing human resource practitioners in the construction industry is the fact that the sector often needs a particular set of skills that can be difficult to find. Aside from the difficulty in getting the right skills, it was also noted that construction teams are temporary, there are unexpected changes in resource demands during construction, and the industry's professional and managerial abilities continue to evolve. These are all crucial challenges to the effective management of the construction workforce.

The problem of getting the right skills has become persistent within the construction industry (Dainty et al., 2007; Yankov & Kleiner, 2001). Construction projects are unique, implying that the knowledge and methods required for each project might differ. However, lessons learnt on a project are transferable to other projects for more effective project delivery. The problem of a skills shortage that has continued to bedevil the industry is a pointer to the need to efficiently manage and retain the few available skills to ensure the proper transfer of knowledge gained from a project to others in the future (Dainty et al., 2007). Aside from skill shortages, studies have noted that construction workers are not given enough training and are often not motivated to perform as expected. For instance, Othman et al. (2012) submitted that inadequate training is a key challenge affecting the effective management of the construction workforce in Malaysia. The story is not different in countries like India, Iran, Nigeria, and South Africa, where issues relating to inadequate training have continued to hinder the effective management of construction employees (Aghimien et al., 2023; Ameh & Daniel, 2017; Samuel & Timmaraju, 2015; Tabassi & Abu Bakar, 2009). In the view of Tabassi and Abu Bakar (2009), the training of construction workers can be improved through a continuous effort by company owners to invest in the short- and long-term development of their workers and by government support through incentives and policies that encourage self-learning such as creating certification of fitness for occupation.

The construction industry has been described as an industry with diverse participants coming together to ensure projects are delivered successfully. While this diversity in the industry makes the industry unique, it can also be a source of nightmare for human resource practitioners if not adequately managed. Gunjan (2021) noted that the construction industry houses people of diverse ages, gender, ethnicity, language, marital status, and beliefs, among others. It is often challenging to bring together the view of this diverse workforce, and as such, effectively, this set of various workers becomes challenging. This situation is made worse by discrimination, prejudice, and ethnocentrism that are common within the construction domain (Chan, 2005; Harold & Kumar, 2012). However, Haizelden et al. (2019) have noted that the productivity of construction organisations depends on how well human resource managers can manage their diverse workforce.

In Canada, the Construction Sector Council (CSC) (2003) observed four key challenges deterring the effectiveness of workforce management. These are:

(1)  trying to match the forecasted demand for a capable and qualified skilled workforce with the future needs of the industry;
(2)  ensuring that a flexible, consistent and responsive apprenticeship system is created within construction organisations;
(3)  ensuring that an innovative training system is in place to maintain available skills; and
(4)  ensuring ease of mobility of workers to meet the demand for these across the country.

As earlier noted, the construction industry itself is challenged by several issues, some of which are related to its human resources. The challenges identified by CSC (2003) can, therefore, be linked to industry-specific issues such as an ageing workforce, shortage of required skills, poor image of the industry, which makes it a less viable choice of career, inadequate investment in training and poor health and safety conditions in the industry among others. The situation is these same developing countries like India, Nigeria, Pakistan, and South Africa where diversity, nature of the construction environment, high labour turnover, unsafe working environment, working conditions, employers and government demands have all been observed (Aghimien et al., 2022; Ameh & Daniel, 2017; Hanif & Imran, 2017; Orga & Ogbo, 2012; Samuel & Timmaraju, 2015).

Several other challenges truncating the effectiveness of workforce management in the construction industry have been noted in past studies. Othman et al. (2012) in Malaysia observed issues relating to ineffective communication, poor teamwork, poor personnel evaluation, and poor reward system. In India, Samuel and Timmaraju (2015) observed challenges such as ineffective recruiting and retaining systems, inadequate competencies, unfavourable working environment, gender equality and conflict resolution, among others. Also, in India, Sethi and Kataria (2017) observed that poor planning, overreliance on the transient workforce, the image of the construction industry, poor work–life balance, health and safety hazards, and abdication of workforce management function to the project manager are some of the key challenges faced by large construction organisations. In Pakistan, Hanif and Imran (2017) noted similar challenges are deterring the success of human resource practitioners in managing the construction workforce. Issues relating to skill shortage, inadequate strategy to retain trained and experienced construction workers, and poor transfer of knowledge within construction organisation, especially when such knowledge gained was not promoted by the management of the organisation.

Based on the studies above, it is evident that the challenges facing construction workforce management are numerous and similar in most countries' construction industry. Furthermore, most of these problems emanate from issues facing the construction industry itself. As such, addressing the issues facing the industry can be the first step towards attaining effective workforce management in the construction industry. Below are some of the key challenges, as noted in past studies:

(1) Difficulty in ensuring gender equality.
(2) Difficulty in motivating employees.
(3) Difficulty in recruiting the right talent.
(4) Difficulty in retaining skilled workforce/high labour turnover.
(5) Difficulty in training employees.
(6) Evolving nature of professional and managerial abilities.
(7) Inflexible work structure.
(8) Inflexible working hours.
(9) Insatiable client demands.
(10) Lack of communication between managers and employees.
(11) Managing the problem of knowledge transfer.

(12)  Managing the work-life balance of employees.
(13)  Mobile workforce/Temporary nature of construction teams.
(14)  Organisational and cultural diversity.
(15)  Over-reliance on transient workers.
(16)  Poor conflict resolution.
(17)  Poor performance evaluation.
(18)  Poor reward and compensation system.
(19)  Poor succession planning.
(20)  Poor teamwork among employees.
(21)  Skill shortage.
(22)  The challenge of creating the healthy and safe working environment.
(23)  Unfavourable government policies and legislation.
(24)  Unfavourable working conditions.

## Improving the Effectiveness of Workforce Management in the Construction Industry

The importance of managing the construction workforce for better project delivery and organisational performance has been reiterated in past studies. Ghatta et al. (2022) noted that workforce management factors can impact construction projects' cost and time performance. Pinto and Holt (1988) noted that effective workforce management is a recipe for project success. It, therefore, becomes crucial to find the ways of improving workforce management in the industry to ensure better industry performance. Molaney (1997) hinted that construction organisations that seek to succeed must put strategies in place to effective management their workforce. These strategies will be shaped by the company's vision, culture and structure, its technologies, workers' diversity and skill availability. In the quest to ensure the successful completion of sustainable projects, Othman et al. (2012) identified some important factors to improve workforce management which significantly impacts successful project delivery. These factors include improved communication between workers and human resource managers, the use of well-trained project managers, ensuring the adequate workforce is on a project, ensuring team participation, regular evaluation of workers and managers, and providing effective training to workers and human resource managers.

Malani and Kambetar (2013) mentioned that workforce management in construction relies on critical success factors such as hiring the right talent, ensuring the right process is used, developing employee skills, motivation and retention, building a culture of innovation, and putting succession plans in place. Similarly, Sethi and Kataria (2017) suggested that for effective workforce management within the construction industry, organisations must consider several factors. These include creating a workforce diversity policy that is clearly communicated within the company, providing training, ensuring job roles are clearly defined, and adopting flexible schemes that will improve workers' work–life balance. Studies have earlier noted the important role of employee work-life balance in the overall success of project delivery (Dlamini et al., 2019; Lingard et al., 2007). As such, Aghimien et al. (2022) suggested using factors such as leave, health and wellness, and work flexibility, among others, in improving workers' work and life relationships and effectively managing them in the process. Aghimien et al. (2023) noted that the success of workforce management in construction is dependent on the readiness of organisation owners and human resource practitioners to put measures in place to promote a safe and healthy working environment, address diversity and improve the working conditions of their workers through flexible work. Deloitte's (2020) report noted that adopting strategies designed to improve their workforce's working condition tend to positively impact not just the employees but also the organisation.

Based on the aforementioned, it is evident that construction organisations need to formulate strategies that will help them manage their workforce effectively. Also, some requirements must be in place for these organisations to succeed in managing their workforce. Some of these success factors are summarised below:

(1) Clearly defined job roles.
(2) Create and implement a workforce diversity policy.
(3) Employ the required number of workers to avoid overloading of few available workers.
(4) Encourage team participation.
(5) Ensure regular evaluation of workers and managers.
(6) Improve working conditions of workers through flexible schemes.
(7) Improve communication between workers and managers.
(8) Promote a safe and healthy working environment.
(9) Promote a culture of innovation among workers.
(10) Promote work–life balance.
(11) Provide training for workers and managers.
(12) Put measures in place to address diversity issues.
(13) Put measures in place to ensure retention and proper succession.
(14) Tailor-made motivation systems.
(15) Use of trained personnel.

## Summary

The construction industry worldwide is important to the economic growth of the countries where they operate. Other industries feel the importance of this industry as construction produces the structures needed by most other industries to operate successfully. The construction industry depends greatly on the input of people who serve as the industry's workforce. The importance of the construction workforce has led to significant studies on how they are managed within the industry. These studies have focussed on occupational health and safety, workforce and information management in construction, workforce management and sustainable construction process, and construction workforce education and development. However, despite these studies, managing the construction workforce has proven to be challenging over time due to factors relating to the nature of the industry itself. Challenges such as skill shortage, unhealthy working environment, and poor image of the industry, among others, have made the construction industry unappealing to young prospective workers. Also, while the construction industry is rich in diversity, this has been a major source of problems for workforce management. To improve workforce management and attain better-performing construction organisations, careful recruitment, effective training, providing a safe working environment, putting policies to promote diversity, and ensuring innovativeness, among others, are essential.

# References

Aboramadan, M., Albashiti, B., Alharazin, H., & Dahleez, K. A. (2019). Human resources management practices and organisational commitment in higher education – The mediating role of work engagement. *International Journal of Educational Management, 34*(1), 154–174.

Aghimien, D. O, Aigbavboa, C. O., Oke, A. E., & Thwala, W. D. (2020). Mapping out research focus for robotics and automation in construction-related studies. *Journal of Engineering Design and Technology, 18*(5), 1063–1079.

Aghimien, D. O., Aigbavboa, C. O., Oke, A. E., & Thwala, W. D. (2021). *Construction digitalisation – A capability maturity model for construction organisations.* Routledge, UK.

Aghimien, D., Aigbavboa, C. O., Thwala, W. D., Chileshe, N., & Dlamini, B. J. (2022). Help, I am not coping with my job! – A work-life balance strategy for the Eswatini construction industry. *Engineering, Construction and Architectural Management*, ahead-of-print. https://doi.org/10.1108/ECAM-11-2021-1060.

Aghimien, L. M., Aigbavboa, C. O., Anumba, C. J., & Thwala, W. D. (2023). A confirmatory factor analysis of the challenges of effective management of the construction workforce in South Africa. *Journal of Engineering, Design and Technology, 21*(4), 1134–1152.

Agyekum, K., Kukah, A. S., & Amudjie, J. (2022). The impact of COVID-19 on the construction industry in Ghana: The case of some selected firms. *Journal of Engineering, Design and Technology, 20*(1), 222–244.

Aigbavboa, C. O., Aghimien, D. O., Thwala, W. D., & Ngozwana, N. (2022). Unprepared industry meet pandemic: COVID-19 and the South Africa construction industry. *Journal of Engineering Design and Technology, 20*(1), 183–200.

Aktar, A., & Pangil, F. (2018). Mediating role of organisational commitment in the relationship between human resource management practices and employee engagement: Does black box stage exist? *International Journal of Sociology and Social Policy, 38*(7–8), 606–636.

Aladwan, K., Bhanugopan, R., & D'Netto, B. (2015). The effects of human resource management practices on employees' organisational commitment. *International Journal of Organizational Analysis, 23*(3), 472–492.

Alfes, K., Shantz, A., Bailey, C., & Soane, E. (2013). The link between perceived human resource management practices, engagement and employee behaviour: A moderated mediation model. *The International Journal of Human Resource Management, 24*(2), 1–22.

Ameh, O. J., & Daniel, E. I. (2017). Human resource management in the Nigerian construction firms: Practices and challenges. *Journal of Construction Business and Management, 1*(2), 46–53.

Ameyaw, E. E., Pärn, E., Chan, A. P. C., Owusu-Manu, D., Edward, D. J., & Darko, A. (2017). Corrupt practices in the construction industry: Survey of Ghanaian experience. *Journal of Management in Engineering, 33*(6), 1–11.

Amri, T., & Marey-Pérez, M. (2020). Impact of Covid-19 on Oman's construction industry. *Technium Social Sciences Journal, 9,* 661–670.

Anaman, K. A., & Osei-Amponsah, C. (2007). Analysis of the causality links between the growth of the construction industry and the growth of the macroeconomy in Ghana. *Journal of Construction Management and Economics, 25,* 951–96.

Armstrong, M., & Murlis, H. (2007). *Reward management: A handbook of remuneration strategy and practice* (5th ed.). Kogan Page.

Arndt, C., Davies, R., Gabriel, S., Harris, L., Makrelov, K., Modise, B., Robinson, S., Simbanegavi, W., van Seventer, D., & Anderson, L. (2020). Impact of Covid-19 on the South African economy. https://sa-tied.wider.unu.edu/sites/default/files/pdf/SA-TIED-WP-111.pdf (accessed 10 August 2020).

Ayodele, E. O., & Alabi, O. M. (2011). Abandonment of construction projects in Nigeria: Causes and effects. *Journal of Emerging Trends in Economics and Management Sciences, 2*(2), 142–145.

Beer, M., Spector, B., Lawrence, P., Quinn Mills, D., & Walton, R. (1984). *Managing human assets.* The Free Press.

Bertelsen, S., & Koskela, L. (2004). *Construction beyond lean: A new understanding of construction management.* Proceedings of the International Group Lean Conference, August 2004, Elsinore, Denmark.

Bilau, A. A., Ajagbe, M. A., Kigbu, H. H, & Sholanke, A. B. (2015). Review of shortage of skilled craftsmen in small and medium construction firms in Nigeria. *Journal of Environment and Earth Science, 5*(15), 98–110.

Bowen, H. R. (1953). *Social responsibilities of the businessman.* Harper and Row.

Boxall, P., & Macky, K. (2009). Research and theory on high-performance work systems: Progressing the high-involvement stream. *Human Resource Management Journal, 19*(1), 3–23.

Chan, A. (2005). The challenges of human resource management. Retrieved on July 11, 2020 from http://ezinearticles.com

Chan, P., Clarke, L., & Dainty, A. (2011). The dynamics of migrant employment in construction: can supply of skilled labour ever match demand? In Ruhs & B. Anderson (Eds.). *Who needs migrant workers? Labour shortages, immigration and public policy* (pp. 225–255). Oxford: Oxford University Press.

Chand, M. (2010). The impact of HRM practices on service quality, customer satisfaction and performance in the Indian hotel sector. *The International Journal of Human Resource Management, 21*(4), 551–566.

Chandler, G. N., & McEvoy, G. M. (2000). Human resource management, TQM, and firm performance in small and medium-size enterprises. *Entrepreneurship Theory and Practice, 25,* 43–57.

Cheng, T., Venugopal, M., Teizer, J., & Vela, P. A. (2011). Performance evaluation of ultra-wideband technology for construction resource location tracking in harsh environments. *Automation in Construction, 20*(8), 1173–1184.

Chitkara, K. (2004). *Construction project management, planning, scheduling and controlling* (4th ed.). Tata McGraw Hill.

Construction Sector Council. (2003). Construction Industry Human Resource Challenges and Responses, Ottawa, Ontario.

Dainty, A. R. J, Harty, T. E., & Neale, R. H. (2000). Improving employee resourcing within large construction organisations. In A. Akintoye (Ed.), 16th Annual ARCOM Conference, Glasgow Caledonian University, 6–8 September 2000.

Dainty, A., Ison, S. G., & Root, D. (2004). Bridging the skills gap: A regionally driven strategy for resolving the construction labour market crisis. *Engineering, Construction and Architectural Management, 11*(4), 275–283.

Dainty, A., Green, S., & Bagilhole, B. (2007). *People and culture in construction.* Taylor and Francis.

Deloitte. (2020). *The social enterprise at work: Paradox as a path forward.* https://www2.deloitte.com/content/dam/Deloitte/at/Documents/human-capital/at-hc-trends-2020.pdf

DeNisi, A. S., & Smith, C. E. (2014). Performance appraisal, performance management, and firm-level performance: A review, a proposed model, and new directions for future research. *The Academy of Management Annals, 8*(1), 127–179.

Department of Statistics Malaysia. (2020). *Malaysia economic performance second quarter 2020.* Department of Statistics Malaysia Official Portal. www.dosm.gov.my/v1/index.php?r=column/cthemeByCatandcat=100andbul_id=NS9TNE9yeHJ1eHB6cHV1aXBNQlNUZz09andmenu_id=TE5CRUZCblh4ZTZMODZIbmk2aWRRQT09 [Accessed on 14 April 2023].

Dessler, G. (2015). *Human resource management* (14th ed.). Pearson Education.

Dixit, S., Pandey, A. K., Mandal, S. T., & Bansal, S. (2017). A study of enabling factors affecting construction productivity: Indian scenario. *International Journal of Civil Engineering and Technology, 8*(6), 741–758.

Dlamini, B., Oshodi, O. S., Aigbavboa, C., & Thwala, A. (2019). *Work-life balance practices in the construction industry of Swaziland.* Proceedings of 11th Construction Industry Development Board (CIDB) Postgraduate Research Conference, Johannesburg, South Africa, 28–30 July.

Druker, J., White, G., Hegewisch, A., & Mayne, L. (1996). Between hard and soft HRM: Human resource management in the construction industry. *Construction Management and Economics, 14*(5), 405–416.

Durdyev, S., & Ismail, S. (2012). Pareto analysis of on-site productivity constraints and improvement techniques in construction industry. *Scientific Research and Essays, 7*(4), 824–833.

Edgar, F., & Geare, A. (2005). HRM practice and employee attitudes: Different measures – different results. *Personnel Review, 34*(5), 534–549.

Egan, J. (1998). *Rethinking construction,* London: HMSO Publisher.

Elkhalifa, A. A. (2012). *The Construction and Building Materials Industries for Sustainable Development in Developing Countries: Appropriate and Innovative Building Materials and Technologies for Housing in Sudan* [PhD thesis]. University of Camerino, Italy.

Erlick, M., & Grabelsky, J. (2005). Standing at the crossroads: The building trade in the 21 century. *Labor History, 46*(4), 421–445.

European Commission. (2020). *Construction sector.* https://ec.europa.eu/growth/sectors/construction_en

Farnham, D. (2000). *Employee relations in context* (2nd ed.). CIPD.

Fox, P. W. (2003). *Construction industry development: Analysis and synthesis of contributing factors.* An unpublished Thesis submitted for the degree of Doctor of Philosophy to the School of Construction Management and Property Faculty of Built Environment and Engineering Queensland University of Technology, Queensland, Australia.

Gamil, Y., & Alhagar, A. (2020). The impact of pandemic crisis on the survival of construction industry: A case of COVID-19. *Mediterranean Journal of Social Sciences, 11*(4), 122–128.

Ghatta, M. S., Bassioni, H. A., & Gaid, E. F. (2022). Human resources management influence on projects performance: A study of contractors' professionals working on construction projects in Egypt. *IOP Conference Series: Earth and Environmental Science, 1056,* 1–9.

Grimshaw, D., & Rubery, J. (2007). Economics and HRM. In P. Boxall, J. Purcell, & P. Wright (Eds.), *Oxford handbook of human resource management.* Oxford University Press.

Guest, D. (1989). Personnel and HRM: Can you tell the difference? *Personnel Management, 21*(1), 48–51.

Guest, D. E. (1987). Human resource management and industrial relations. *Journal of Management Studies*, *14*(5), 503–21.

Gunjan, S. (2021). Workforce diversity. Retrieved on June 25, 2021 from www.business-managementideas.com/humanresource-management-2/workforce-diversity/20385

Guz, A. N., & Rushchitsky, J. J. (2009). Scopus: A system for the evaluation of scientific journals. *International Applied Mechanics*, *45*(4), 351–362.

Haizelden, J., Marasini, R., & Daniel, E. (2019). An analysis of diversity management in the construction industry: A case study of a main contractor. In C. Gorse & C. J. Neilson (Eds.), Proceedings of the 35th Annual ARCOM Conference, 2-4 September 2019, Leeds, pp. 465–474.

Hanif, M., & Imran, M. (2017). Prevalent problems of HR practices in organisations and their solution: Pakistani context. *Science International (Lahore)*, *29*(2), 481–488.

Har, W. C., Tan, B. I., Loke, S., & Hsien, L. V. (2010). The impact of HRM practices on KM: A conceptual model. *Australian Journal of Basic and Applied Sciences*, *4*(12), 5281–6291.

Harmon, J., Fairfield, K. D., & Wirtenberg, J. (2010). Missing an opportunity: HR leadership and sustainability. *People and Strategy*, *33*(1), 16–21.

Harold, A. P., & Kumar, V. R. (2012). Managing workforce diversity: Issues and challenges, SAGE Open, 2(2), 1–15.

Haupt, T. C., & Harinarain, N. (2016). The image of the construction industry and its employment attractiveness. *Acta Structilia*, *23*(2), 79–108.

Heimgartner, J. (2020). *Long-Term effects of COVID-19 in the construction industry*. www.engineering.com/BIM/ArticleID/20445/Long-Term-Effects-of-COVID-19-in-the-Construction-Industry.aspx

Hillebrandt, P., & Cannon, J. (1990). Growth and diversification. In *The modern construction firm*. Palgrave Macmillan.

Huemann, M., Keegan, A., & Turner, T. R. (2007). Human resource management in the project – oriented company: A review. *International Journal of Project Management*, *25*, 315–325.

Huselid, M. A. (1995). The impact of human resource management practices on turnover, productivity, and corporate financial performance. *Academy of Management Journal*, *38*, 635–672.

Huselid, M. A., & Becker, B. E. (2011). Bridging micro and macro domains: Workforce differentiation and strategic human resource management. *Journal of Management*, *37*(2), 421–428.

Ibrahim, R., Roy, M. H., Ahmed, Z. U., & Imtiaz, G. (2010). Analysing the dynamics of the global construction industry: Past, present and future. *Benchmarking: An International Journal*, *17*(2), 232–252.

Imperatori, B. (2017). People Engagement and new fashions in HRM practices: Social responsibility, digital transformation, happiness and well-being. In *Engagement and disengagement at work*. Springer Briefs in Business. Springer.

International Labor Organization (ILO). (2001). *The construction industry in the twenty-first century: Its image, employment prospects and skill requirements*. ILO. www.ilo.org/public/english/standards/relm/gb/docs/gb283/pdf/tmcitr.pdf

Kazaz, A., & Ulubeyli, S. (2009). Strategic management practices in Turkish construction firms. *Journal of Management in Engineering*, *25*(4), 185–194.

Kinnie, N., & Swart, J. (2016). Human resource management and organisational performance: In search of the HR advantage. In T. Redman, A. Wilkinson, & T. Dundon (Eds.), *Contemporary human resource management: Text and cases* (5th ed.). Pearson Publishing.

Lange, J. E., & Mills, D. Q. (1979). *Construction industry: Balance wheel of the economy*. Lexington Books.

Lingard, H., Brown, K., Bradley, L., Bailey, C., & Townsend, K. (2007). Improving employees' work-life balance in the construction industry: Project alliance case study. *Journal of Construction Engineering and Management*, *133*(10), 807–815.

Loosemore, M., Dainty, A. R. J., & Lingard, H. (2003). *Human resource management in construction projects – Strategic and operational approaches.* Taylor and Francis.

Malani, Z. A. K., & Kambetar, A. R. (2013). Management of human resource in construction industry. *International Journal of Engineering Research and Technology, 6*(2), 353–362.

Marchington, M., & Wilkinson, A. (2005). *Human resource management at work: People management and development* (3rd ed.). Chartered Institute of Personnel and Development.

Marescaux, E., De Winne, S., & Sels, L. (2013). HR practices and HRM outcomes: The role of basic need satisfaction. *Personnel Review, 42*(1), 4–27.

Maseko, C. (2017). Literature on theory and practice on unethical practices in the construction of projects: A case of an emerging economy. *Risk Governance and Control: Financial Markets and Institutions, 7*(4), 214–224.

McGrath-Champ, S., Rosewarne, S., & Rittau, Y. (2011). From one skill shortage to the next: The Australian construction industry and geographies of a global labour market. *Journal of Industrial Relations, 53*(4), 467–485.

Mengistu, D. G., & Mahesh, G. (2020). Challenges in developing the Ethiopian construction industry. *African Journal of Science, Technology, Innovation and Development, 12*(4), 373–384.

Mitchell, A. (2020). *CLC Statement on payment and contracts.* https://www.construction-leadershipcouncil.co.uk/news/clc-statement-on-payment-and-contracts

Molaney, W. F. (1997). Strategic planning for human resource management in construction. *Journal of Management in Engineering, 13*(3), 49–56.

Mondy, R. W., & Noe, R. M. (1996). *Human resource management* (6th ed.). Prentice Hall.

Naidu, S., & Chand, A. (2014). A comparative analysis of best human resource management practices in the hotel sector of Samoa and Tonga. *Personnel Review, 43*(5), 798–815.

National Bureau of Statistics. (2020). *Nigerian Gross Domestic Product Report (Q3).* National Bureau of Statistics PDF. www.nigerianstat.gov.ng/

Navon, R. (2005). Automated project performance control of construction projects. *Automation in Construction, 14,* 467–476.

Nazir, F. A., Edwards, D. J., Shelbourn, M., Martek, I., Thwala, W. D. D., & El-Gohary, H. (2020). Comparison of modular and traditional UK housing construction: A bibliometric analysis. *Journal of Engineering, Design and Technology, 19*(1), 164–186.

Ogunmakinde, O. E., Sher, W., & Maund, K. (2019). Challenges of the Nigerian construction industry: A systematic review. In *IISBE forum of young researchers in sustainable building,* Prague, Czech Republic, 1 July.

Ogunsemi. (2015). *Value for money in construction projects: The quantity surveyor's quest.* 71st Inaugural Lecture delivered by Prof. D. R. Ogunsemi at the 2500 Capacity Auditorium, Federal University of Technology, Akure, Ondo State.

Ojo, A. O., & Raman, M. (2019). Role of green HRM practices in employees' pro-environmental it practices. In Á. Rocha, et al. (Eds.), *WorldCIST'19, AISC 930* (pp. 678–688).

Olatunji, S. O., Oke, A. E, Aghimien, D. O., & Seidu, S. A. (2016). Effect of construction project performance on economic development of Nigeria. *Journal of Economics and Sustainable Development, 7*(12), 42–149.

Olawumi, T. O., & Chan, D. W. M. (2018). A scientometric review of global research on sustainability and sustainable development. *Journal of Cleaner Production, 183,* 231–250.

Olsen, D., Tatun, M., & Defnall, C. (2012). *How industrial contractors are handling skilled labor shortages in the United States.* 48th ASC Annual International Conference Proceeding, Birmingham City University, UK. April 11–14.

Orga, C. C., & Ogbo, A. I. (2012). Evaluating the challenges of human resource management in Nigeria. *European Journal of Business and Management, 4*(13), 78–85.

Othman, I., Idrus, A., & Napiah, M. (2012). Human resource management in the construction of a sustainable development project: Towards successful completion. *WIT Transactions on Ecology and the Environment, 162*, 169–180.

Park, C.-S., & Kim, H.-J. (2013). A framework for construction safety management and visualisation system. *Automation in Construction, 33*, 95–103.

Paul, C. A., Aghimien, D. O., Ibrahim, A. D., & Ibrahim, Y. M. (2021). Measures for curbing unethical practices among construction industry professionals: Quantity surveyors' Perspective. *Construction Economics and Building, 21*(2), 1–17.

Pearce, D. (2003). *The social and economic value of construction: The construction industry's contribution to sustainable development*. www.ncrisp.org.uk

Pfeffer, J. (1994). *Competitive advantage through people – Unleashing the power of the workforce*. Harvard Business School Press.

Pfeffer, J. (1998). Seven practices of successful organisation. *California Management Review, 40*(2), 96–124.

Pinto, J. K., & Holt, G. D. (1988). Variations in critical success factors over the stages in the project life cycle. *Journal of Management, 14*(1), 5–18.

Prusak, L. (2001). Where did knowledge management come from? *IBM Systems Journal, 40*(4), 1002–1006.

Ramos-Rodríguez, A.-R., & Ruíz-Navarro, J. (2004). Changes in the intellectual structure of strategic management research: A bibliometric study of the strategic management journal, 1980–2000. *Strategic Management Journal, 25*, 981–1004.

Redman, T., & Mathews, P. B. (1998). Service quality and human resource management: A review and research agendas. *Personnel Review, 27*(1), 57–77.

Rezgui, Y., & Zarli, A. (2006). Paving the way to the vision of digital construction: A strategic roadmap. *Journal of Construction Engineering and Management, 132*(7), 767–776.

Robinson, G., Leonard, J., & Whittington, T. (2021). Future of construction: A global forecast for construction to 2030. https://resources.oxfordeconomics.com/hubfs/Africa/Future-of-Construction-Full-Report.pdf

Rubery, J., Carroll, M., Cooke, F., Grugulis, I., & Earnshaw, J. (2004). Human resource management and the permeable organisation: The case of the multiclient call Centre. *Journal of Management Studies, 41*(7), 1199–1222.

Saka, N., & Lowe, J. (2010). *An assessment of linkages between the construction sector and other sectors of the Nigerian economy*. The Construction, Building and Real Estate Research Conference of the Royal Institution of Chartered Surveyors Held at Dauphine Université, Paris, 2–3 September.

Saks, A., & Gruman, J. A. (2010). Organisational socialisation and newcomer engagement. In Albrecht (Ed.), *Handbook of employee engagement: Perspectives, issues, research and practice*. Edward Elgar.

Samuel, C., & Timmaraju, K. (2015). Initial assessment of human resources management challenges in the Indian construction sector. *International Journal of Earth Sciences and Engineering, 8*(5), 256–258.

Schultz, T. W. (1961). Investment in human capital. *American Economic Review, 51*, 1–17.

Sethi, S., & Kataria, N. (2017). The human resource management challenges in construction projects in a large construction company. *International Journal of Development Research, 7*(2), 11775–11779.

Shuck, B., Reio, G., & Rocco, S. (2011). Employee engagement: An examination of antecedent and outcome variables. *Human Resource Development International, 14*(4), 427–445.

Sierra, F. (2022). COVID-19: Main challenges during construction stage. *Engineering, Construction and Architectural Management, 29*(4), 1817–1834.

Siew, R. Y. J. (2014). Human resource management in the construction industry – Sustainability competencies. *Australasian Journal of Construction Economics and Building, 14*(2), 87–103.

Snell, S., & Bohlander, G. (2012). *Managing human resources* (16th ed.). Cengage Learning.

Spooner, K., & Kaine, S. (2010). Defining sustainability and human resource management. *International Employment Relations Review, 16*(2), 70–81.

Statista Research Department. (2019). China's construction industry contribution share to GDP 2018 to 2021. *Statista Research Department.* www.statista.com/statistics/1068213/china-construction-industry-gdp-contribution-share/#:~:text=China's%20construction%20industry%20contribution%20share%20to%20GDP%202018%20to%202021andtext=In%202018%2C%20the%20construction%20industry,a%20five%20percent%20annual%20growth

Storey, J. (1995). *Human resource management: A critical text.* Routledge.

Tabassi, A. A., & Abu Bakar, A. H. (2009). Training, motivation, and performance: The case of human resource management in construction projects in Mashhad, Iran. *International Journal of Project Management, 27*(5), 471–480.

The Office of National Statistics. (2020). Construction output in Great Britain: April 2020. https://www.ons.gov.uk/businessindustryandtrade/constructionindustry/bulletins/constructionoutputingreatbritain/april2020

Tucker, R. L., Haas, C. T., Glover, R. W., Alemany, C. H., Carley, L. A., Eickmann, J. A., Rodriguz, A. M., & Shields, D. (1999). *Craft workers' experiences with and attitudes towards multiskilling* [Report No. 3]. Center for Construction Industry Studies, The University of Texas at Austin, Austin, TX.

Van Eck, N. J., & Waltman, L. (2014). Visualising bibliometric networks. In Y. Ding, R. Rousseau, & D. Wolfram (Eds.), *Measuring scholarly impact: Methods and practice.* Springer.

Vatan, M. (2017). Evolution of construction systems: Cultural effects on traditional structures and their reflection on modern building construction. In G. Koç & B. Christiansen (Eds.), *Cultural influences on architecture.* IGI Global.

Vitharana, V. H. P., De Silva, G. H. M. J., & De Silva, S. (2015). Health hazards, risk and safety practices in construction sites – A review study. *Engineer: Journal of the Institution of Engineers, Sri Lanka, 48*(3), 35–44.

Wells, J. (1985). The role of construction in economics growth and development. *Habitat International, 9*(1), 55–70.

Werner, A. (2017). Introduction to human resource management. In Nel & Werner (Eds.), *Human resource management* (10th ed.). Oxford University Press.

Windapo, A. O., & Cattell, K. (2013). The South African construction industry: Perceptions of key challenges facing its performance, development and growth. *Journal of Construction in Developing Countries, 18*(2), 65–79.

Wirtenberg, J., Harmon, J., Russell, W. G., & Fairfield, K. D. (2007). HR's role in building a sustainable enterprise: Insights from some of the world's best companies. *Human Resource Planning, 30*(1), 1–13.

World Economic Forum. (2016). *Shaping the future of construction. A breakthrough in mindset and technology.* www3.weforum.org/docs/WEF_Shaping_the_Future_of_Construction_full_report__.pdf

Wright, P. M., Gardner, T. M., & Moynihan, L. M. (2003). The impact of HR practices on the performance of business units. *Human Resource Management Journal, 13*(3), 21–36.

Yan, X., Li, H., Li, A. R., & Zhang, H. (2017). Wearable IMU-based real-time motion warning system for construction workers' musculoskeletal disorders prevention. *Automation in Construction, 74*, 2–11.

Yankov, L., & Kleiner, B. H. (2001). Human resources issues in the construction industry. *Management Research News, 24*(3/4), 101–105.

Zhai, X., & Liu, A. (2009). A framework for investigating the relationship of human resource practices and performance of the Chinese construction enterprises. In A. Dainty (Ed.), *Proceedings of the 25th Annual ARCOM Conference*, 7–9 September 2009, Nottingham, UK, pp. 675–864.

Zhai, X., Liu, A. M. M., & Fellows, R. (2014). Role of human resource practices in enhancing organisational learning in Chinese construction organisation. *Journal of Management in Engineering*, *30*(2), 194–20.

Zheng, X., Le, Y., Chan, A. P. C., Hu, Y., & Li, Y. (2016). Review of the application of social network analysis (SNA) in construction project management research. *International Journal of Project Management*, *34*, 1214–1225.

Zingoni, T. (2020). Deconstructing South Africa's construction industry performance. *Mail and Guardian*. https://mg.co.za/opinion/2020-10-19-deconstructing-south-africas-construction-industry-performance/#:~:text=The%20South%20African%20con-struction%20sector,for%20construction%20in%20the%20country

# Chapter 3

# Construction Workforce Management in the Fourth Industrial Revolution

## Abstract

The current era of the fourth industrial revolution has attracted significant research on the use of digital technologies in improving construction project delivery. However, less emphasis has been placed on how these digital tools will influence the management of the construction workforce. To this end, using a review of existing works, this chapter explores the fourth industrial revolution and its associated technologies that can positively impact the management of the construction workforce when implemented. Also, the possible challenges that might truncate the successful deployment of digital technologies for effective workforce management were explored. The chapter submitted that implementing workforce management-specific digital platforms and other digital technologies designed for project delivery can aid effective workforce management within construction organisations. Technologies such as cloud computing, the Internet of Things, big data analytics, robotics and automation, and artificial intelligence, among others, offer significant benefits to the effective workforce management of construction organisations. However, several challenges, such as resistance to change due to fear of job loss, cost of investment in digital tools, organisational structure and culture, must be carefully considered as they might affect the successful use of digital tools and by extension, impact the success of workforce management in the organisations.

*Keywords*: Digitalisation; digital technologies; digital transformation; fourth industrial revolution; innovation; workforce management

## Introduction

With the recent wave of the fourth industrial revolution, organisations are transforming their business models through digital tools to increase revenues and create value opportunities. This process is known as digitalisation (Kalavendi, 2017).

Construction Workforce Management in the Fourth Industrial Revolution Era, 41–74

Copyright © 2024 by Lerato Aghimien, Clinton Ohis Aigbavboa and Douglas Aghimien

Published under exclusive licence by Emerald Publishing Limited

doi:10.1108/978-1-83797-018-620241003

In construction, digitalisation which involves using digital technologies, tends to change the construction and business process and how human resource systems are handled. Lumi (2020) affirmed that digitalisation is an essential technological change that significantly impacts organisations' workforce management. In the view of Balabanova and Balabanov (2020), digitalising business functions can ensure labour productivity growth and improve the organisation's competitiveness. For instance, the use of data-driven technologies such as big data analytics and cloud computing can help human resource departments analyse the personalities and behavioural patterns of construction workers, especially during recruitment and selection, training and development, performance evaluation as well as compensation (Chamorro-Premuzic et al., 2017; Garcia-Arroyo & Osca, 2019). García de Soto et al. (2019) also noted that as technology advances, there will come a time when conventional construction and robotic technologies will coexist. The result of this coexistence will be higher job variability and new roles both at the managerial and operational levels.

Unfortunately, the recent unprecedented attention garnered by the fourth industrial revolution and its associated digital technologies has not changed construction organisations' slow digital transformation (Aghimien et al., 2021; Turk, 2021). This slow transformation results in poor performance and a lack of innovativeness in construction organisations (Agarwal et al., 2016), which negatively impacts the workforce. While several studies have explored the application of digital technologies to construction activities, their benefits, challenges, and impact on construction activities (Li et al., 2017; Oke et al., 2021), how these technologies impact the management of the construction workforce is unknown. As a result, this chapter explores the fourth industrial revolution and its associated technologies that can positively impact the management of the construction workforce when implemented. The chapter also explored the challenges that might truncate the successful deployment of digital technologies for effective workforce management.

## The Fourth Industrial Revolution and Construction

The term 'fourth industrial revolution', also known as industry 4.0, was first coined in 2011 at the Hannover Fair (Lu, 2017; Roblek et al., 2016). According to Bahrin et al. (2016), this industrial revolution was portrayed as an emerging structure wherein manufacturing companies adopted pervasive information and communication tools to improve their already automated production process. The fourth industrial revolution preceded three prior revolutions, hence the name. The first industrial revolution, which saw the transition from an agrarian economy to mechanical production through water and steam-powered engines, happened between the 1700s and mid-1800s. The second industrial revolution saw the introduction of electrical energy for mass production. This revolution happened in the early 1900s, with Henry Ford being a profound name due to his production line, which produced cars for public use. The third industrial revolution happened in the late 1960s and saw the introduction of information technology and electronics. This introduction led to the automation and optimisation of production processes (Bienhaus & Haddud, 2018; Schwab, 2017).

The current fourth industrial revolution is characterised by cyber-physical systems that integrate digital, physical, and biological technologies to improve production (Lu, 2017; Schwab, 2017). Speringer and Schnelzer (2019) noted that this industrial revolution is a pragmatic transition driven by technology and the digital age. Studies have also noted that the fourth industrial revolution depicts the improvement in automation and digitisation of the manufacturing process. This improvement allows communication between products and their environment while ensuring a digital value chain is created (Dallasega et al., 2018; Oesterreich & Teuteberg, 2016). Consequently, the fourth industrial revolution is not limited to automation but extends to digitising every aspect of a business. In essence, this industrial revolution cut across the acquisition of a contract through its procurement, the production process and the final product delivery to the consumer (Roblek et al., 2016).

The fourth industrial revolution is characterised by emerging digital technologies like the Internet of Things (IoT), intelligent sensors, digital twins, Unmanned Aerial Vehicles (UAVs), robotics, cloud computing, big data analytics, information modelling, artificial intelligence (AI), augmented and virtual realities among others (Aghimien et al., 2021). Bhattacharya and Momaya (2021) noted that this industrial revolution also focusses on organisational management through digital technologies that can assist organisations in connecting their tools, services, facilities, products, and customers to collect and distribute information in real time. To this end, Vaidya et al. (2018) submitted that the main requirement of this industrial revolution is the ability to monitor data in real-time using available digital tools. It also entails improving the overall performance of available machines by altering them into self-learning and self-aware machines through integrating emerging cyber-physical systems. Lastly, it involves being able to track the status of products as well as their position. The ultimate goal of the fourth industrial revolution is to attain a higher level of automation and maximise productivity while ensuring the operational process is efficient (Lu, 2017).

The fourth industrial revolution driven by physical, biological, and digital technologies (Li et al., 2017; Schwab, 2017) has revolutionalised many sectors of the economy of countries worldwide. Aghimien et al. (2021) noted the significant transformation in manufacturing, finance, agriculture, education, and construction. However, the slow adoption of these emerging technologies has been noted in the construction industry of developed and developing countries worldwide (Alaloul et al., 2020; Oke et al., 2018). Earlier, Dallasega et al. (2018) asserted that this industrial revolution had found its way into other industries, including construction, despite starting from manufacturing. However, unlike manufacturing, the construction industry still struggles with several issues that make development and increased productivity difficult. As such, Osunsanmi et al. (2018) contend that the dynamic nature of the construction industry has contributed to the slow adoption of the fourth industrial revolution concept within the industry. To this end, there has been a continuous call for the digitalisation of the construction industry through emerging digital technologies that promise better productivity, improved quality, and customer satisfaction.

Digitalisation is applying digital technology in business operations (Kalavendi, 2017). Bahl (2015) described it as an innovation that combines technology, business strategy, data, and design to change how business operates. From the business perspective, Gartner (2016) described digitalisation as using digital tools to change business models while creating a new stream of income and opportunities that add value to the business. In construction, Aghimien et al. (2021) conceptualised digitalisation as using digital technologies to deliver tangible and intangible services within construction organisations to achieve a strategic edge over rivals and boost service quality. Lipsmeier et al. (2020) and Plekhanov and Netland (2019) described digitalisation as a disruptor of core business functions associated with organisation-wide modernisation efforts affecting all structures, systems, and processes. Digitalisation is driven by digital technologies, which according to Rouse (2017), are electronic technologies capable of generating, storing, and processing data using binary codes. According to Dimick (2014), these digital technologies can be viewed from three facets: software, communication equipment, and technology equipment. In today's business climate, organisations are under increasing pressure to undergo digital transformation by adopting these digital technologies to deliver their services. This is especially true for construction organisations, as clients now expect a certain level of digitalisation (Hassaini et al., 2017).

Past studies have shown the benefits of digitalisation of organisational activities. According to Oke et al. (2023), adopting the concept of digitalisation through digital technologies allows organisations to achieve meaningful growth and be sustainable. Other studies have noted that organisations (construction inclusive) stand to gain increased productivity and profitability, competitive advantage, enhanced flexibility, enhanced sustainability, better information management, improved safety, quality, and increased responsiveness (Alaloul et al., 2020; de Andrade Régio et al., 2016; Sepasgozar & Davis, 2018). Albeit these benefits promised by digital technologies, their slow adoption is still prominent in construction. There are numerous reasons why construction may be experiencing this slow adoption. Among many other factors, these include a workforce with a limited preference for emerging technologies (Aghimien et al., 2021; Oke et al., 2023). More so, the construction industry is splintered, with numerous stakeholders involved, and it is rife with widespread opposition to change (Froese, 2010; Sepasgozar et al., 2016).

Based on the preceding, it is evident that the fourth industrial revolution offered promising benefits to the construction industry and the services the industry delivers. However, for the industry to enjoy these benefits, a shift from traditional ways of doing things is needed to a digitalised approach. To do this, among other factors, the industry must be ready to adopt digital technologies that will help improve the management of its workers and how they deliver their services to the client.

## Overview of Technological Advancement in Construction Workforce Management

The current digital era has resulted in the emergence of digital labour and digital workplaces (Calvard & Jeske, 2018). Digitalisation is altering human interaction and communication and how organisations function (Halid et al., 2020). Deloitte (2017) noted that organisations have grown interested in how to improve human resource services through the use of digital tools. As a result, digital/electronic human resource management has continued to gain traction within many organisations. According to Marler and Parry (2016), electronic human resource management is a set of technological configurations that drives traditional human resource management functions through managing and coordinating data, information, and interaction within and across organisational boundaries. In the view of Bondarouk and Ruël (2009), this electronic management of human resources is simply the convergence of workforce and technological activities to generate value. In a much earlier description, Ruël et al. (2004) described it as implementing human resource practices, policies, and activities in organisations through thoughtful and well-planned support of web technology-based platforms. Ma and Ye (2015) noted that electronic management of human resources can be operational, relational, and transformational. The operational deals with maintaining records of the workforce, while the relational deals with the recruiting process, and the transformational deals with the advancement of the workers in accordance with the strategic decisions of the organisation. Zhou et al. (2021) concluded that the digital management of the workforce is designed to increase the efficiency and performance of traditional workforce management activities by utilising digital technologies and suitable data.

With the increase in digitalisation, the world has become more data-driven, with the rising possibilities of analysing people's data to support decision-making. Exponential technology advances have made it possible for human resource practitioners or units to gather, store and access massive amounts of employee data, which are collected in large, and often unstructured datasets together with other organisational data, from which insights can be generated to help the organisation and its processes (Angrave et al., 2016; Shah et al., 2017; van den Heuvel & Bondarouk, 2017). There is a growing believe that human resource analytics is a possible solution to ensure and improve the data-driven management of workers, aid workforce management to attain its strategic potential, and help achieve competitive advantage (Marler & Boudreau, 2017). It has been noted that through data analytics, large complex volumes of data are turned into useful information, and this can be used to support workforce management's decision-making process by helping to make more accurate and data-driven decisions (Rasmussen & Ulrich, 2015). Data-driven decisions are based on data and facts rather than personal experience or intuition (McAfee & Brynjolfsson, 2012; Rasmussen & Ulrich, 2015).

Advancement in high-powered computing technology has led to the emergence of diverse data analytics techniques such as AI and machine learning (ML), which are ideally suited for managing and extracting information from massive, linked datasets and big data (Kitchin, 2014). These analytical tools can be descriptive, predictive, or prescriptive (Kitchin, 2014). Descriptive analytics aims to understand past behaviours and outcomes and to analyse and identify relationships and trends (Fitz-enz, 2010; Ulrich & Dulebohn, 2015). It aids in distinguishing past trends and compares them over a period of time or with others. In the context of workforce management, at this stage, the focus is usually on cost reduction and process improvement. On the other hand, predictive analysis attempts to predict the future through historical and current data. At this level, the focus is on the probabilities and potential impact. The prescriptive analysis is all about decision-making options and workforce optimisation (Fitz-enz & Mattox, 2014).

Through technological advancement in managing their workforce, organisations can now make logical forward-looking decisions informed by the data analysed. Unfortunately, while this potential might be evident, the poor adoption of the needed digital technologies within organisations operating in the construction industry might serve as a barrier to effectively implementing digital management of the workforce. Though the construction industry is labour-intensive, it is slow in adopting digital technologies that can help improve its labour productivity and service efficiency. Also, there is a deficiency in the body of knowledge regarding how emerging technological advancements are used to improve construction workforce management. This lack of studies to illuminate the impact of emerging digital technologies on construction workforce management is detrimental to embracing digital tools and the possible digital transformation of the construction industry. This situation is worsened by the fact that the construction industry in many countries has been characterised by poor management of its workforce, which has led to the unappealing characteristics that the industry has adorned among young professionals (Mengistu & Mahesh, 2020; Ngwenya & Aigbavboa, 2017).

## Bibliometric Perspective of Workforce Management and the Fourth Industrial Revolution

Due to the scarcity of studies on how the fourth industrial revolution technologies impact construction workforce management, it became necessary to review a broad range of existing studies that have explored this concept. To this end, a bibliometric review, a quantitative approach for text mining scientific publications (Hawkins, 2001), was adopted. The bibliographic data used for the review were extracted from the Scopus database due to the recent momentous attention garnered by this database in the field of science (Aghimien et al., 2020; Guz & Rushchitsky, 2009). The search for related literature was conducted using keywords such as 'digital technologies' OR digitalisation OR 'digital transformation' AND 'Workforce management', OR 'human resource management' OR 'employee management'. These keywords were searched in journal articles, conference proceedings and book series published between 2012 and 2023, and 540 documents were revealed from across diverse fields of study. Studies from 2012 were targeted based on past submissions that digitalisation, a product of the fourth industrial revolution, only became popular after the 2011 Hannover fair in Germany. In terms of area of study, only engineering and computer science documents were retained to get works closely related to construction. The publication language was English alone. At the end of the refinement, 143 documents were retained from the initial 540 for further review.

The documents came from 45 countries, with the Russian Federation having the highest number of documents ($f = 28$) with 53 citations. This is followed by China ($f = 22$ documents, 242 citations) and Germany ($f = 20$ documents, 214 citations). Careful observation showed only one document from an African country (South Africa). This study was by Naidoo and Ndlovu (2021), which assessed the ambivalent relationship between users and digital human resource management using a case study approach. The qualitative study explored users' competing views about digital human resource management. This observation of only one document from the continent shows an opportunity for researchers in this area to contribute significantly to the body of knowledge on the impact of digital technologies on workforce management from the African perspective.

In terms of contribution, the work of Li et al. (2018) on a capability perspective of digital transformation by small and medium entrepreneurs has garnered attention, with 228 citations recorded. Also significant is the work of Mechtcherine et al. (2019), who, to address the low productivity and shortage of skilled workers in construction, explored large-scale digital concrete construction from the perspective of 3D printing. This document has so far gained 115 citations. Fareri et al. (2020) also estimated the impact of the fourth industrial revolution on job profiles and skills through text mining. The study provided a framework for estimating the fourth industrial revolution readiness of organisations' human capital, which is fast, adaptable and reusable. The article has also received 72 citations since its publication.

In understanding the area of focus of these extracted documents in relation to the issue under review, a visualisation of the keywords was conducted using the visualisation of similarities viewer (VOSviewer) software. The 143 documents extracted had 1,326 keywords, subsequently reduced to 53 using a minimum threshold of four co-occurring keywords. These 53 co-occurring keywords are regrouped into four themes, as seen in Table 3.1, and they show the area of focus of digital technologies and workforce management research in construction-related domains.

Cluster 1 – The first cluster has 15 keywords, including human resource management, digital technologies, digital economy, AI, project managers, employment, personnel training, e-learning, risk assessment, risk management, health and safety, and human engineering, among others. This cluster points to studies relating to the use of digital technologies for effective learning and risk management of organisations' workforce.

Cluster 2 – The second cluster revealed 14 keywords, such as decision-making, quality control, productivity, automation, project management, life cycle, construction projects, virtual reality, augmented reality, building information modelling, data handling, and information analysis, among others. This cluster points to studies relating to the use of digital technologies for effective project management and decision-making.

Cluster 3 – The third cluster revealed 13 keywords, including digitalisation, competition, information system, information use, change management, knowledge management, personnel management, and management systems, among others. This cluster points to studies relating to the use of digital information systems for effective personnel management.

Cluster 4 – The last cluster revealed 11 keywords, including digital transformation, information management, metadata, big data, data visualisation, the IoT, resource allocation, and natural resource management. This cluster points to studies relating to data and information processing for effective resource allocation.

Table 3.1.   Co-occurring keywords

| Keyword | $f$ | TLS | Keyword | $f$ | TLS |
|---|---|---|---|---|---|
| **Cluster 1** | | | **Cluster 2** | | |
| Human resource management | 116 | 397 | Project management | 16 | 79 |
| Digital technologies | 29 | 90 | Construction industry | 10 | 56 |
| Artificial intelligence | 12 | 55 | Architectural design | 8 | 47 |
| Managers | 12 | 53 | Decision making | 8 | 28 |
| Personnel training | 12 | 52 | Life cycle | 8 | 49 |
| E-learning | 11 | 49 | Automation | 5 | 17 |
| Digital economy | 10 | 40 | Data handling | 5 | 44 |
| Employment | 7 | 43 | Productivity | 5 | 23 |
| Manufacture | 7 | 22 | Augmented reality | 4 | 23 |
| Project managers | 5 | 24 | Building information modelling | 4 | 21 |
| Health and safety | 4 | 14 | Construction projects | 4 | 20 |
| Human engineering | 4 | 14 | Information analysis | 4 | 36 |
| Organisation | 4 | 10 | Quality control | 4 | 25 |
| Risk assessment | 4 | 14 | Virtual reality | 4 | 25 |
| Risk management | 4 | 17 | | | |
| **Cluster 3** | | | **Cluster 4** | | |
| Digitalisation | 22 | 90 | Digital transformation | 33 | 134 |
| Information systems | 14 | 66 | Information management | 23 | 121 |
| Information use | 14 | 68 | Human resources management | 17 | 63 |
| Industry 4.0 | 13 | 55 | Natural resources management | 8 | 55 |
| Competition | 7 | 43 | Resource allocation | 8 | 55 |
| Knowledge management | 5 | 12 | Internet of things | 7 | 34 |
| Management information systems | 5 | 30 | Metadata | 7 | 39 |
| Change management | 4 | 11 | Personnel management | 6 | 34 |
| Economic and social effects | 4 | 24 | Big data | 5 | 18 |
| Industrial revolutions | 4 | 27 | Data visualisation | 4 | 18 |
| Management systems | 4 | 23 | | | |

Following the bibliometric review, it can be said that the adoption of the fourth industrial revolution digital tools in relation to workforce management in construction-related fields has been researched from four broad categories vis:

(1)  digital technologies for effective learning and risk management of organisations' workforce;
(2)  digital technologies for effective project management and decision-making;
(3)  digital information systems for effective personnel management; and
(4)  data and information processing for effective resource allocation.

These broad areas give insight into the possible influence of digital technologies on construction organisations' workforce management. From the extracted documents, Achchab and Temsamani (2022) noted that in recent times, human resource professionals within diverse organisations have focussed on optimising the combined effort of man and machine to gain a simple, unified, and spontaneous working environment. This is because such an environment allows these professionals the time for creativity, intelligence, and empathy to deliver an enhanced candidate and employee experience. Also, da Silva et al. (2022) noted that digital technologies would influence workforce management in areas such as competence, learning and training, recruitment and selection, rewards, performance management, and talent management, among others. Similarly, Talend (2021) have noticed that digitalisation can reshape human resource management practices, including recruiting and selecting employees, compensation, performance evaluation, and training and developing employees' skills and capabilities.

## Types of Digital Technologies for Effective Construction Workforce Management

Based on the above sections, it is evident that the workforce management domain has experienced significant transformation through technological advancement and emerging digital information systems. To this end, electronic and digital human resources management, human resource analytics, human resources information system, virtual human resources management and intranet-based human resources management have all become common phrases within the workforce management space. However, it is essential to note that as organisations (particularly in construction) continue to embrace emerging digital technologies, the workforce management department may benefit from this adoption. While several digital technologies have been noted to be useful to the successful delivery of construction projects, not all will directly impact the management of the construction workforce. Based on this notion, this section X-rayed the different digital technologies peculiar to construction that can aid the effective management of the workforce in construction organisations.

### *Cloud Computing*

Cloud computing has been described as networked computers designed to offer information technology services to users in an on-demand environment using the

Internet (Adjei et al., 2021). This technology has been described as an extensive distributed computing model in which a pool of configurable computing resources, such as networks, servers, storage, applications, and data, are utilised and managed with minimal effort (Rawai et al., 2013; Sun et al., 2012). Bello et al. (2021) further described the advent of cloud computing as a paradigm shift in how organisations and individuals manage and use computing hardware and software.

Cloud computing services are broadly categorised into Infrastructure as a Service (IaaS), Platform as a Service (PaaS), and Software as a Service (SaaS) (Almishal & Youssef, 2014). The IaaS model allows clients to outsource computing resources from a service provider. These outsourced resources include servers, networks, storage, memory, operating system, and firewalls (Tadapaneni, 2020). In this case, the client or user is not responsible for the computing resources but fully controls the virtual platforms (Sareen, 2013). IaaS offers personalisation of services to suit client's requirements, reduced maintenance costs, and secure data storage that can be retrieved or recovered even with the failure of host allocation (Mukundha & Vidyamadhuri, 2017). The PaaS model allows the client to design and develop their applications in accordance with the infrastructure of the service providers. By so doing, the client has control over their designed application but not the operating systems, hardware, and network infrastructure (Rawai et al., 2013). This category of cloud computing allows the client to use the host's environment for their applications, which will be monitored but not controlled by the host. The advantage of using PaaS is that it allows the creation of agile applications using standard and reliable technologies. It optimises the productivity and development time of required applications (Mukundha & Vidyamadhuri, 2017). The SaaS model allows clients to rent and use applications within the cloud service provider's infrastructure. The provider updates and administers these services (Sareen, 2013). In essence, the client will use the application but cannot control the operating system, hardware and network infrastructure on which the application operates (Garyaev & Rybakova, 2018; Rawai et al., 2013). SaaS eliminates the time needed to develop applications since they are already available. More so, the application is flexible and scalable and updating them is done by the cloud service providers (Mukundha & Vidyamadhuri, 2017).

Workforce management has recently faced issues such as improving efficiency, saving costs, and providing timely responses. Cloud computing offers possible solutions to these issues (Dai et al.,2015). The use of cloud computing promises cost-effectiveness, simple access to employees' information, high computing power and storage, easy performance management, efficient recruitment process, attendance management, and salary management, all of which contribute to the workforce management department's productivity (Chandra, 2020; Johnson et al., 2016). Moreover, the technology can merge the link between internal and external management and between senior and lower-level management (Hao, 2017). Also, the cloud-based system includes distinctive features such as video-based information analysis systems for talent management and intelligent career prediction systems (Hjort et al., 2018; Palee et al., 2020). Thus, cloud computing offers workforce management departments within construction organisations the opportunity to effectively manage their workforce while staying competitive within the dynamic construction environment.

## Internet of Things

The IoT can be described as all the objects that can be recognised and incorporated into communication networks, both in the physical and digital worlds (International Telecommunications Union, 2012). Simply put, IoT enables people and things to connect using communication networks. Rad and Ahmada (2017) described IoT as the interconnectivity of networks via smart systems that can interact using sensors and actuators with minimal human interaction. Yang et al. (2013) noted that the objective of IoT is to effectively share data in real time amongst autonomous entities in a network. McDonald (2017) submitted that IoT within construction organisations can assist with resource monitoring (i.e. man, material and machine). This can be achieved by using smart wearables, which can track workers' locations, progress and safety. More so, sensors can help monitor construction activities and maintenance needs of structures in real-time. Ghimire et al. (2017) proposed a situational awareness framework wherein IoT can be used to manage projects in real time. The framework was designed to allow organisations to implement IoT for planning, monitoring and control, and the intelligent update of construction activities using field data. This helps improve the delivery of projects. Mahmud et al. (2018) have noted that IoT can be used in conjunction with other digital technologies like UAVs, augmented reality, and radio frequency identification (RFID) tags among others. This fusion allows remote operation on construction sites, sending information & hazard alerts, and security control for materials.

Mohanty and Mishra (2020) observed that IoT within organisations, particularly in relation to workforce management, allows organisations to effectively manage objectivity, productivity and privacy transparently without prejudice. Some studies have noted that the use of IoT within an organisation will have a ripple effect on workforce management in terms of enhanced flexibility, improved staff engagement, enhanced transparency, less human error, increased data speed and volume, and better productivity (Kremer, 2022). Also, IoT has reportedly streamlined all phases of the recruitment process, resulting in better hiring decisions and the selection of the best candidates (Gaur et al., 2019; Moyeenudin & Anandan, 2020). It enhances employee training and development by collecting information that can be used to tailor training programs and spot qualification gaps and training inadequacies in real time (Gaur et al., 2019; Mohanty & Mishra, 2020). Other benefits offered by the use of IoT within organisations include ease of documenting every part of employee experience, improving performance management, monitoring the health of workers, and assisting with the development of a productive and sophisticated workforce without the need for time-wasting processes (El-Aziz et al., 2020; Gaur et al., 2019).

## Artificial Intelligence

AI, sometimes called Machine Intelligence, is the term for the development of machines, robots, or computer programs that exhibit behaviour that is thought to be intelligent in a comparable way to that of humans (Kaplan, 2016; Tecuci, 2012).

Newton (2018) described AI as the ability of computing systems to carry out tasks normally requiring intelligent human intervention. According to Tambe et al. (2019), AI enables a computer to carry out activities that typically require human intellect. Clavero (2018) submitted that AI gathers and analyses large datasets to develop patterns and trends. This is achieved through machine power to model human intelligence and ML to profer faster and more accurate solutions to existing problems. Jia et al. (2018) noted that AI aims to create 'thinking machines' that can eventually replace humans as the standard for intelligence. As a result, one may claim that AI is a digital human or a digital clone of a human.

Lately, AI has been presented as an essential tool for workforce management (Tambe et al., 2019). It has been effectively used in workforce management activities such as employee development, deployment, recruitment and selection, turnover, performance assessment, and emotional engagement level (Karatop et al., 2015; Moon et al., 2010). AI may also be used in payroll, where it aids in calculating and establishing employee salary criteria (Mehrabad & Brojeny, 2007). More so, studies have noted that job engagement, commitment, better job performance, employee retention, lower workers-related overhead costs, higher productivity, efficient decision-making, and increased employee satisfaction are all advantages of integrating AI into organisations' workforce management (Castellacci & Vinas-Bardolet, 2019). Manoharan et al. (2009) found the impact of AI in training where it enhances the training process by aiding in identifying individuals who require improvement and the necessary level of development.

Additionally, AI enables organisations to reach a bigger pool of candidates in the recruitment process. When the pool of candidates has been narrowed down, interviewing them becomes quicker and simpler thanks to cutting-edge technologies like asynchronous video interviews (Torres & Mejia, 2017). As a result, the paperwork required throughout the recruiting process is reduced (Dickson & Nusair, 2010).

### *Big Data Analytics*

Big data refers to 'information asset characterised by high volume, velocity and variety that require specific technology and analytical methods for its transformation into value' (de Mauro et al., 2016, p. 127). Also, a dataset is referred to as big data when such data cannot be documented, secured, managed, analysed, and processed using every regular device (Chahal & Gulia, 2016; Manyika et al., 2011). Analysing these large datasets using appropriate analytical approaches becomes important. This can be achieved through the concept of big data analytics, which entails using technology to process Big Data in real time and unearthing pertinent information that can assist organisations in becoming market leaders (McAfee & Brynjolfsson, 2012; Rüßmann et al., 2015). The different emerging digital technologies available to construction organisations, coupled with the continuous complexity of construction projects, have led to the emergence of big data from construction projects which organisations can leverage to make data-driven decisions that will benefit the organisations and the projects they deliver (Aghimien et al., 2019; Bagheri et al., 2015).

Within workforce management, big data analytics can support organisational decision-making founded on a data-driven strategy (Angrave et al., 2016; Shah et al., 2017). While big data in workforce management encompasses employees, clients, and transactional information in an organisation, when this data is analysed using Big Data Analytics, applying workforce management practices becomes easier, allowing firms to make better decisions and reap greater rewards (Rabhi et al., 2019). According to Evans and Kitchin (2018), using big data analytics to observe and substantially reconfigure new methods to regulate the workforce is the cornerstone of operational advancements. The advancement of workers' potential, assisting in candidate screening and searching, providing human resource staff with access to all pertinent data, enabling them to communicate with anyone at any time, enabling smarter decision-making regarding workers and workforce management practices, and increasing the likelihood of success in forecasting, while favouring tactical decision-making are all additional benefits of big data analytics observed in past studies (Hamilton & Sodeman, 2020). Thus, construction organisations stand a lot to gain by investing and adopting big data analytics within their organisation. Not only would this technology help improve the delivery of projects through swift data-driven decision-making, but it will also improve the management of the construction workforce and, by so doing, improve organisational productivity and competitiveness.

## *Blockchain Technology*

Blockchain technology is a distributed ledger system that allows decentralisation, transparency, and data integrity (Seo et al., 2017). Sakho et al. (2019) described blockchain technology as a distributed database that can be decentralised and tracked, safe, dependable, integrated, peer-to-peer protocol, and digital encryption technology. The distributed database in blockchain technology serves as a 'ledger' to permanently and verifiably record transactions between two entities (Iansiti & Lakhani, 2017). Blockchain technology guarantees data security (Sakho et al., 2019; Seo et al., 2017). This name derives from the notion that each transaction's data is logged at regular intervals as a 'block', which is added to the 'chain', producing an indestructible ledger called 'blockchain' (San et al., 2019). Blockchain technology is gradually becoming popular in construction. This is because blockchain technology offers solutions to the age-long problem of poor productivity, none compliance with regulations, ineffective collaboration as well as poor payment practices that have bedevilled the construction industry for a long period (Akinradewo et al., 2022; San et al., 2019).

Blockchain technology in workforce management applies to documentation, recruitment and selection, and performance management (Martin, 2021). Examples of the application of blockchain technology in workforce management include the blockchain-based recruitment management system and the blockchain-based human resource management system, as noted by Onik et al. (2018). Implementing blockchain technology in workforce management is a disruptive force since organisations frequently struggle with hiring competent workers because people falsify their talents, obligations, date of employment, designations, academic qualifications, organisations worked at, and awards obtained (Sakran, 2019). Spence (2018) noted that blockchain technology may be used to check the credentials of prospective workers. More so, traditional ways of processing information have several limitations, such as the risk of being erroneous, losing data, being expensive, and needing a lengthy time to validate data (Rhemananda et al., 2021). Blockchain technology may resolve these issues (Spence, 2018). According to PricewaterhouseCoopers, PwC (2017), blockchain technology can examine and analyse candidates' credentials, competencies, and productivity. Verifying employee credentials minimises expenses and delays while increasing credibility and recruitment automation (Han, 2017). Lukic et al. (2018) affirmed that blockchain technology saves time and costs of hiring while also improving the quality and simplicity of validating employees' data, centralising career profiles, and relatively easy capturing and tracking of career advancements.

Eliaçık (2022) noted that blockchain technology offers effective data management and can assist the human resource department in managing sensitive employees' data. It was noted that as organisations continue to grow with several branches, sensitive human resource department data such as salary, healthcare, financial, performance and disciplinary records, among others, becomes susceptible to exploitation. Blockchain technology offers the protection and security to keep these data safe. There are other advantages of using blockchain technology in workforce management, including the ability to create smart contracts, secure transactions, eliminate fraud, secure data, and aid with compliance and audits (Spence, 2018). Kişi (2022) outlined the benefits of blockchain, including aiding the development of career networks in an online, safe, and distributed manner. It also offers adequate, quicker, and less expensive credential verifications, workers' performance evaluations, conducting interviews in a metaverse, and enables efficient job matching.

### *Robotics and Automation*

The construction industry is a highly labour-intensive sector with a high rate of accidents (Kurien et al., 2018). Cai et al. (2018) observed that the ageing population and lack of safety have led to a decreased number of young workers on construction sites. In addition, Aghimien et al. (2021) noted that the construction industry has become unappealing to most young people due to the industry's unattractiveness resulting from frequent site accidents. The construction industry has one of the highest site injuries and fatalities yearly records (Chan & Aghimien, 2022; Lipscomb et al., 2006). This labour shortage and lack of safety among the few available workers have led to the clamour among researchers and practitioners on the need to leverage machines and robots to replace human effort in construction (Aghimien et al., 2021; Cai et al., 2018).

Automation through robots is not a new concept. Many manufacturing and service sectors have continued adopting this technology to increase productivity. According to Vähä et al. (2013), automation involves using regulated systems and information technologies to minimise the use of human effort in producing goods and services. Mistri and Rathod (2016) described it as a self-regulating technique using computerised machines to carry out numerous tasks. Similarly, Joshi and

Shah (2015) presented construction automation as the utilisation of machine and electronic equipment in the construction industry to attain automatic operation or control so that the possible exposure, schedule, or effort of humans can be minimised while still sustaining and improving the productivity and quality of the project's deliveries.

Despite the constant research into health and safety issues on construction sites and the provisions of measures to reduce accident occurrence, site accidents are still recorded at the highest rate (Chan & Aghimien, 2022). To overcome the traditional limitations of manual efforts, automated safety monitoring is considered one of the most promising approaches that allow continuous and accurate observation of construction site conditions (Park et al., 2017). Due to the complex environment of construction sites, it is incredibly challenging for safety inspectors to continuously monitor and manually identify all incidents that may expose workers to safety risks. Consequently, Fang et al. (2016) suggested automated methods to identify workers under safety management risks based on location data acquired from sensing systems, including Bluetooth, Ultra-Wideband, global positioning system, RFID, laser scanning, video camera, and magnetic proximity sensing.

Aghimien et al. (2022) noted that to perform work in dangerous conditions, robots can be used to improve operation and safety. Due to the complex nature of construction sites, the use of robots in construction will minimise the use of human beings, thus reducing the risk to workers (Bahrin et al., 2016). This becomes very important to the human resource department responsible for their workers' occupational health and safety. Sklar (2015) submitted that commercial systems robots such as Semi-Automated Mason are being used for buildings to enhance productivity. This Semi-Automated Mason is a robotic bricklayer with the functional purpose of laying approximately 800–1200 bricks daily, while a skilled bricklayer can lay about 300–500 bricks daily. According to Kasperzyk et al. (2017), this robot is not invented to replace humans as it still requires construction workers to tidy up the mortar and place bricks in difficult areas such as corners. Furthermore, automation via building information modelling is the key to enhancing the effectiveness and efficiency of safety management, while the development of Safety Information Modelling is the key prerequisite (Chan et al., 2016). Digital and physical technologies such as three-dimensional printing, robotics and UAVs offer a safer method of delivering construction projects (Bahrin et al., 2016), which impacts workforce management's occupational health and safety function (Akinlolu et al., 2020).

## *Mobile Applications*

The pervasiveness of phones has increased to the point where businesses increasingly offer services through mobile platforms (Laukkanen, 2016). The increasing use of mobile platforms, and the prevalence of mobile phones and mobile internet, make mobile applications an important medium for obtaining services (Shankar & Datta, 2019). According to Phyoung and Young (2003), a mobile application is an internet application that works effectively in a mobile computer environment. The benefits of using mobile applications include accessibility, localisation and affordability (Huang et al., 2015). As a result of these advantages, organisations are increasingly utilizing mobile applications to manage their workforce (Shankar & Nigam, 2022). Through these mobile application platforms, workforce management practices are revolutionised. Such a revolution increases job satisfaction, boosts efficiency, and enables communication from anywhere and at any time (Sukumar & Giridharan, 2014). Additionally, mobile applications assist the human resource department in becoming proactive in implementing each significant element of workforce management, such as recruitment, performance and development. In carrying out workforce management practice of occupational health and safety, using smart wearables linked with mobile applications can help monitor frontline workers and ensure proper management of their health and well-being during construction activities (Choi et al., 2017).

## Key Opportunities in Digital Technologies Deployment for Construction Workforce Management

Adopting and implementing digital technologies within construction organisations will impact various aspects and functions of the organisation. This section explores the different workforce management-related practices that the use of digital technologies in construction organisations can influence.

### *Smart Recruitment*

The conventional methods for hiring workers have been ineffective in simultaneously reaching a larger geographic area (Halid et al., 2020). However, using technology has made the recruiting process more efficient and successful by disseminating information adequately (Nawaz, 2019). Through digital platforms, jobs can now be listed, and candidates can be traced for thousands of opportunities in multiple regions (Neeraj, 2018). In recruiting the right worker for a job, some organisations (construction inclusive) adopt online channels such as job boards, corporate recruiting sites and social media websites in their recruitment techniques (Allen et al., 2007). This process, known as e-recruitment, covers all recruitment practices performed using different electronic means and the Internet (Brandão et al., 2019). It allows organisations to attract many applicants at a low cost. More so, with various preliminary online procedures, applicants that do not match the vacant position criteria are excluded (Brandão et al., 2019; Faliagka et al., 2012). The approach offers organisations the benefits of lower recruitment costs, less administrative burden, easier applicant screening, shorter recruiting phases, constant access for job seekers to applicable job ads regardless of geographic location, and flexibility (Faliagka et al., 2012; Samson & Agrawal 2020).

### *Improved Training*

The use of digital tools promises a positive impact on the training and development of workers, and organisations have started adopting digital platforms to achieve this workforce management practice of improving the capabilities and careers of their workforce (Shafiq & Hamza, 2017). Versatility and accessibility,

increased training velocity, modifiability, interactive feedback, decreased training costs, variety of teaching techniques, quick distribution of training materials,
return on investment, shortened timeframes and improved training adaptability
are all advantages of using digital technology in training (Jayabalan et al., 2021;
Perez & Foshay, 2002). Online meeting platforms allow a more technical approach
to training that enhances the experience of new workers. In addition, implementing technology allows for more effective training of new employees while allowing
them to access onboarding and training programs anywhere. For instance, with
cloud computing and storage, employees can access recordings of training sessions anywhere. Also, digital classrooms allow human resource practitioners to
quickly train many employees and assess their progress through computerised
testing programmes (Neeraj, 2018). Furthermore, cyber-physical systems, augmented, virtual and mixed realities, are beneficial learning tools for construction
workers (Akanmu et al., 2020; Aziz et al., 2010; Ikuabe et al., 2022).

### *Improved Productivity*

Employee productivity is the degree to which an employee produces work.
Samson and Agrawal (2020) argued that integrating digital technologies into
workforce management can increase employee productivity. This increased productivity can be attributed to, among other factors, the notion that employees
can work remotely from any location due to technological advances. It boosts
employee performance by increasing flexibility. Due to advances in digital technology, employees can now focus on more strategically important tasks. Marler
and Parry (2016) noted that these technological advancements increase productivity by automating and replacing low-value administrative tasks with higher-
added value. More so, digital tools like blockchain technology, for instance,
lessen the bureaucracy and administrative strain on human resource professionals
(Al-Shameri & Omar, 2022).

### *Improved Data Management*

Technology has transformed how human resource departments gather, analyse,
and interpret data. As a result, human resource managers now have direct access
to important data required for critical decision-making. This ease of data accessibility fosters knowledge acquisition and allows for flexibility in the workplace
(Fenech et al., 2019). In contrast to conventional workforce management, using
digital technologies to improve workforce management has enabled firms to
keep and document workers' data for lengthy periods in a simple and error-free
manner. Furthermore, digital tools allow for more advanced analytical capabilities for data processing via algorithms. Such advanced analytical capabilities improve and facilitate the transmission of information in an organisation
(Al-Shameri & Omar, 2022). Other benefits of digital tools in workforce management include transparency of data set, easier data classification and reclassi-
fication, and a faster rate of data recovery (Al-Shameri & Omar 2022; Fındıklı &
Bayarçelik 2015).

## Cost Savings

Digital technology reduces costs relating to the management of workers through expediting processes and information management (Iqbal et al., 2019). Khairullina (2021) asserted that organisations could save money by using digital technology to accelerate processes and data gathering. Relatively, by implementing digital tools, organisations can save time and money. This cost savings can be in hiring and selecting candidates, enabling the business to maintain its competitiveness regarding human resource function (Samson & Agrawal, 2020). Also, using digital platforms now allows cost-effective training of workers (Neeraj, 2018).

## Improved Communication

Emerging digital tools have significantly altered how employees communicate with one another and their employers. More lines of communication have emerged as a result of these emerging technologies. By removing communication barriers, organisations can alter employee experiences, resulting in innovation, productivity, and development (Negi & Kaur, 2019). According to Cohen (2010), E-communication promotes interactivity and communication between workers and the human resource department. FitzPatrick and Valskov (2014) submitted that interactivity makes communication more efficient and practical. These technologies enhance employee communication and, by extension, increase employee productivity.

## Increased Employee Engagement and Participation

Organisations' digital tools can influence workforce management regarding employee participation in organisational activities. Digital technologies allow the automation of dull and repetitive duties, giving workers more time to focus on significant activities and engagement (Deloitte, 2017). Furthermore, to ensure employee involvement, the human resource department can get recommendations, reactions, and viewpoints on employee and employee-centric aspects faster using online surveys and reviews (Galgali, 2017). Also, introducing digital platforms in an organisation will allow workers to use technology-based self-service software that encourages employee participation (Venterink, 2017). This creates a substantial shift from the traditional workforce management strategies and activities adopted within organisations to a more digitalised approach.

## Strategic Decision-Making and Problem-Solving

According to Fedorova et al. (2019), digital tools in workforce management eliminate repetitive activities, lower the possibility of human error, and empower professionals to address critical problems, enabling them to apply their expertise and knowledge more efficiently to solve problems in the organisation. Managing enormous employee data, which is the foundation for strategic decision-making, has made the task of human resource practitioners more challenging. However, the effective analysis and simplicity of producing data that supports strategic decision-making have been made possible by digital tools (Jäger & Petry, 2018). There is no gainsaying that digital tools in workforce management can enable managers to make strategic decisions. As such, Voermans and Van Veldhoven (2007) noted that digital tools in workforce management are a strategic driver of important organisational decisions. These digital tools in workforce management allow for faster and more informed decisions, which adds value to the organisation.

### Efficiency in Performance Management

Some organisations use automated, self-service, and electronic workforce management systems to promote the performance management process. This is done to achieve the ultimate objective of influencing employee behaviour to enhance performance (Rondeau, 2018). Managers can easily assess employees' performance, collect and write performance reports, and provide comprehensive feedback to workers through these digital systems (Cardy & Miller, 2005). Organisations with automated performance appraisal management use various performance assessment tools to evaluate goals and interpret outcomes and other employee data. This helps to reduce the paperwork and lessens the time and cost burden on organisations. Additionally, human resource analytic systems make it easier to collect, record, and retrieve a range of performance data from different sources and provide managers with better knowledge required to identify and resolve employee performance problems regarding behaviour and results (Sharma & Sharma, 2017).

### Improved Accuracy in Compensation

The use of technology in the compensation process has made it possible for human resource managers to play a substantial role in managing compensation for their employees. These managers can access more comprehensive data, resulting in more efficient and precise compensation plans (Tripathi & Singh, 2017). Additionally, employers can make expenditure plans, ensure that compensation designation decisions are acceptable, and show how incentive frameworks impact the employees and the organisation. Moreover, digital platforms promote flexible benefits and compensation packages that allow workers to change their benefits packages as their need changes (Gueutal & Falbe, 2005).

### Enhanced Trust

Employees' trust in their organisation is proportional to their perceived fairness of the workforce management system (Iqbal et al., 2019). Bissola and Imperatori (2013) noted that digital tools in workforce management impact organisational trust while influencing employee trust in the human resource department. Bondarouk et al. (2017) submitted that employees now trust organisational procedures and systems due to the growing use of digital tools. This is because digital tools in workforce management make processes more explicit and more transparent.

After all, all employees can easily access these processes on a digital database. Bissola and Imperatori (2013) noted that Views on the workforce management system's clarity and transparency affect impersonal trust because employees presume that the organisation has an accurate, trustable, and transparent performance recognition system.

### *Improved Occupational Health and Safety*

Occupational health and safety are also crucial aspects of workforce management, particularly in the construction industry, which has been characterised as a dangerous industry for workers (Akinlolu et al., 2020; Cai et al., 2018; Chan & Aghimien, 2022). Digital technologies offer significant benefits in ensuring the safety of construction workers. These technologies include; robotics and automation, warning systems, UAVs, sensors, laser scanners, building information modelling, wearable sensing devices, RFIDs, and quick response codes. These technologies can be integrated into the project from the design stage to reduce potential construction hazards and facilitate workplace safety (Bahrin et al., 2016; Karakhan & Alsaffar, 2019). For instance, building information modelling has an integrated safety management framework, which detects possible hazards before work starts and recommends risk reduction steps (Zhang et al., 2013). In addition, it allows construction site workers to record near-hits, allowing managers and supervisors to identify and minimise possible occupational hazards (Shen & Marks, 2015). More so, smart wearables help managers monitor employees' job activities and health. Through this monitoring, actions can be taken when necessary (Manning, 2017).

## Envisaged Challenges for Construction Organisations in Deploying Digital Technologies for Effective Workforce Management

Emerging technologies continue to offer significant benefits to construction organisations' delivery of projects and management of their workforce. However, the successful deployment of these technologies in the quest for effective management of workers can be challenged by several factors. This section explored some of the challenges for construction organisations deploying digital technologies for effective workforce management.

One of the major risks associated with technology adoption in many organisations is the fear of job loss. This fear leads to resistance to using digital technologies among workers and unions. The resistance to technology adoption within the construction industry has been attributed to the fear that these technologies will replace humans and render people jobless (Mzekandaba & Pazvakav, 2018). The Price Waterhouse Coopers (PwC) reports in 2018 noted that many jobs in developing nations might seize to exist with the advent of emerging technologies. However, Windapo (2016) earlier proposed that instead of pondering on the jobs to be lost, the question should be what types of jobs are these and what else could best replace these jobs. To this end, there have been studies stating that contrary to the popular opinion that technology leads to job loss, the use of pervasive digital tools will open up new markets for new skills and help people improve their skills, particularly in areas of managing these technologies for optimum production (Muro, 2017).

Integrating digital tools into existing workforce management system can be difficult due to compatibility issues (Troshani et al., 2011). Aside from compatibility, the complexity of the digital tool can be an issue for the effective adoption of digital tools for effective workforce management. This is because the way the digital tool is constructed impacts the results. If the program is not user-friendly, it increases the administration work for managers rather than decreasing it. If employees have trouble using and understanding the implemented digital tool, it will interfere with their performance (Rahman & Aydin, 2019). As a result, the complexity of digital tools intended for effective workforce management might make user adoption difficult.

More so, given that the introduction of digital workforce management requires an internal promoter, the organisational structure of an existing workforce management department may play a role in its acceptance. The motivation, aptitude, and capability to implement digital workforce management will be very low if an organisation's structure is not formalised, systematic and strategic to accept these technologies (Strohmeier & Kabst, 2009). In the same vein, Pollitt (2006) asserted that the internal culture of an organisation may influence the successful implementation of electronic platforms for managing the organisation's workers. As a result, it is unlikely that an organisation will implement digital tools for workforce management if its culture does not support digital technology adoption.

Also, studies have noted that many human resource practitioners lack the necessary skills to use digital tools to manage the workforce effectively (Dhanpat et al., 2020). Similarly, employees lack the technical understanding and abilities to implement digital tools (Denver et al., 2018). Furthermore, Guechtouli (2010) identified a shortage of people with information technology abilities or knowledge as a hurdle to implementing digital workforce management. As a result, if employees lack the requisite skills and competence, implementing digital workforce management may be unsuccessful. According to Banerji (2013), training and adapting to a new system is cumbersome and time-consuming. This is a concern because employee training is a significant aspect of adopting digital technologies, especially when people have been working in an organisation for a long time and need to learn how to do things differently, which they are hesitant or unable to accomplish without training. According to Mishra (2009), insufficient training can weaken the system's value and generate resistance to the system among the very personnel and supervisors who are expected to help in its usage. Therefore, without adequate training, workers may be hesitant to adopt digital tools that can aid workforce management, and it can also be inferred that because the training procedure is excessively drawn out, organisations may be discouraged from offering training to their workers.

Subramaniyan et al. (2019) remarked that the transition in technology in the modern world of work had exacerbated issues linked to data loss and leakage due to ambiguous data ownership. The problem with digital workforce management systems is security and privacy, as other workers can input their personal details, private information, and payroll system, and other employees may be able to update their personal details (Joseph & Ezzedeen, 2009). Additionally, if strict measures are not implemented, data can be readily available to everyone, and anyone can access key data and utilise it however they see fit without any authorisation (Devika & Prakash, 2018). The nature of the construction industry and the adequacy of technology infrastructure may deter digital technology adoption for effective workforce management. The hardware and software programs required to run the entire organisation make up the technology infrastructure (Al-Dmour et al., 2013). Oliveira and Martins (2009) assert that an organisation's current technological infrastructure influences whether or not such an organisation is ready to accept new technologies. Therefore, adopting digital tools for workforce management will be challenging if a strong technology infrastructure does not already exist in the organisations. More so, the internet service and technological infrastructure play a major role in adopting digital tools for workforce management. This is because digital tools for workforce management systems are integrated with the existing technology infrastructure. Poor technological infrastructure may make people uneasy and anxious, discouraging them from adopting new technology (Masum, 2015).

Technology implementation within an organisation requires a substantial financial investment. This large financial requirement can significantly impede the successful and continuous implementation of digital tools that can aid workforce management (Devika & Prakash, 2018). The financial investment includes the cost of getting the necessary technologies, maintaining them, and training employees to use these technologies. Also, personal interactions between employees can decrease due to the development of virtual networks through web-based human resource portals or intranets (Devika & Prakash, 2018; Punithavathi & Sugavaneswari, 2016). Also, Bondarouek and Ruel (2009) noted that one of the factors that may limit the rapid and widespread dissemination of digital tools in workforce management practices is the imprecise and ambiguous outcomes of its implementation. This is due to human resource personnel's lack of technological expertise, insufficient research and lack of digital skills, which drives them to embrace too ambitious objectives that are most likely to fail (Ghosh & Tripathi, 2018).

Based on the above, the envisaged challenges for construction organisations in deploying digital technologies for effective workforce management are summarised below:

(1) Complexity of technology.
(2) Data access, security, and privacy.
(3) Decreased face-to-face interactions.
(4) Existing workforce management structure.
(5) Fear of job loss.
(6) Inadequate financial resources.
(7) Inadequate technology infrastructure.
(8) Integration with existing systems.
(9) Lack of clear vision and clear goals for digitalising workforce management.
(10) Lack of top management support.

(11) Lack of user training.
(12) Nature of construction tasks.
(13) Organisational culture.
(14) Skills and knowledge gaps.
(15) Unfavourable legislation and regulations.

## Summary

This chapter explores the fourth industrial revolution and the digital technologies that can positively impact the management of the construction workforce when implemented. The chapter also unearths the possible challenges that might impede the successful deployment of digital technologies for effective workforce management. It was found that deploying workforce management-specific digital platforms and other digital technologies designed for project delivery can aid effective workforce management within construction organisations. Technologies such as cloud computing, IoT, big data analytics, robotics and automation, AI, and blockchain technology offer significant benefits to the effective workforce management of construction organisations. Impacts such as smart recruitment, better training, improved compensation administration, improved performance management and employee engagement, among others, are expected when digital tools are implemented within an organisation. However, several challenges, such as resistance to change due to fear of job loss, cost of investment in digital tools, organisational structure and culture, must be carefully considered as they might affect the successful use of digital tools and, by extension, impact the success of workforce management in the organisations. The next chapter explores workforce management theories, models, and practices.

## References

Achchab, S., & Temsamani, Y. K. (2022). Use of artificial intelligence in human resource management: Application of machine learning algorithms to an intelligent recruitment system. *Lecture Notes in Networks and Systems, 249*, 203–215.
Adjei, J., Adams, S., & Mamattah, L. (2021). Cloud computing adoption in Ghana; accounting for institutional factors. *Technology Society, 65*, 1–9.
Agarwal, R., Chandrasekaran, S., & Sridhar, M. (2016). *Imagining construction's digital future.* Capital Project and Infrastructure, McKinsey and Company. https://www.mckinsey.com/capabilities/operations/our-insights/imagining-constructions-digital-future
Aghimien, D. O., Aigbavboa, C. O., & Oke, A. E., & Thwala, W. D. (2021). *Construction digitalisation – A capability maturity model for construction organisations.* Routledge, UK.
Aghimien, D. O., Oke, A. E., & Aigbavboa, C. O. (2019). A review of the application of data mining for sustainable construction in Nigeria. *Energy Procedia, 158*, 3240–3245.
Aghimien, D., Ikuabe, M., Aghimien, L. M., Aigbavboa, C., Ngcobo, N., & Yankah, J. (2022). PLS-SEM assessment of the impediments of robotics and automation deployment for effective construction health and safety. *Journal of Facilities Management*, ahead-of-print https://doi.org/10.1108/JFM-04-2022-0037

Aghimien, E. I., Aghimien, L. M., Petinrin, O. O., & Aghimien, D. O. (2020). High-performance computing for computational modelling in built environment-related studies – A scientometric review. *Journal of Engineering Design and Technology*, *19*(5), 1138–1157.

Akanmu, A. A., Olayiwola, J., Ogunseiju, O., & McFeeyers, D. (2020). Cyber-physical postural training system for construction workers. *Automation in Construction*, *117*, 1–12.

Akinlolu, M., Haupt, T. C., Edwards, D. J., & Simpeh, F. (2020). A bibliometric review of the status and emerging research trends in construction safety management technologies. *International Journal of Construction Management*, *22*(14), 2699–2711.

Akinradewo, O. I., Aigbavboa, C. O., Edwards, D. J., & Oke, A. E. (2022). A principal component analysis of barriers to the implementation of blockchain technology in the South African built environment. *Journal of Engineering, Design and Technology*, *20*(4), 914–934.

Alaloul, W. S., Liew, M. S., Zawawi, N. A. W. A., & Kennedy, I. B. (2020). Industrial revolution 4.0 in the construction industry: Challenges and opportunities for stakeholders. *Ain Shams Engineering Journal*, *11*(1), 225–230.

Al-Dmour, R. H., Love, S., Bi, Z., & Al-Zu'bi, M. F. (2013). Factors influencing the adoption of hris applications: A literature review. *International Journal of Management and Business Studies*, *3*(4), 9–26.

Allen, D. G., Mahto, R. V., & Otondo, R. F. (2007). Web-based recruitment: Effects of information, organisational brand, and attitudes toward a web site on applicant attraction. *The Journal of Applied Psychology*, *92*(6), 1696–1708.

Almishal, A., & Youssef, A. E. (2014). Cloud service providers: A comparative study. *International Journal of Computer Applications and Information Technology*, *5*(2), 46–52.

Al-Shameri, A. S. A. S., & Omar, S. S. B. (2022). *HR digitalization as a critical HR practice to navigate through Covid-19 for the improvement of the employee job performance*. Proceedings of the International Conference on Industrial Engineering and Operations Management, Istanbul, Turkey, March 7–10.

Angrave, D., Charlwood, A., Kirkpatrick, I., Lawrence, M., & Stuart, M. (2016). HR and analytics: Why HR is set to fail the big data challenge. *Human Resource Management Journal*, *26*(1), 1–11.

Aziz, Z., Anumba, C. J., & Pena-Mora, F. (2010). Using context-aware wireless technologies to support teaching and learning in built environment. *International Journal of Construction Education and Research*, *6*(1), 18–29.

Bagheri, B., Yang, S., Kao, H. A. & Lee, J. (2015). Cyber-physical systems architecture for self-aware machines in industry 4.0 environment. *IFAC Conference*, *38*(3), 1622–1627.

Bahl, M. (2015). *Asia rising: Digital driving. Cognizant – Keep challenging*. https://www.the-digital-insurer.com/wp-content/uploads/2016/01/635-asia-rising-digital-driving-codex1403.pdf

Bahrin, M. A. K., Othman, M. F., Nor, N. H., & Azli, M. F. T. (2016). Industry 4.0: A review on industrial automation and robotic. *Jurnal Teknologi (Sciences and Engineering)*, *78*(6–13), 137–143.

Balabanova, I. O., & Balabanov, I. P. (2020). The use of digital technology in personnel management (HRM). *Advances in Economics, Business and Management Research*, *128*, 2821–2826.

Banerji, S. C. (2013). A study of issues and challenges of implementation of information technology in HRM. *Global Journal of Management and Business Studies*, *3*(4), 435–440.

Bello, S. A., Oyedele, L. O., Akinade, O. O., Bilal, M., Delgado, J. M. D., Akanbi, L. A., Ajayi, A. O., & Owolabi, H. A. (2021). Cloud computing in construction industry: Use cases, benefits and challenges. *Automation in Construction*, *122*, 1–18.

Bhattacharya, S., & Momaya, K. S. (2021). Actionable strategy framework for digital transformation in AECO industry. *Engineering, Construction and Architectural Management*, *28*(5), 1397–1422.

Bienhaus, F., & Haddud, A. (2018). Procurement 4.0: Factors influencing the digitisation of procurement and supply chains. *Business Process Management Journal, 24*(4), 965–984.

Bissola, R., & Imperatori, B. (2013). Facing e-HRM: The consequences on employee attitude towards the organisation and the HR department in Italian SMEs. *European Journal of International Management, 7*(4), 450–468.

Bondarouk, T., Parry, E., & Furtmueller, E. (2017). Electronic HRM: Four decades of research on adoption and consequences. *The International Journal of Human Resource Management, 28*(1), 98–131.

Bondarouk, T. V., & Ruël, H. J. M. (2009). Electronic human resource management: Challenges in the digital era. *The International Journal of Human Resource Management, 20*(3), 505–514.

Brandão, C., Silva, R., & dos Santos, J. V. (2019). Online recruitment in Portugal: Theories and candidate profiles. *Journal of Business Research, 94*, 273–279.

Cai, S., Ma, Z., Skibniewski, M., Guo, J., & Yun, L. (2018). Application of automation and robotics technology in High-Rise building construction: An overview. In *Proceedings of the 35th International Symposium on Automation and Robotics in Construction*, Berlin, Germany, 20–25 July.

Calvard, T. S., & Jeske, D. (2018). Developing human resource data risk management in the age of big data. *International Journal of Information Management, 43*, 159–164.

Cardy, R. L., & Miller, J. S. (2005). eHR and performance management: A consideration of positive potential and the dark side. In H. G. Gueutaland & D. L. Stone (Eds.), *The brave new world of eHR: human resource management in the digital age*. Jossey-Bass.

Castellacci, F., & Vinas-Bardolet, C. (2019). Internet use and job satisfaction. *Computers in Human Behavior, 90*, 141–152.

Chahal, H., & Gulia, P. (2016). Big data analytics. *Research Journal of Computer and Information Technology Sciences, 4*(2), 1–4.

Chamorro-Premuzic, T., Akhtar, R., Winsborough, D., & Sherman, R. A. (2017). The datafication of talent: How technology is advancing the science of human potential at work. *Current Opinion in Behavioural Sciences, 18*, 13–16.

Chan, A. P., Javed, A. A., Lyu, S., Hon, C. K., & Wong, F. K. (2016). Strategies for improving safety and health of ethnic minority construction workers. *Journal of Construction Engineering and Management, 142*(9), 05016007.

Chan, W. W. M., & Aghimien, D. O. (2022). Safe working cycle: Is it a panacea to combat construction site safety accidents in Hong Kong? *Sustainability, 14*(2), 1–17.

Chandra, S. (2020). A study on impact of cloud-based computing on performance of human resources in selected IT industry in Odisha. *International Journal of Scientific and Technology Research, 9*(1), 2719–2723.

Choi, B., Hwang, S., & Lee, S. (2017). What drives construction workers' acceptance of wearable technologies in the workplace? Indoor localisation and wearable health devices for occupational safety and health. *Automation in Construction, 84*, 31–41.

Clavero, J. (2018). *Artificial intelligence in construction: The future of construction*. https://esub.com/artificial-intelligence-construction-future-construction/

Cohen, E. (2010). *CSR for HR: A necessary partnership for advancing responsible business practices*. Greenleaf Publishing Limited.

da Silva, L. B. P., Soltovski, R., Pontes, J., Treinta, F. T., Leitão, P., Mosconi, E., de Resende, L. M. M., & Yoshino, R. T. (2022). Human resources management 4.0: Literature review and trends. *Computers and Industrial Engineering, 168*, 1–20.

Dai, L., He, Y., & Xing, G. (2015) The construction of human resource management cloud service platform. *Intelligent Information Management, 7*, 1–6.

Dallasega, P., Rauch, E., & Linder, C. (2018). Industry 4.0 as an enabler of proximity for construction supply chains: A systematic literature review. *Computers in Industry, 99*, 205–225.

De Andrade Régio, M. M., Gaspar, M. R. C., Do Carmo Farinha, L. M., & De Passos Morgado, M. M. A. (2016). Forecasting the disruptive skillset alignment induced by the forthcoming industrial revolution. *Romanian Review Precision Mechanics, Optics and Mecatronics, 49,* 24–29.

de Mauro, A., Greco, M., & Grimaldi, M. (2016). A formal definition of big data based on its essential features. *Library Review, 65*(3), 122–135.

Deloitte. (2017). Deloitte Global Human Capital Trends - Rewriting the rules for a digital age. https://www2.deloitte.com/cn/en/pages/human-capital/articles/global-human-capital-trends-2017.html

Denver, M., Gibson, M., Tonderayi, N., & Severino, M. (2018). Human resource management practices: A case of SMES in Zimbabwe. *International Journal of Economics, Commerce and Management, 6*(8), 483–497.

Devika, A., & Prakash, H. (2018). E-HRM: Opportunities and challenges. *International Journal of Applied Research, 4*(4), 129–133.

Dhanpat, N., Buthelezi, Z. P., Joe, M. R., Maphela, T. V., & Shongwe, N. (2020). Industry 4.0: The role of human resource professionals. *SA Journal of Human Resource Management, 18,* 1–11.

Dickson, D., & Nusair, K. (2010). An HR perspective: The global hunt for talent in the digital age. *Worldwide Hospitality and Tourism Themes, 2*(1), 86–93.

Dimick, S. (2014). *Adopting digital technologies: The path for SMEs.* The Conference Board of Canada, Ottawa, ON, pp. 1–13.

El-Aziz, R., El-Gamal, S., & Ismail, M. (2020). Mediating and moderating factors affecting readiness to IoT applications: The banking sector context. *International Journal of Managing Information Technology, 12*(4), 1–26.

Eliaçık, E. (2022). *Is HR ready for blockchain?* https://dataconomy.com/2022/06/22/blockchain-in-hr/#:~:text=Blockchain%20technology%20can%20aid%20in,hacks%20of%20important%20personnel%20records

Evans, L., & Kitchin, R. (2018). A smart place to work? Big data systems, labour, control and modern retail stores. *New Technology, Work and Employment, 33*(1), 44–57.

Faliagka, E., Tsakalidis, A., & Tzimas, G. (2012). An integrated e-recruitment system for automated personality mining and applicant ranking. *Internet Research, 22*(5), 551–568.

Fareri, S., Fantoni, G., Chiarello, F., Coli, E., & Binda, A. (2020). Estimating Industry 4.0 impact on job profiles and skills using text mining. *Computers in Industry, 118,* 1–19.

Fedorova, A., Zarubina, A., Pikulina, Y., Moskovskikh, A., Balandina, T., & Gafurova, T. (2019). Digitalization of the human resource management: Russian companies case. In *Proceedings of SOCIOINT 2019 - 6th International Conference on Education, Social Sciences and Humanities,* Istanbul, Turkey, 24–26 June, pp. 1227–1230.

Fenech, R., Baguant, P., & Ivanov, D. (2019). The changing role of human resource management in an era of digital transformation. *Journal of Management Information and Decision Sciences, 22*(2), 166–175.

Fındıklı, M., & Bayarçelik, E. (2015). Exploring the Outcomes of Electronic Human Resource Management (E-HRM)? *Procedia - Social and Behavioral Sciences, 207,* 424–431.

Fitz-enz, J. (2010). *The New HR analytics – Predicting the economic value of your company's human capital investments.* American Management Association.

Fitz-enz, J., & Mattox, J. (2014). *Predictive analytics for human resources.* Wiley.

FitzPatrick, L., & Valskov, K. (2014). *Internal communications: A manual for practitioners.* Springer.

Froese, T. M. (2010). The impact of emerging information technology on project management for construction. *Automation in Construction, 19*(5), 531–538.

Galgali, P. (2017). *Digital transformation and its impact on organisations' human resource management.* IOR and Stakeholder Management, MCM, School of Communication and Information, Rutgers University, USA.

García de Soto, B., Agustí-Juan, I., Joss, S., & Hunhevicz, J. (2019). Implications of Construction 4.0 to the workforce and organisational structures. *International Journal of Construction Management*, 1–13.

Garcia-Arroyo, J., & Osca, A. (2019). Big data contributions to human resource management: A systematic review. *The International Journal of Human Resource Management*, *32*(10), 1–27.

Gartner. (2016). *Digitalisation*. Gartner Glossary. https://www.gartner.com/en/information-technology/glossary/digitalization

Garyaev, N., & Rybakova, A. (2018). Cloud interaction technologies in the design and construction. *MATEC Web of Conferences*, *170*, 1–6.

Gaur, B., Shukla, V. K., & Verma, A. (2019). Strengthening people analytics through wearable IoT device for real-time data collection. In *International conference on automation, computational and technology management*, London, UK, 24–26 April, Spp. 555–560.

Ghimire, S., Luis-Ferreira, F., Nodehi, T., & Jardim-Goncalves, R. (2017). IoT based situational awareness framework for real-time project management. *International Journal of Computer Integrated Manufacturing*, *30*(1), 74–83.

Ghosh, V., & Tripathi, N. (2018). Cloud computing and e-HRM. In M. Thite, *e-HRM* (1st ed.) Routledge.

Guechtouli, M. (2010). E-HRM's Impact on an environmental scanning process: How can technology support. *International Journal of Technology and Human Interaction*, *6*(3), 53–66.

Gueutal, H. G., & Falbe, D. L. (2005). HR: Trends in delivery methods. In H.G. Gueutal & D. L. Stone (Eds.), *The brave new world of eHR*. Jossey-Bass.

Guz, A. N., & Rushchitsky, J. J. (2009). Scopus: A system for the evaluation of scientific journals. *International Applied Mechanics*, *45*(4), 351–362.

Halid, H., Yusoff, Y. M., & Somu, H. (2020). The relationship between digital human resource management and organizational performance. *Advances in Economics, Business and Management Research*, *141*, 96–99.

Hamilton, R. H., & Sodeman, W. A. (2020). The questions we ask: Opportunities and challenges for using big data analytics to strategically manage human capital resources. *Business Horizons*, *63*(1), 85–95.

Han, Y. J. (2017). Blockchain-verified credentials could change the game of hiring. https://news.bloomberglaw.com/daily-labor-report/blockchain-verified-credentials-could-change-the-game-of-hiring?context=article-related

Hao, Y. (2017). Research on strategic human resource management of enterprises based on cloud computing. *Advances in Intelligent Systems Research*, *156*, 107–112.

Hassaini, R., El Bouzekri El Idrissi, Y., & Abouabdellah, A. (2017). Software project management in the era of digital transformation. In A. El Abbadi & B. Garbinato (Eds.), *Networked Systems. NETYS 2017. Lecture Notes in Computer Science* (p. 10299). Springer.

Hawkins, D. T. (2001). Bibliometrics of electronic journals in information science. *Information Research*, *7*(1), 1.

Hjort, A., Henriksen, K., & Elbæk, L. (2018). Player-driven video analysis to enhance reflective soccer practice in talent development. *International Journal of Game-Based Learning*, *8*(2), 29–43.

Huang, E. Y., Lin, S. W., & Fan, Y. C. (2015). MS-QUAL: Mobile service quality measurement. *Electronic Commerce Research and Applications*, *14*(2), 126–142.

Iansiti, M., & Lakhani, K. (2017). The truth about blockchain. *Harvard Business Review*, *95*(1), 1–11.

Ikuabe, M., Aigbavboa, C., Anumba, C., Oke, A., & Aghimien, L. (2022). Confirmatory factor analysis of performance measurement indicators determining the uptake of CPS for facilities management. *Buildings*, *12*(466), 1–15.

International Telecommunications Union, ITU – Y.2060. (2012). *ITU – Y.2060: Overview of the Internet of things. Recommendation ITU-T Series Y: Global Information Infrastructure, Internet Protocol Aspects and Next-Generation Networks.* https://www.itu.int/rec/T-REC-Y.2060-201206-I

Iqbal, N., Ahmad, M., & Allen, M. M. C. (2019). Unveiling the relationship between e-HRM, impersonal trust and employee productivity. *Management Research Review*, *42*(7), 879–899.

Jäger, W., & Petry, T. (2018). Digital HR: Ein Überblick. In T. Petry, W. Jäger [Hrsg.], *Digital HR: Smarte und agile Systeme, Prozesse und Strukturen im Personalmanagement* (pp. 27–99). Haufe Lexware.

Jayabalan, N., Makhbul, Z. K. M., Senggaravellu, S. N., Subramaniam, M., & Ramly, N. A. B. (2021). The impact of digitalization on human resource management practices in the automotive manufacturing industry. *Journal of Southwest Jiaotong University*, *56*(5), 524–537.

Jia, Q., Guo, Y., Li, R., Li, Y., & Chen, Y. (2018). A conceptual artificial intelligence application framework in human resource management. In *8th International Conference on Electronic Business*, Gulin, China, 2–6 December.

Johnson, R. D., Lukaszewski, K. M., & Stone, D. L. (2016). The evolution of the field of human resource information systems: Co-evolution of technology and HR processes. *Communications of the Association for Information Systems*, *38*(1), 533–553.

Joseph, R. C. & Ezzedeen, S. R. (2009). E-government and e-HRM in the public sector. In T. Torres-Coronas & M. Arias-Oliva (Eds.), *Encyclopaedia of human resources information systems: Challenges in e-HRM*. IGI Global.

Joshi, D., & Shah, R. (2015). Automation in construction industry. *International Journal of Advanced Research in Engineering, Science and Management*, 1–5.

Kalavendi, R., (2017). *Digitisation and digitalisation: The two-letter difference*. https://medium.com/@ravisierraatlantic/digitization-digitalisation-the-2-letter-difference-59b747d42ade

Kaplan, J. (2016). *Artificial Intelligence: What everyone needs to know*. Oxford University Press.

Karakhan, A., & Alsaffar, O. (2019). Technology's role in safety management. *Professional Safety Journal*, *64*(1), 43–45.

Karatop, B., Kubat, C., & Uygun, O. (2015). Talent management in manufacturing system using fuzzy logic approach. *Computers and Industrial Engineering*, *86*, 127–136.

Kasperzyk, C., Kim, M., & Brilakis, I. (2017). Automated re-prefabrication system for buildings using robotics. *Automation in Construction*, *83*, 184–195.

Khairullina, K. (2021). *Modernization of HR services driven by digitalization: Example of Russian Railways*. Master Thesis submitted to the School of Engineering Science, Lappeenranta-Lahti University of Technology LUT, Finland.

Kişi, N. (2022). Exploratory research on the use of blockchain technology in recruitment. *Sustainability*, *14*(16), 10098.

Kitchin, R. (2014). The real-time city? Big data and smart urbanism. *Geo Journal*, *79*, 1–14.

Kremer, K. (2022). HR practices in the context of the Internet of Things. *Strategic Management*. *27*(1), 34–42.

Kurien, M., Kim, M., Kopsida, M., & Brilakis, I. (2018). Real-time simulation of construction workers using the combined human body and hand tracking for robotic construction worker system. *Automation in Construction*, *86*, 125–137.

Laukkanen, T. (2016). Consumer adoption versus rejection decisions in seemingly similar service innovations: The case of the Internet and mobile banking. *Journal of Business Research*, *69*(7), 2432–2439.

Li, G., Hou, Y., & Wu, A. (2017). Fourth industrial revolution: Technological drivers, impacts and coping methods. *Chinese Geographical Science*, *27*(4), 626–637.

Li, L., Su, F., Zhang, W., & Mao, J.-Y (2018). Digital transformation by SME entrepreneurs: A capability perspective. *Information Systems Journal*, *28*(6), 1129–1157.

Lipscomb, H. J., Dement, J. M., Nolan, J., & Patterson, D. (2006). Nail gun injuries in apprentice carpenters: Risk factors and control measures. *American Journal of Industrial Medicine, 49*(7), 505–513.

Lipsmeier, A., Kühn, A., Joppen, R., & Dumitrescu, R. (2020). Process for the development of a digital strategy. *Procedia CIRP, 88,* 173–178.

Lu, Y. (2017). Industry 4.0: A survey on technologies, applications, and open research issues. *Journal of Industrial Information Integration, 6,* 1–10.

Lukic, J., Salkic, H., & Ostojic, B. (2018). New job positions and recruitment of employees shaped by blockchain technologies. In 4th International Scientific – Business Conference, Belgrade, Serbia, 13 December.

Lumi, A. (2020). The impact of digitalisation on human resources development. *Prizren Social Science Journal, SHIKS, 4*(3), 39–46.

Ma, L., & Ye, M. (2015). The role of electronic human resource management in contemporary human resource management. *Open Journal of Social Sciences, 3,* 71–78.

Mahmud, S. H., Assan, L., & Islam, R. (2018). Potentials of Internet of Things (IoT) in Malaysian construction industry. *Annals of Emerging Technologies in Computing, 2*(4), 44–52.

Manning, E. (2017). *Six questions exploring the direction of wearable safety technology on the jobsite.* https://www.constructionbusinessowner.com/technology/iot-wearables-construction-industry

Manoharan, T. R., Muralidharan, C., & Deshmukh, S. G. (2009). An integrated fuzzy multi-attribute decision-making model for employees' performance appraisal. *International Journal of Human Resource Management, 22*(3), 722–745.

Manyika, J., Chui, M., Brown, B., Bughim, J., Dobbs, R., Roxburgh, C., & Byers, A. H. (2011). *Big Data: The next frontier for innovation, competition, and productivity.* https://www.mckinsey.com/business-functions/mckinsey-digital/our-insights/big-data-the-next-frontier-for-innovation#

Marler, J., & Parry, E. (2016). Human resource management, strategic involvement and e-HRM technology. *The International Journal of Human Resource Management, 27*(19), 2233–2253.

Marler, J. H., & Boudreau, J. W. (2017). An evidence-based review of HR Analytics. *The International Journal of Human Resource Management, 28*(1), 3–26.

Martin, D. (2021). *Role of technology in human resource management.* https://www.the-humancapitalhub.com/articles/role-of-technology-in-human-resource-management

Masum, A. (2015). Adoption factors of electronic human resource management (e-HRM) in banking industry of Bangladesh. *Journal of Social Sciences, 11*(1), 1–6.

McAfee, A., & Brynjolfsson, E. (2012). Big Data: The management revolution. *Harvard Business Review, 90*(10), 60–68.

McAfee, A., & Brynjolfsson, E. (2012). Big Data: The management revolution. *Harvard Business Review.* https://hbr.org/2012/10/big-data-the-management-revolution

McDonald, S. (2017). It's time to embrace IoT in construction. *Engineering News-Record.* http://digitaladmin.bnpmedia.com/publication/?m=38305&i=390701&p=12&ver=html5

Mechtcherine, V., Nerella, V. N., Will, F., Näther, M., Otto, J., & Krause, M. (2019). Large-scale digital concrete construction – CONPrint3D concept for on-site, monolithic 3D-printing. *Automation in Construction, 107,* 1–16.

Mehrabad, M. S., & Brojeny, M. F. (2007). The development of an expert system for effective selection and appointment of the jobs applicants in human resource management. *Computers & Industrial Engineering, 53*(2), 306–312.

Mengistu, D. G., & Mahesh, G. (2020). Challenges in developing the Ethiopian construction industry. *African Journal of Science, Technology, Innovation and Development, 12*(4), 373–384.

Mishra, A. (2009). E-HRM Challenges and Opportunities. In *Torres-Coronas and Arias-Olvia editions of Encyclopaedia of Human Resources Information Systems: Challenges in e-HRM*, IGI Global.

Mistri, P. S., & Rathod, H. A. (2016). Remedies over barriers of automation and robotics for construction industry. *International Journal of Advanced Research in Engineering, Science and Management, 21*(3), 1–4.

Mohanty, S., & Mishra, P. C. (2020). Framework for understanding Internet of Things in human resource management. *Revista Espacios, 41*(12), 25–36.

Moon, C., Lee, J., & Lim, S. (2010). A performance appraisal and promotion ranking system based on fuzzy logic: An implementation case in military organizations. *Applied Soft Computing Journal, 10*(2), 512–519.

Moyeenudin, H. M., & Anandan, R. (2020). IoT implementation at global enterprises for progressive human resource practices. *Proceedings of First International Conference on Mathematical Modelling and Computational Science: ICMMCS 2020*. Springer Nature.

Mukundha, C., & Vidyamadhuri, K. (2017). Cloud Computing models: A survey. *Advances in Computational Sciences and Technology, 10*(5), 747–761.

Muro, M., Liu, S., Whiton, J., & Kulkarni, S. (2017). *Digitalisation and the American Workforce*. Metropolitan Policy Program Report, Brookings Institute, USA.

Mzekandaba, S., & Pazvakav, R. (2018). *Tech to contribute to job losses in SA*. https://www.itweb.co.za/content/o1Jr5qxEE5YvKdWL

Naidoo, R., & Ndlovu, S. W. (2021). Ambivalent relations between users and digital HRM. In Proceeding of the virtual 27th Annual Americas Conference on Information Systems, 9–13 August, pp. 1–11.

Nawaz, N. (2019). Artificial Intelligence interchange human intervention in the recruitment process in Indian Software Industry. *International Journal of Advanced Trends in Computer Science and Engineering, 8*(4), 1433–1442.

Neeraj. (2018). Role of digitalization in human resource management. *International Journal of Emerging Technologies and Innovative Research, 5*(1), 284–288.

Negi, P., & Kaur, J. (2019). The digital workplace: Implications for human resource management. *International Journal of Management, Technology and Engineering, 9*(2), 1491–1500.

Newton, J. (2018). Artificial intelligence in the construction industry. *International Journal of Civil Engineering and Technology, 9*(13), 957–962.

Ngwenya, L. M., & Aigbavboa, C. (2017). Improvement of productivity and employee performance through an efficient human resource management practice. *Advances in Intelligent Systems and Computing, 498*, 727–737.

Oesterreich, T. D., & Teuteberg, F. (2016). Understanding the implications of digitisation and automation in the context of industry 4.0: A triangulation approach and elements of a research agenda for the construction industry. *Computers in Industry, 83*, 121–139.

Oke, A. E., Aghimien, D. O., Aigbavboa, C. O., & Koloko, N. (2018). Challenges of digital collaboration in the South African construction industry. In *Proceedings of the International Conference on Industrial Engineering and Operations Management*, Bandung, Indonesia, March 6–8, pp. 2472–2482.

Oke, A. E., Aliu, J., & Onajite, S. A. (2023). Barriers to the adoption of digital technologies for sustainable construction in a developing economy. *Architectural Engineering and Design Management*. ahead-of-print. https://doi.org/10.1080/17452007.2023.2187754

Oke, A. E., Farouk, K. A., Abdel-Tawab, M., Abubakar, A. S., Albukhari, I., & Kingsley, C. (2021). Barriers to the implementation of cloud computing for sustainable construction in a developing economy. *International Journal of Building Pathology and Adaptation*, ahead-of-print. https://doi.org/10.1108/IJBPA-07-2021-0098

Oliveira, T., & Martins, M. R. (2009). *Determinants of information technology adoption in Portugal.* Proceedings of the International Conference on e-Business, Milan, Italy, 7–10 July, pp. 264–270.

Onik, M. H., Miraz, M. H., & Kim, C. S. (2018). *A recruitment and human resource management technique using Blockchain technology for Industry 4.0.* In Proceedings of the Smart Cities Symposium, Manama, Bahrain, pp. 11–16.

Osunsanmi, T. O., Aigbavboa, C. O., & Oke, A. E. (2018). Construction 4.0: The future of South Africa construction industry. *World Academy of Science, Engineering and Technology International Journal of Civil and Environmental Engineering, 12*(3), 206–212.

Palee, P., Wannapiroon, P., & Nilsook, P. (2020). The architecture of intelligent career prediction system based on the cognitive technology for producing graduates to the digital manpower. *International Journal of Advanced Computer Science and Applications, 11*(12), 115–121.

Park, J., Kim, K., & Cho, Y. K. (2017). Framework of automated construction-safety monitoring using cloud-enabled BIM and BLE mobile tracking sensors. *Journal of Construction Engineering and Management, 143*(2), 05016019.

Perez, S., & Foshay, R. (2002). Adding up the distance: Can developmental studies work in a distance learning environment? *T.H.E. Journal, 29*(2), 19–24.

Phyoung, J. K., & Young, J. N. (2003). *Mobile agent system architecture for supporting mobile market application service in mobile computing environment.* In 2003 International Conference on Geometric Modeling and Graphics, London, UK, pp. 149–153.

Plekhanov, D., & Netland, T. (2019). Digitalisation stages in firms: Towards a framework. In *Proceedings of the 26th EurOMA Conference*, Helsinki, Finland, 17–19 June 2019.

Pollitt, D. (2006). E-HR brings everything together at KPN. *Human Resource Management International Digest, 14*(1), 34–35.

PricewaterhouseCoopers, PwC. (2017). How blockchain technology could impact HR and the world of work. https://www.pwc.co.uk/issues/futuretax/assets/blockchain-can%20impact-hr.pdf

Punithavathi, I., & Sugavaneswari, P. M. (2016). Electronic human resource management: Challenges in the digital era. *An International Journal of Interdisciplinary Studies, 20*, 505–514.

Rabhi, L., Falih, N., Afraites, A., & Bouikhalene, B. (2019). Big data approach and its applications in various fields: Review. *Procedia Computer Science, 155*, 599–605.

Rad, B. B., & Ahmada, H. A. (2017). Internet of Things: Trends, opportunities, and challenges. *International Journal Computer Science Network Security, 17*(7), 89–95.

Rahman, M., & Aydin, E. (2019). Organisational challenges and benefits of e-HRM implementations in governmental organisations: Theoretical shift from toe model. *International Journal of Economics and Administrative Studies*, 127–142.

Rasmussen, T., & Ulrich, D. (2015). Learning from practice: How HR analytics avoids being a management fad. *Organizational Dynamics, 44*(3), 236–242.

Rawai, N. M., Fathi, M. S., Abedi, M., & Rambat, S. (2013). Cloud computing for green construction management. In *3rd International Conference on Intelligent System Design and Engineering Applications*, Hong Kong, China, 16–18 January, pp. 432–435.

Rhemananda, H., Simbolon, D. R., & Fachrunnisa, O. (2021). Blockchain technology to support employee recruitment and selection in industrial revolution 4.0. In P. K. Pattnaik, M. Sain, A. A. Al-Absi, & P. Kumar (Eds.), *Proceedings of International Conference on Smart Computing and Cyber Security, Lecture Notes in Networks and Systems, 149*, Springer, Singapore.

Roblek, V., Meško, M., & Krapež, A. (2016). A complex view of industry 4.0. *Sage Open, 6*(2), 1–11.

Rondeau, K. V. (2018). e-Performance and reward management. In M. Thite (Ed.), *e-HRM – Digital approaches, directions and applications.* Routledge, UK.

Rouse, M. (2017). *Meaning of digitalization.* http://whatis.techtarget.com/definition/digitization

Ruël, H., Bondarouk, T., & Looise, J. (2004). E-HRM: Innovation or irritation. An explorative empirical study in five large companies on web-based HRM. *Management Revue, 15*(3), 364–381.

Rüßmann, M., Lorenz, M., Gerbert, P., & Waldner, M. (2015). *Industry 4.0: The future of productivity and growth in manufacturing industries.* Boston Consulting Group 2015 Report.

Sakho, S., Zhang, J., Mbyamm Kiki, M. J., Kouassi Bonzou, A., & Essaf, F. (2019). Privacy protection issues in blockchain technology. *International Journal of Computer Science and Information Security, 17*(2), 124–131.

Sakran, T. (2019). Educational tips for the detection of resume padding. *International Journal on Policy and Information, 7*(2), 31–41.

Samson, H., & Agrawal, V. (2020). Effectiveness of digitalization in HRM: An emerging trend. *Journal of Critical Reviews, 7*(4), 4082–4088.

San, K. M., Choy, C. F., & Fung, W. P. (2019). The potentials and impacts of blockchain technology in construction industry: A literature review. *IOP Conference Series: Materials Science and Engineering, 495,* 012005.

Sareen, P. (2013). Cloud computing: Types, architecture, application, concerns, virtualization and role of IT governance in cloud. *International Journal of Advanced Research in Computer Science and Software Engineering, 3*(3), 533–538.

Schwab, K. (2017). *The fourth industrial revolution* (1st ed.). Crown Business.

Seo, Y. H., Song, J. H., & Kong, Y. I. (2017). *Blockchain technology: Prospect and implications in perspective of industry and society.* Software Policy & Research Institute.

Sepasgozar, S. M. E., & Davis, S. (2018). Construction technology adoption cube: An investigation on process, factors, barriers, drivers and decision makers using NVivo and AHP analysis. *Buildings, 9*(7), 1–31.

Sepasgozar, S. M., Loosemore, M., & Davis, S. R. (2016). Conceptualising information and equipment technology adoption in construction: A critical review of existing research. *Engineering, Construction and Architectural Management, 23*(2), 158–176.

Shafiq, S., & Hamza, S. M. (2017). The effect of training and development on employee performance in private company, Malaysia. *International Journal of Education, Learning and Training, 2*(2), 42–56.

Shah, N., Irani, Z., & Sharif, A. M. (2017). Big data in an HR context: Exploring organizational change readiness, employee attitudes and behaviors. *Journal of Business Research, 70,* 366–378.

Shankar, A., & Nigam, A. (2022). Explaining resistance intention towards mobile HRM application: The dark side of technology adoption. *International Journal of Manpower, 43*(1), 206–225.

Shankar, A., & Datta, B. (2019). Measuring mobile commerce service quality: A review of literature. In P. Duhan & A. Signh (Eds.), *M-Commerce* (1st ed.). Apple Academic Press.

Sharma, A., & Sharma, T. (2017). HR analytics and performance appraisal system: A conceptual framework for employee performance improvement. *Management Research Review, 40*(6), 684–697.

Shen, X., & Marks, E. (2015). Near-miss information visualisation tool in BIM for construction safety. *Journal of Construction Engineering and Management, 142*(4), 1–10.

Sklar, J. (2015). Robots lay three times as many bricks as construction workers. *MIT Technology Review.* https://www.technologyreview.com/2015/09/02/10587/robots-lay-three-times-as-many-bricks-as-construction-workers/

Spence, A. (2018). *Blockchain and Chief Human Resource Officer.* Blockchain Research Institute, Mountain View. https://www.blockchainresearchinstitute.org/project/blockchain-and-the-chief-human-resources-officer/

Speringer, M., & Schnelzer, J. (2019). Differentiation of industry 4.0 models: The 4th industrial revolution from different regional perspectives in the Global North and Global South. In Regional Academy on the United Nations (RAUN) (Eds.), *Innovations for development: Towards sustainable, inclusive, and peaceful societies.* http://www.ra-un. org/uploads/4/7/5/4/47544571/1_unido_differentiation_of_industry_4.0_models.pdf

Strohmeier, S., & Kabst, R. (2009). Organizational adoption of e-HRM in Europe: An empirical exploration of major adoption factors. *Journal of Managerial Psychology, 24*(6), 482–501.

Subramaniyan, S., Thite, M., & Sampathkumar, S. (2019). Information security and privacy in e-HRM. In M. Thite (Ed.), *e-HRM: Digital approaches, directions and applications.* Routledge.

Sukumar, M., & Giridharan, K. S. (2014). Development and challenges in mobile human resource management arena. *Elysium Journal, 1*(2), 1–6.

Sun, D. W., Chang, G. R., Gao, S., Jin, L. Z., & Wang, X. W. (2012). Modelling a dynamic data replication strategy to increase system availability in cloud computing environments. *Journal of Computer Science and Technology, 27*(2), 256–272.

Tadapaneni, N. A. (2020). Cloud computing security challenges. *International Journal of Innovations in Engineering Research and Technology, 7*(6), 1–6.

Talend, (2021). *How does big data work for HR analytics?* https://www.talend.com/resources/big-data-hr-analytics/

Tambe, P., Cappelli, P., & Yakubovich, V. (2019). Artificial intelligence in human resources management: Challenges and a path forward. *California Management Review, 61*(4), 15–42.

Tecuci, G. (2012). Artificial intelligence. *Wires Computational Statistics, 4*(2), 168–180.

Torres, E. N., & Mejia, C. (2017). Asynchronous video interviews in the hospitality industry: Considerations for virtual employee selection. *International Journal of Hospitality Management, 61*, 4–13.

Tripathi, R. T., & Singh, P. J. (2017). A study on innovative practices in digital human resource management. In National Seminar on Digital Transformation of Business in India: Opportunities and Challenges, 24–25 March, Dehradun, India.

Troshani, I., Jerram, C., & Hill, S. (2011). Exploring the public sector adoption of HRIS. *Industrial Management & Data Systems, 111*(3), 470–488.

Turk, Z. (2021). Structured analysis of ICT adoption in the European construction industry. *International Journal of Construction Management, 23*(5), 756–762.

Ulrich, D., & Dulebohn, J. H. (2015). Are we there yet? What's next for HR? *Human Resource Management Review, 25*, 188–204.

Vähä, P., Heikkilä, T., & Kilpeläinen, P. (2013). Extending automation of building construction – Survey on potential sensor technologies and robotic applications. *Automation in Construction, 36*, 168–178.

Vaidya, S., Ambad, P., & Bhosle, S. (2018). Industry 4.0 A glimpse. *Procedia Manufacturing, 20*(11–12), 233–238.

van den Heuvel, S., & Bondarouk, T. (2017). The rise (and fall?) of HR analytics: A study into the future application, value, structure, and system support. *Journal of Organizational Effectiveness: People and Performance, 4*(2), 157–178.

Venterink, J. (2017). *Practical future developments in e-HRM, HR SSC's and employee involvement* [Master thesis]. Submitted to University of Twente, Netherlands.

Voermans, M., & Van Veldhoven, M. (2007) Attitude towards E-HRM: An empirical study at Philips. *Personnel Review, 36*(6), 887–902.

Windapo, A. (2016). Skilled labour supply in the South African construction industry: The nexus between certification, quality of work output and shortages. *SA Journal of Human Resource Management, 14*(1), 1–8.

Yang, L., Yang, S. H., & Plotnick, L. (2013). How the Internet of Things technology enhances emergency response operations. *Technological Forecasting and Social Change, 80*, 1854–1867.

Zhang, S., Teizer, J., Lee, J., Eastman, C. M., & Venugopal, M. (2013). Building information modelling (BIM) and safety: Automatic safety checking of construction models and schedules. *Automation in Construction, 29*, 183–195.

Zhou, Y., Liu, G., Chang, X., & Wang, L. (2021). The impact of HRM digitalization on firm performance: Investigating three-way interactions. *Asia Pacific Journal of Human Resources, 59*, 20–43.

# Chapter 4

# Workforce Management Theories, Models, and Practices

## Abstract

The construction workforce plays a crucial role in the successful delivery of any construction project and, eventually, the performance of any construction organisation. Effectively managing these workforces becomes crucial. However, past studies have shown that workforce management within the construction industry has been on the back foot, with workers being seen as resources required to deliver construction projects. This situation begs the need for a construction workforce management model that can be tailored to an organisation's situation and adopted to manage workers and improve organisational performance effectively. To this end, this chapter reviewed existing workforce management theories, models, and practices to develop a suitable approach towards managing the construction workforce. Ultimately, a strategic workforce management with a classical view using a soft workforce management approach that embraces employees' empowerment and development through trust was proposed. Five major practices that best suit the soft workforce management approach were identified as key constructs in the proposed construction workforce management model.

*Keywords*: Construction workers; human resource management; personnel management; motivation; workforce; workforce management

## Introduction

In the quest to develop a construction workforce management model that construction organisations can adopt to improve how they manage their workers, this chapter explored existing workforce management theories, models, and practices. The chapter begins with a review of motivational theories and relates these theories to the construction context. Ultimately, the need for effective motivation of construction workers was proposed considering the importance of these workers

Construction Workforce Management in the Fourth Industrial Revolution Era, 75–102
Copyright © 2024 by Lerato Aghimien, Clinton Ohis Aigbavboa and Douglas Aghimien
Published under exclusive licence by Emerald Publishing Limited
doi:10.1108/978-1-83797-018-620241004

to the success of every construction project. The chapter also reviewed existing theories and models relating to workforce management. This review determined the ideal theory and model to underpin the proposed construction workforce management model. Also, the related practices ideal for this proposed model were uncovered, and these practices serve as the key constructs in the proposed construction workforce management model. The chapter ends with a summary of the reviewed theories, models, and practices.

## Motivation in Workforce Management

The outset of employee motivation may be traced back to the works of motivational theorists like Abraham Maslow, who postulated the needs hierarchy theory, Frederick Herzberg's two-factor theory, Douglas McGregor's X and Y theory, and Victor Vroom's expectancy theory. Although these theories were propounded long ago, their underlining principles are paramount for any organisation's continued success. After appointing and training employees, they must be motivated to achieve organisational objectives. Moreover, in designing employee compensation packages, employee expectations should be considered by ascertaining the extrinsic and intrinsic needs of the individuals within given organisational policies and procedures.

The theory of motivation has evolved, starting from a hedonistic view that considers man as a lover of pleasure and hater of pain to the contemporary motivation concept. To understand what motivates employees and how employees should be motivated, two sets of related motivation theories will be explored. First is the content or need theories which deal with identifying people's needs in relation to their strengths and goals set towards actualising their needs. The second set of theories are the process theories which concentrate on how behaviour is initiated, directed, and sustained. These theories also recognise the relationship among the dynamic variables which make up motivation.

### *Content Theories*

Content theories emphasise the needs of people as a means of motivation. These theories were designed to unearth the inherent factors influencing individuals' behaviour. Within this context of content theories lies Maslow's hierarchy of needs, McClelland's need theory, Alderfer's Existence, Relatedness, and Growth (ERG) Theory and Herzberg's two-factor theory.

#### *1. Maslow's Hierarchy of Needs*

Maslow's hierarchy of needs suggests the basic five levels of need, depicted in a pyramidal hierarchy. These needs are:

(1) physiological;
(2) safety;
(3) love and belonging;
(4) esteem; and
(5) self-actualisation.

Each need requires fulfilment before an individual can move to the next need (Maslow, 1943). According to Benson (2008), at the bottom of the pyramid are physiological needs which include the basic needs for survival, such as food, clothing, shelter, and water. The safety and social needs come next once the basic needs are fulfilled. The safety needs can be financial security and protection from emotional and physical harm, while the social needs entail longing for love, friendship and belonging. The esteem needs are the next, encompassing responsibility, promotion, job status, and respect from co-workers. At the top of the pyramid, the self-actualisation needs. At this stage, a wholly satisfied individual can be found. Maslow's needs theory allows managers to know and understand the different types of employees' needs within the organisation and how to motivate them. Also, organisations that understand the need of their employees can gratify these needs by adopting tailored made strategies such as creating a conducive working environment, engaging individuals to take up new challenges at work, promoting healthy work relationships, and rewarding and recognising their efforts.

## 2. ERG Theory

The ERG theory emerged from Maslow's hierarchy of needs. Alderfer (1989) reformed the hierarchy from five to three and called them ERG needs. The existence needs comprise physiological and material desires. In an organisational context, the need for compensation, benefits, and conducive working conditions will be categorised in this section. These needs are likened to Maslow's physiological and safety needs. The relatedness needs are evident in the interpersonal relationships with other workers. This relationship is mostly dependent on mutual understanding among workers, and these needs are compared to the safety, social, and some of the self-esteem needs in Maslow's need hierarchy theory. The growth needs are related to an individual's personal growth at work. It requires individuals to work to the best of their abilities and, at the same time, develop new capabilities. The growth needs relate to Maslow's self-actualisation and some of his self-esteem needs (Wanous & Zwany, 1977).

The ERG theory reflects intrinsic factors that aid employees in taking specific actions (Ivancevich et al., 2008). Managers can use this as a tool to improve performance in the workplace. Alderfer (1989) also theorised two concepts, namely satisfaction-progression and frustration-regression. Satisfaction-progression is similar to Maslow's needs theory, whereby fulfilling one need allows an individual to move up the pyramid to satisfy the succeeding needs. However, the frustration-regression denotes that when individuals become frustrated with trying to fulfil their needs at a particular level, the previous lower-level needs will resurface. The individual will regress to satisfy more basic needs. In an organisational setting, while the ERG components will aid the managers with a workable approach to motivating employees, the frustration-regression component allows the organisation to redirect employee behaviour, though the higher-order needs are temporarily frustrated.

## 3. McClelland's Needs Motivation Theory

In the 1960s, McClelland submitted that every individual has three types of emotional needs: achievement, power, and affiliation. The need for achievement refers to the drive to excel and to achieve set goals. In contrast, the need for affiliation indicates the need for interpersonal relations, and the need for power denotes the desire to be influential and control others. According to Gibson et al. (1979), McClelland's theory portrays the learning concept, which indicates that behaviour results in optimum satisfaction of the individual's needs. The theory's focal point is that needs can be greater than before or be suppressed through social norms, self-concept, and past experiences. Hence, needs can be 'learned', and compensated behaviour tends to recur more frequently.

Employee needs differ; as such, their motivation and performance will vary based on their capabilities and need for achievement (Kreitner & Kinicki, 2008). Individuals who yearn for achievement are jaded by unchallenging work tasks, but tasks that are too challenging may instil the fear of failure in them. High achievers tend to take up tasks that are at a moderately difficult level. This allows them to execute and accomplish the task successfully without any problems. Individuals with a high need for power desire a high sphere of influence and authority within the organisation. When the need is gratified, such employees thrive in high-level positions. These sets of employees will fearlessly execute, direct, and ensure that employees carry out organisational goals. More so, managers who are kind, approachable and give supportive feedback have the power to influence employees with a high need for affiliation to give better performance in their jobs.

## 4. Herzberg's Two-Factor Theory

Herzberg (1959) suggested that the result of some job factors is satisfaction, while other job factors avert dissatisfaction. It was further noted that when an employee is not satisfied, it does not mean such an employee is dissatisfied. It only implies that such an employee derives no satisfaction. Similarly, when an employee is not dissatisfied, it does not imply that satisfaction has been attained. The theory proposed two crucial factors essential for employers to note, and they are: (1) hygiene factors and (2) motivational factors.

Hygiene factors are essential factors within organisations. They do not yield long-term satisfaction, but their absence may lead to dissatisfaction. Hygiene factors are extrinsic factors; when adequately given, they pacify employees, thus preventing dissatisfaction. They include:

(1) *Pay* – the composition of pay or salary should be suitable and sensible. It must be on the same competitive level as those in the same sector.
(2) *Company and administrative policies* – the business's policies should be flexible, authentic and clear. They should include flexible working hours, dress codes, breaks, and holidays.
(3) *Fringe benefits* – such as medical aid, benefits for family members, and worker assistance programmes should be provided for staff.
(4) *Physical working conditions* – such as safe, tidy, and hygienic working conditions.
(5) *Status* – the status of the staff should be recognised, acquainted and maintained within the organisation.

(6) *Interpersonal relationships* – employee relationships should be suitable and acceptable among colleagues, superiors, and subordinates. There should be no disputes or humiliation.
(7) *Job Security* – employees must be provided with job security by the organisation.

On the other hand, when adopted, the motivational factors would produce employee satisfaction. These factors are essential in the workplace because they motivate employees to perform their job and enhance performance. Motivational factors are intrinsic, and they include:

(1) *Recognition* – management should praise and recognise the staff for their work achievements.
(2) *Sense of achievement* – ensuring employees have a feeling of accomplishment. There must be some kind of productiveness in the workplace.
(3) *Growth and opportunities for promotion* – an organisation must have possibilities for development to motivate staff members to perform well.
(4) *Responsibility* – employees must be accountable for their jobs. Management should give them ownership of the job and minimise control; however, they should maintain responsibility.
(5) *Work meaningfulness* – the work the employee does should be meaningful, interesting, and challenging.

In summary, Herzberg's two-factor theory requires managers within organisations to effectively implement hygiene factors to avoid employee dissatisfaction. Also, these managers must create a stimulating and rewarding work environment for employees to attain employees' motivation and better performance. This theory emphasises job enrichment to motivate workers and maximises the employees' skills and abilities, focussing on motivational factors that can enhance work quality.

## Process Theories

Process theories view motivation as a conscious human decision process. These theories are more concerned with the psychological and behavioural processes people adopt. Process theories strive to understand the thought processes of individuals demonstrating motivated behaviour. By understanding the thought process of these individuals, the actions, interactions, and context that motivate their behaviour can be understood. Common process theories include expectancy theory, equity theory, goal-setting theory, and reinforcement theory.

### 1. Expectancy Theory

In the 1960s, Vroom proposed the expectancy theory as a substitute for the content models. This theory was designed under four assumptions. Firstly, it is assumed that the first individuals join an organisation with expectations based on their needs, experience and motivations. These factors influence how they act within the organisation. Also, people's behaviour is assumed to be equivalent to their conscious choices. In other words, individuals can exhibit those behaviours suggested by their expectancy calculations. The third assumption denotes that individuals have different wants (e.g. job security, good salary, progression, and a challenge). Lastly, there is the assumption that individuals will settle for alternatives to optimise personal gain outcomes (Vroom, 1964). Based on these assumptions, Vroom's expectancy theory suggests that the motivation of employees is dependent on three vital elements, namely:

(1) Expectancy – which is the effort put into the organisation or activities.
(2) Instrumentality – which is seen from the aspect of the performance of the employee leading to expected outcomes.
(3) Valence – which is related to the reward for the performance. Most employees will be concerned with finding the reward favourable.

The theory considers the multiplier effect of each element. This implies that there will be greater motivation when:

- effort (expectancy) results in acceptable performance;
- performance (instrumentality) is rewarded; and
- the rewards (valence) are extremely favourable.

Motivation will not be attained if any of the three elements are absent. In other words, if employees think their efforts will result in performance, the performance should yield the rewards they expect. However, the motivation will decrease or be zero if the expected rewards are lower than expected (Lunenburg, 2011). It is of utmost importance for management to identify each employee's different goals and expectations. This will aid management in motivating each one according to personal preferences and choices.

## 2. Equity Theory

Adams's equity theory is based on the concept that people are driven by fairness. The equity theory says that the degree of equity or inequity individuals perceive in their work positions influences their job performance and satisfaction (Adams, 1965). This means that equity happens when the ratio of output to inputs of an individual is equal to the proportion of output to inputs of a fellow employee. On the other hand, inequity happens when an employee observes that the outcome of their effort is not commensurate with the outcomes and efforts of other employees within the organisation. Inequity can be divided into two categories – under-reward and over-reward. Under-reward happens when individuals think that they have put in more effort than the other employee, yet they get the same reward or receive a lower reward for the same attempt as the other employee. The reverse is the case with over-reward. Simply put, equity theory says that if employees perceive inequity in how they are rewarded for their effort in comparison with their peers, they will most likely adjust their efforts to make the situation fair in their eyes (Cropanzano, 1993). As such, the greater the perceptions of equity (fairness) in employees, the more driven they will be. But if they perceive unfairness, they will be demotivated (Carrell & Dittrich, 1978).

According to the equity theory, inputs and outputs should be clearly defined. Inputs are an individual's contribution to the organisation. They include the number of working hours, commitment exhibited, enthusiasm, work experience, personal sacrifices, responsibilities, loyalty, and the flexibility of individuals to take on responsibilities on short notice. Outputs can be defined as the rewards an individual receives for inputs to the organisation. These outputs can be intrinsic or extrinsic. They include salary, bonus, pension fund, annual holiday allowance, company car scheme, company shares, recognition, promotion, performance appraisals, the flexibility of work arrangements, sense of achievement, training, and development.

It is important to note that the equity theory showed that employees do not view equity in isolation; they compare their situation with others. The theory indicates four possible referents for comparison:

(1) *Self-inside* – the individuals' experience in their present organisation;
(2) *Self-outside* – the experience of the individual with other organisations;
(3) *Others-inside* – others within the present organisation of the individual; and
(4) *Others-outside* – others outside the organisation of the individual.

Albeit the source of referent an employer uses for comparison, the employees may try to decrease the perceived inequity in various ways (Greenberg, 1991; Schmidt & Marwell, 1972). To this end, managers can use three key strategies for motivating employees based on this theory. Firstly, organisations should be honest with employees. Transparency and honesty about pay structures will give employees an understanding of their pay grade, leading to employees' trusting the organisation. Secondly, companies should avoid underpaying their employees. Employees who are underpaid may resort to stealing from the company or deliberately underperforming. Thirdly, organisations must avoid overpaying employees as a means of motivation. Overpaying employees is a short-term solution to increasing performance because employees will start believing that they deserve a high salary and therefore decrease their work performance. In addition, overpaying certain employees means that some employees are being underpaid.

## 3. Goal-Setting Theory

Edwin Locke propounded the goal-setting motivation theory in the 1960s. This theory indicates that setting goals is fundamentally associated with task performance. The theory further suggests that specific and challenging goals, coupled with feedback, enhance the performance of tasks (Locke, 1968). Simply put, goals indicate and guide an employee on what is required and the effort needed to achieve it (Locke & Latham, 1990). The theory comprises:

(1) clarity – the goal must be clear and specific;
(2) challenge – the goal must be realistic as an easy or tedious goal is demotivating;

(3) commitment – from the beginning, employees must comprehend and accept the goals;
(4) feedback – it is imperative that employees obtain feedback timeously. This will help keep track of the goals; and
(5) task complexity – set realistic timescales and subdivide the goals with a regular review process (Locke, 1968).

Goal setting aims to enhance performance by increasing and regulating the effort of employees, to have efficient work behaviours. It is also designed to clarify employees' roles and duties and encourage the development of goal-attainment action plans (Locke, 1968). It is, therefore, imperative that managers assign specific and challenging goals, ensure employee acceptance of these organisational goals, and provide frequent, specific performance-related feedback to ensure the attainment of the set goals. A methodical way to utilise the goal-setting theory is by implementing a management-by-objectives programme. Objective management emphasises setting tangible, verifiable and measurable goals in a participatory manner (Locke, 1968).

### *Application of Motivation Theories in the Construction Industry*

The use of motivational techniques within the construction sector has been slow-paced (Ngwenya et al., 2018). Previous studies reveal that the motivational theories adopted in traditional management organisations have been implemented only to enhance productivity within the construction industry (Aina, 2000; Borcherding & Laufer, 1981; Shrader, 1972). According to Aina (2014), the construction industry has mostly favoured three motivation pathways: the negative and positive 'KITA' (Kick in the Ass) approach, the carrot and stick approach, and Maslow's and Herzberg's need theories of motivation. It was observed that the roots of motivational techniques in the construction industry stem from Maslow's and Herzberg's theories of motivation (Aina, 2014). The financial incentives adopted within the sector mirror Maslow's physiological needs and Herzberg's hygiene factors, while semi- and non-financial incentives confirm the importance of Maslow's higher needs. However, the peculiarities of the construction industry have made the wholesale adoption of these theories possible.

In connecting Maslow's theory of need with the construction industry, Schrader (1972) observed that employees in construction could satisfy their physiological needs when employed, thus confirming that these needs are less essential. Agreeably so, people who are employed have met their basic needs and are now only driven by greater needs. Furthermore, the study by Schrader (1972) observed that Maslow's self-actualisation needs are relatable within the construction industry; however, some aspects were faulted. For instance, artisans may prefer working their trade instead of being promoted and having supervisors' responsibilities. In addition, Wilson's (1979) empirical study of motivation in the construction industry indicated that safety and belonging needs were the biggest motivators of construction workers. Mckenzie and Harris (1984) later tabulated their findings against Maslow's hierarchy and concluded that Maslow's hierarchy of lower needs partially explain motivation in construction. In light of Herzberg's theory, the study by Yap (1992) found that a clear boundary between hygiene and motivating factors could not be confirmed when applying Herzberg's theory to labour-only subcontractors. The study further highlighted that the two distinct factors of the theory do not reflect the feelings of construction workers. The difference between both factors is rather unclear in practice.

Over time, studies on motivation within the construction domain have continued to clamour for change in how managers motivate the construction workforce. It has been noted that the majority of managers in construction do not comprehend the concept of motivation and therefore do not have a suitable strategy to increase productivity through effective motivation. Haseltine (1976) stated that satisfaction already exists within construction. However, further development is required for management. Management should develop good employee attitudes, administer praise, show respect, and satisfy self-fulfilled needs. In this light, the study by Maloney and McFillen (1983) echoed the significance of managing work team factors. The study suggested that construction teams could be motivated by effectively managing:

(1) stability of employment;
(2) work-team staffing;
(3) team building;
(4) goal-setting; and
(5) incentives.

These can enhance employee productivity and satisfaction (Maloney & McFillen, 1983). Furthermore, Hancock (2006) provided the basis for the role of managers in motivating employees. It was recommended that managers must understand:

(1) some element of human behaviour and motivational theories;
(2) factors that influence behaviour;
(3) employee motivators and demotivators;
(4) the uniqueness of the construction industry or project when designing motivational programmes; and
(5) the needs of the workers in construction.

## Related Workforce Management Theories and Models

According to Armstrong and Taylor (2014), the management of human resources encompasses the employment and management of people within organisations. It strives to increase an organisation's effectiveness and capacity to achieve its goals through effectively and efficiently using its available workforce. With its high importance in attaining organisational and employee performance and creating a competitive advantage for organisations (Cascio & Bailey, 1995), human resources management is built upon several theories from which several models have emerged.

A model simplifies a statement, proposition, or hypothesis. This can be in the form of an organisational chart, which reduces a complicated idea to a visually comprehensible statement. They can help design formulae or hypotheses (Stoner et al., 1999). Conversely, a theory is 'a coherent group of assumptions put forth to explain the relationship between two or more observable facts and to provide a sound basis for predicting future events' (Stoner et al., 1999, p. 8). While a model is an explicit part of a theory, a theory is an implicit aspect of a model. However, the existence of both concepts gives meaning to how a concept is viewed and implemented. Several theories and models exist within and outside the human resources management domain that shape the practices used in managing the workforce within an organisation. The most common theories and models are subsequently discussed.

### Universalistic Theory

A universalistic perspective is one of the theoretical perspectives adopted in past studies to examine the effectiveness of human resource practices on organisations' performance (Busienei et al., 2013; Chang & Huang, 2005). Promoters of the universalistic approach are always micro-analytic (Busienei et al., 2013). They believe that the practices used in managing the workforce are best viewed piecemeal and that some practices are better than others (Delery & Doty, 1996; Tsui et al., 1997; Wright & Snell, 1991). In other words, the universalistic theory promulgates the idea of best practices and high-performance work practices. Universalistic perspectives argue that a universal linear relationship exists between a dependent variable (organisation performance) and an independent variable (human resources management practice) across the population of any firm (Osterman, 1994; Pfeffer, 1998). It is believed that through the adoption of specific practices, changes within an organisation can be attained (Zheng et al., 2007). The promoters of this view opined that the 'best practice' of workforce management is universal and can be adopted within any organisation to attain high levels of organisational performance. From the perspective of employees, Innes and Wiesner (2012) described the universalistic approach as the idea that practices involved in managing human resources linearly influence the knowledge of employees, their skills, and their abilities.

Although this theory appears to be simple and easy to imbibe, studies have shown that the theory tends to give a myopic view of the real situation surrounding workforce management practices and organisational performance. For instance, Martin-Alcazar et al. (2005) noted that this theory's promoters do not dedicate time to understanding the interdependence or the integration of diverse practices. Similarly, other studies have noted that the promoters of this view tend to assess a single practice at a time and understand how these practices affect organisational performance or employees' attitude to work. The problem with this is that the process of assessing each human resource practice separately will not consider the likelihood of interdependence or relatedness among workforce management practices, the combination of which can promote high levels of organisational performance (Al-Emadi & Schwabenland, 2015; Delery & Doty, 1996; Khawaja et al., 2014).

## Contingency Theory

Contingency theory was noted as the main approach needed for studying organisations (Child, 1977). According to Wood (1979), the theory is simply the notion that there is no single best way of organising. Although this theory has come under several criticisms as to its functionalism (Bowey, 1976; Elger, 1975; Silverman, 1970), the laudable justification for its usage has been observed in some studies. For instance, Burns and Stalker (1966) posited that the form of management adopted within an organisation depends on the situation that such an organisation wants to meet and that no single set of principles exists for a good organisation. Thus, Wood (1979) concluded that the right organisation is contingent on specific factors such as the environment, and available technology, among others.

Regarding managing humans in organisations, Harney (2016) noted that unlike the universalistic theory, which suggests that workforce management practices directly impact an organisation's performance, contingency theory suggests interactions rather than direct relationships. To be effective, workforce management practices within an organisation must align with other organisational elements, including the external environment. This suggestion was drawn from Legge's (1978) submission that workforce management practices are largely influenced by an organisation's environment and the circumstances surrounding such an organisation. Harney (2016) further asserted that the contingency decision of an organisation could broadly be understood from the direction of the external and internal fit. The external fit is the situation whereby management practices adopted within an organisation are expected to align with the organisation's strategy or environmental conditions. In this case, the 'best fit' approach whereby workforce management practices are expected to concur with the organisation's cost, quality, and innovation, among others, is sought. While the external fit is required, exhibiting the internal fit to attain the goal of workforce management practices within the organisation is crucial. In essence, it can be deduced that the management of an organisation's workforce in the view of the contingency theory is not a 'one-size-fits-all' approach. The practices to be adopted in a given situation and for a given purpose may differ from what will be adopted by the same organisation in a different scenario.

## Configuration Theory

Fiss et al. (2013, p. 1) stated that 'the notion of configuration – that the whole is best understood from a systemic perspective and should be viewed as a constellation of interconnected elements – is arguably one of the central ideas in organisation studies'. The submission of MacDuffie's (1995) research in the automobile industry further amplifies this notion as a holistic assessment of issues revealing a unique pattern of factors. Fiss et al. (2013) noted that the configuration theory gained recognition as an organisational theory in the 70s and 80s, as evident in the studies of Child (1977) and Mintzberg (1983). Significant contributions regarding this theory also emerged in the 90s, as seen in the work of Doty et al. (1993) and

Ketchen et al. (1993). However, in recent times, no significant improvement has been evident in this theory, and as such, the theory has failed to live up to its full potential in organisational studies (Fiss et al., 2013). The configuration theory is seen as the combination of several approaches in terms of views and models to assess a problem holistically and then come up with several factors that might be responsible for the assessed problem. Ultimately, the configuration theory is a complementary or mixed approach involving utilising the views and systems of more than one approach to achieve answers.

### Resource-Based Theory

The resource-based view (RBV) provides a platform for organisations to assess the strategic fit between an organisation's unique resources and the attainment of sustained competitive advantage can be achieved and sustained (Eisenhardt & Martin, 2000; Teece et al., 1997). Das and Teng (2001) noted that the RBV is based on the notion that an organisation can only gain a competitive advantage when such an organisation can effectively manage its internal resources. Previous studies have noted that the RBV believes that every organisation possesses a significant amount of heterogeneously distributed resources, the differences of which persist over time (Amit & Schoemaker, 1993; Mahoney & Pandian, 1992). This belief of the RBV has given rise to the assumption that once an organisation has resources with high value that is uncommon among their competitors, and that cannot be imitated nor substituted by another, such an organisation can achieve a sustainable competitive advantage. This is because these resources can be used to implement new strategies that are value-oriented and that cannot be easily duplicated by their competitors (Eisenhardt & Martin, 2000). This theory has, however, been criticised by researchers such as Teece and Pisano (1994). They submitted that the foundation of the RBV is not strong enough to support attaining a sustainable competitive advantage. Despite this criticism, the RBV has been used to create a significant explanation for the concept of workforce management. According to Barney (1995), in the RBV, workforce management strives to deliver added value through the strategic development of an organisation's human resources that are rare, hard to imitate and difficult to substitute.

### Ability–Motivation–Opportunity Theory

The AMO focus majorly on how workers perform within an organisation. Appelbaum et al. (2000) posited that workers' performance can be determined using the AMO theory. Employees' performance is believed to be shaped by increased abilities, motivation and opportunity to participate. This realisation provides the platform for developing workforce management systems that meet the employees' interests based on their required skills, the necessary motivation, and job delivery (Appelbaum et al., 2000; Boxall & Purcell, 2003). According to Bos-Nehles et al. (2013), the AMO theory can predict employees' performance because while employees need the ability to carry out their assigned tasks, they also need motivation for these tasks and the opportunity provided to carry out these tasks.

According to Yang et al. (2014), this theory has gained traction among many academics because this perspective, if effectively adopted, can increase job satisfaction and commitment and reduce employee stress levels. This ultimately affects the organisation's performance positively.

### Strategic Theory

One common perspective gaining popularity owing to the diversity in organisations and their activities is the strategic theory. Guest (1997) noted that although untested in the United Kingdom, it is assumed that a synergy between workforce management practices and an organisation's internal and external context will lead to increased performance. However, classifying the different types of workforce management strategies has gained more focus in the United States. Here, it is presumed that when an organisation has a synergy between its business strategy, organisational structure, and human resource policy, superior performance can be attained. Paauwe and Boon (2009) noted that the concept of workforce management has undergone significant changes, with researchers and business entities modifying the concept to suit their activities. One key aspect noted is the infusion of workforce management with strategic management, where the former is used as a strategic tool to attain business objectives (Delery, 1998; Paauwe & Boon, 2009). This has given rise to the much-discussed strategic workforce management, which, according to Paauwe and Boon (2009), is simply the added value of workforce management to an organisation. Delery and Doty (1996) submitted that an organisation adopting a strategy requires practices different from those required by another organisation adopting alternative strategies. The bottom line is to have a strategy that best fits the organisation's objective.

In attaining this best fit or 'strategic fit', four approaches were discussed by Paauwe (2004) based on Whittington's (1993) generic perspective of strategy. These approaches are:

(1) *Classical approach* – believes that workforce management is designed to maximise human capital to achieve organisational goals. Huselid (1995) opined that this approach attempts to link individual attitude and role behaviour to the performance of an organisation logically and rationally.
(2) *Evolutionary approach* – a process whereby managers try to conform to market demand by selecting appropriate management practices to ensure organisational survival and competitiveness. This approach reveals that the market decides an organisation's success and not the manager's. Thus, the manager is expected to adapt the organisation optimally to the market's demands through appropriate and effective management practices.
(3) *Processual approach* – refers to the gradual development of strategic assets such as knowledge, patents, organisational culture and routines into an organisation's core competencies. The approach sees workforce management function developing and maintaining people-related competencies over a period.

(4) *Systemic approach* – considers the wider social context of an organisation and how it impacts the workforce management practices and policies
adopted within the organisation. This social context differs from country to
industry and from one organisation to another.

### Other Related Theories

Apart from the aforementioned workforce management theories, other related
theories that have been explored within the body of literature are:

(1) *Descriptive theories* – which are considerably non-prescriptive (Armstrong &
Taylor, 2014). They either give guidelines in the areas of human resource
policies and outcomes (Beer et al., 1984) or adopt a systems approach, in
which a description of the relationships between levels in an organisation is
given (Kochan et al., 1986).
(2) *Normative theories* – which are a set of theories that strive to establish a norm
in the form of prescribed best practice. Contrary to the contingency theory,
normative theories take a considerable risk in implying 'one best way' (Guest,
1997).
(3) *Behavioural perspective* – which was developed to shed light on the likely effect
of workforce management practices on employees' behaviour (Wright &
McMahan, 1992). The theory argues that specific workforce management
practices can be employed to prompt and control those employee behaviours
that contribute positively to the organisation's overall performance of the
organisation.
(4) *Social exchange theory* – is another widely used theory in the management
of workers (Whitener, 2001). This theory considers that employees will most
likely interpret workforce management practices to indicate the organisation's support and care for them. The satisfaction with these practices will
see a reciprocating sense of commitment, satisfaction, and trust in the
organisation.

### Harvard Model

Beer et al. (1984) developed the Harvard model at the University of Harvard, from
where it got its name. Boxall (1992) nicknamed the model the Harvard framework,
and most literature has adopted this terminology over time. According to Paauwe
and Boon (2009), the Harvard framework is one of the most common workforce
management models. Significant literature abounds regarding the application of
this model in the public sector owing to its usefulness in determining the changes
in human resource policies on workforce management outcomes (Ackroyd et al.,
2007; Brunetto et al., 2011). According to Beer et al. (1984), organisations experience significant pressure. To withstand these pressures, the management of the
organisation's employees needs to take a much wider, comprehensive and strategic approach. There is now the need for a longer-term perspective in managing

an organisation's employees and considering people as potential organisational assets. According to Armstrong (2003), the Harvard model is premised on the assumption that conventional challenges of workforce management can only be solved when managers develop a perspective of how they wish to see employees' participation within the organisation and their development by the organisation, as well as the policies and practices that may be required to achieve these developments.

According to Paauwe and Boon (2009), the Harvard model starts from a situational perspective. Apart from the market and strategic vision or consideration, the model considers stakeholders' interests. The model shows that the stakeholders' interest (which encompasses major shareholders, management, employee groups, government, community and trade unions) is influenced by some situational factors (such as workforce characteristics, business strategy and conditions, management philosophy, labour market, unions, task technology, laws and societal values). In turn, both the stakeholders' interests and situational factors influence the choice of human resource policy adopted within the organisation. This policy choice includes employee influence, their flow, rewards systems, and work systems. Adopting the right policy will yield specific outcomes, which can be in the form of employee commitment, increased competence congruence and cost-effectiveness. These outcomes go beyond organisational performance and effectiveness and include individual well-being and societal consequences. Paauwe and Boon (2009) noted that the Harvard model could be regarded as both a descriptive and prescriptive framework. This is because, on the one hand, the framework clearly describes the factors that shape the human resource policies adopted within an organisation. On the other hand, it gives a conclusive prescription of what the outcome of the choice of these policies should be if adopted. Furthermore, studies have noted that this model provides the much-needed link between workforce management decisions, the business environment and an organisation's performance. This is because the model provides a more open system model that shows how human resource policy impacts other organisational functions and how stakeholders and situational factors constrain workforce management (Huczynski & Buchanan, 2001; Loosemore et al., 2003).

Some of the advantages of the Harvard model, as noted by Boxall (1992) and Armstrong (2003), include:

(1) its recognition of the role of diverse stakeholder interests;
(2) its recognition of the explicit or implicit trade-offs between owners' and employees' interests and between the different interest groups;
(3) its inclusion of employees' influence, work organisation, and supervisory style into the context of workforce management;
(4) its acknowledgement of varied contextual influences on the management's choice of strategy; and
(5) its emphasis on choice which is not driven by situation or environment.

While these advantages abound, some shortfalls have also been noted in the model. Loosemore et al. (2003) opined that despite acknowledging the influence of certain environmental factors and stakeholders, the nature of the causal chain suggested by the model is not clear. It was noted that the model fails to explain how each of the four identified policy areas (employee influence, human resources flow, rewards systems, and work systems) are affected by the stakeholders' interests and the identified situational factors and how it affects the management of employees in the long term. However, Agyepong et al. (2010) noted that, to a considerable extent, this model informed future developments of the concept of workforce management.

### Matching Model

Armstrong and Taylor (2014) described the matching model, also called the Michigan model as one of the major sources of detailed description of the concept of workforce management. This model was developed by Fombrun, Tichy, and Devanna in 1984 at the Michigan Business School. The name 'matching model' came from the model's submission that the human resource systems within an organisation and the organisation's structure should be managed in a manner consistent with the company's organisational strategy (Fombrun et al., 1984). Paauwe and Boon (2009) observed that the matching model presents a synergy between strategy, organisational structure and human resource policies which occurs in economic, political and cultural forces. With more focus on the functional level of human resource management, the model emphasises a cyclic system in which performance depends on selection, appraisal, rewards and development. From the model, employees' input to attaining organisational objectives needs to be appraised using the right technique, with a reward to be given based on the outcome of the appraisal and the performance of the assessed employee. The model reveals a cyclic process, with each function depending on another to attain an organisation's objectives. Therefore, this model is descriptive as it considers the entire function as a single element needed to achieve high levels of organisation/employee performance (Beer et al., 1984).

### Warwick Model

Agyepong et al. (2010) noted that the Warwick model was developed by Hendry and Pettigrew at the Centre for Corporate Studies and Change at the University of Warwick in 1990 to close the gap in existing workforce management models in terms of reflecting European traditions and management style. The model is designed using five various interrelated elements. These elements are the outer context (macro-environmental forces), inner context (firm-specific or microenvironmental forces), business strategy context, workforce management context and content. Agyepong et al. (2010) observed that by design, the model allows the impact of external factors on internal operations to be analysed. The outer context of the model deals with socio-economic, technical, political-legal and competitive issues. The inner context covers issues around culture, structure, politics/leadership, task technology and business outputs. Thus, to achieve high organisational performance, there must be an alignment between the inner and outer contexts. According to Loosemore et al. (2003), the Warwick model considers the broad context within which workforce management functions. The alignment of the outer and inner context gives rise to the business strategy context, which comprises the business objective, product market and strategy, and the workforce management context comprising the role, definition, organisation, and output. These two contexts (outer and inner) create the workforce management content of workflows, work system, reward systems, and employee relations. This content also gives feedback into the business strategy context, the workforce management context, and the inner context to create a continuous loop.

### Guest Model

In 1997, David Guest developed the Guest model, which shows the relationship between workforce management activities and organisational strategy. Marsden (2002) opined that the core reason for developing this model was that workforce management practices should be designed to drive employees to high quality, flexibility and commitment to their organisation. The model comprises six dimensions: workforce management strategy, practices, and outcomes, behaviour outcomes, performance outcomes, and financial outcomes. The idea that an employee's commitment has a significant bearing on valued business consequences is promoted in this model. It is believed that employee commitment is a key workforce management outcome that involves ensuring that employees are obligated to their organisation and achieve the behavioural outcomes of increased effort, cooperation, and involvement (Guest, 1997; Marsden, 2002). Guest (1997) also submitted that high productivity and its attributed outcomes can only be achieved when a well-defined strategy is adopted within an organisation. This strategy must be directed towards policy goals, integrated into business processes and supported by management at all levels. Marsden (2002) opined that, like the Michigan model, the Guest model is helpful in understanding the relationship between workforce management practices and performance. However, the model is also limited in that it fails to consider the organisation's external factors such as unions, competitors, economic conditions, legal requirements and the socio-cultural environment, among others.

### Hard and Soft Model

Most workforce management models can be classified using McGregor's X and Y theory to understand the viewpoint of those adopting such a model. Where models that follow the X theory concept are classified as 'hard' models, those that adopt the Y theory concept are believed to be 'soft' models. Truss et al. (1997) noted that the first classification of workforce management models into these two forms was done in Guest and Storey's studies. While defining workforce management, Guest (1987) proposed two major dimensions: 'hard-soft' and 'tight-loose' dimensions of managing human resources. In the same vein, Storey (1995) interpreted the perspectives of workforce management in terms of 'hard-soft' and 'strong-weak'. Truss (1997) further noted that most workforce management models are either hard or soft and are based on 'the divergent views of human nature and strategic controls' (p. 70).

The McGregor X theory believes that humans inherently dislike work, and as such, managers tend to adopt strict and tight managerial approaches through close monitoring. This connotes a hard approach towards attaining organisational goals. According to Legge (1989), the hard model employs tight rules and regulations, order, authority and strict supervision in the quest for a controlled working environment. Other studies have also emphasised that hard workforce management models regard the workforce within any organisation just like any other production resource. Therefore, they believe in the strategic management of this workforce so that maximum productivity can be generated (Legge, 1998; Storey, 1995). Guest (1999) also noted that hard workforce management models consider the workers of an organisation to be economic resources of such an organisation, and as such, significant output must be derived through tight control strategies. Truss et al. (1997) further noted that hard models emphasise strategic fit in the sense that workforce management practices and policies are linked to the organisations' strategic objectives and are clear among themselves with the sole purpose of attaining better competitive advantage over the organisations' competitors.

On the other hand, the McGregor Y theory implies that humans can exercise a significant level of self-direction and control in the quest to achieve objectives to which they are committed. Based on this, managers tend to trust their workforce and adopt a participatory management style that allows the workforce to take ownership of what they do and, in the process, do it effectively. This theory is evident in soft workforce management models, which, according to Walton (1985a) and Wood (1996), are likened to the concept of a 'high commitment work system' aimed at achieving commitment among the workforce through self-regulated behaviour and the attainment of a high level of trust within the organisation in a manner whereby behaviour is primarily self-regulated. Gould-Williams and Davies (2005) noted that soft workforce management deals with creating empowerment and development for employees while at the same time trusting and managing them.

Other studies have emphasised that soft workforce management models uphold the assumption that employees will perform better if they are fully committed to the organisation and its objectives (Guest, 1987; Walton, 1985b). Based on the issue of commitment and how it affects the productivity of organisations, Hope (1994, p. 3) submitted that 'employees working under a workforce management system would not merely comply with the organisation's wishes, but positively and effectively commit themselves to the aims and values of their employers, and thereby give added value through their labour'. Truss et al. (1997), therefore, concluded that by adopting soft workforce management models, employees' commitment to their organisation can be derived through the trust of such employees, their training and development, and being given a free hand to take control of their work. This contrasts with the hard model, which believes commitment comes through control. Legge (1998) further identified three major features of a soft workforce management model, namely: (1) flexibility in diverse forms; (2) team building; empowerment and involvement; and (3) culture management.

Thus, it can be said that workforce management models can either be controlled related, as in the case of hard workforce management models or commitment related, as evident in the soft workforce management models.

## Summarising the Reviewed Workforce Management Theories and Models and Determining Existing Practices

In summary, the theories and models reviewed show that workforce management is seen from diverse perspectives. However, while it entails managing workers within an organisation, the goal remains to achieve optimum organisational performance. Construction organisations vary in nature and this variation comes from their set policies, environment, and other features. The practices that would yield substantial results and improved organisational performance within an organisation may not necessarily give the same result when adopted within another organisation (Kandula, 2003). Therefore, viewing workforce management practices strictly in relation to organisational performance, as noted in the universalistic theory, may not be a good approach. On the other hand, Paauwe and Boon (2009) and Yang et al. (2014) noted that while the contingency theory and RBV are both situated at the organisational level, the AMO theory focusses on variables relating to the individuals. This includes employees' skills and competencies, motivation, and participation opportunities. Consequently, as construction organisations strive towards increasing their individual and organisational productivity, it is important to understand that no single workforce management practice can best serve an organisation as the contingency theory proposes.

Strategically managing construction organisations' rare, hard to imitate and hard-to-substitute workforce is important to gain a competitive advantage within the ever-dynamic and difficult construction environment (Yang et al., 2014). Continuously refining the adopted management strategy to suit the organisation's situation and environmental influences must be a top priority for the organisation. Notwithstanding the strategy adopted, it will be most useful to ensure employees can perform their given tasks, that they are adequately motivated to carry out these tasks, and at the same time are allowed to participate as postulated in the AMO theory. Only through this can there be an increase in job satisfaction and commitment, trust in an organisation and its management, and a reduction in the stress level of construction workers (Bos-Nehles et al., 2013; Yang et al., 2014).

The reviewed existing models revealed different approaches towards managing workers in diverse organisations. Studies have noted that the construction industry tends to adopt hard workforce management models whereby workers are treated like any other factor of production with the sole aim of maximising productivity (Druker et al., 1996; Legge, 1998; Storey, 1995). The resultant effect of this approach is the lack of commitment to organisations and high employee turnover being experienced in the industry today. However, the soft workforce management model should be adopted, wherein employees are empowered and developed through trust (Gould-Williams & Davies, 2005). Rooting this soft management model in the classical approach, where worker's attitude and role behaviour are linked to the performance of an organisation logically and rationally

Table 4.1.    Existing Workforce Management Practices.

| Authors | Planning | Recruitment & Selection | Compensation & Benefits | Performance management/ Appraisal | Employee involvement/ empowerment | Training & Development | Employment security | Incentive pays | Information sharing/ information systems | Employee ownership |
|---|---|---|---|---|---|---|---|---|---|---|
| McLagan and Bedrick (1982) | * | * | * | | | * | | | * | |
| Beer et al. (1984) | | | * | | * | | | | | |
| Fombrun et al. (1984) | | * | * | * | | * | | | | |
| Hendry and Pettigrew (1990) | | * | | | | | | | | |
| Mondy and Noe (1996) | * | * | * | | | * | | | * | |
| Schwartz (1999) | | * | * | * | | * | | | | |
| Busienei et al. (2013) | * | * | * | * | * | * | | | | |
| Pfeffer (1994) | | * | * | | * | * | * | * | * | * |
| Guest (1997) | | * | * | * | * | * | * | | | |
| Pfeffer (1998) | | * | * | | * | * | * | | * | |
| Edgar and Geare (2005) | | * | | | | * | | | | |
| AFROSAI-E (2018) | * | * | * | * | * | * | | | | |
| Smriti (2009) | * | * | * | | | * | | | | |
| Dessler (2011) | | * | * | | * | * | | | | |
| Har et al. (2010) | | * | * | * | | * | | | | * |
| Duke and Udono (2012) | * | * | * | | | * | | | | |
| Kumar and Murthy (2013) | | * | * | * | | * | | | | |
| Zhai et al. (2014) | | * | * | | * | * | | | | |
| Naidu and Chand (2014) | * | * | * | | * | * | | | | |
| Aladwan et al. (2015) | | * | * | * | | * | | | | |
| Abu Keir (2016) | | * | * | * | * | * | | | | |
| Abuazoom et al. (2017) | | | * | * | * | * | * | | * | |
| Aboramadan et al. (2020) | | * | * | * | | * | * | | | |
| Ojo and Raman (2019) | | * | * | * | * | * | | | | |
| **Total** | 7 | 21 | 23 | 12 | 12 | 22 | 5 | 1 | 5 | 2 |

| Terms & Job design and re-design | Cross-utilisation/cross training | Symbolic Egalitarianism/minimal status distinction | Wage compression | Promotion from within | Long term perspective | Measurement of practices | Overarching philosophy | Employee/industrial/labour relations | Safety & Health/ Staff wellness | Maintaining (working conditions and welfare) | Motivating | Succession and Retention |
|---|---|---|---|---|---|---|---|---|---|---|---|---|
| * | | | | | | | | * | | | | |
| * | | | | | | | | | | | | |
| * | | | | | | | | | | | | |
| | | | | | | | | * | | | | |
| | | | | | | | | * | * | | | |
| * | * | * | * | * | * | * | * | | | | | |
| * | | | | | | | | | | | | |
| | | * | | | | | | | | | | |
| | | | | | | | | | * | | | |
| | | | | | | | | | * | * | | * |
| | | | | | | | | * | * | * | * | * |
| * | | | | | | | | | | | | |
| * | | | | | | | | | | | | |
| 7 | 1 | 2 | 1 | 1 | 1 | 1 | 1 | 4 | 4 | 2 | 1 | 2 |

*Source*: Author's compilation (2023)

(Huselid, 1995), for a strategic fit will offer significant benefits to construction organisations seeking to attain maximum output from its workers to achieve set organisational objectives.

Also, from the reviewed models, it is evident that existing workforce management models all occur owing to the need to improve the productivity and performance of organisations by effectively managing their workers. So, it is important to note the practices being adopted and the expected outcomes in terms of the organisations performance. It is worth mentioning at this stage that names given to these workforce management practices and their expected outcomes differ from model to model. Over time, studies have continued to change the choice of words to describe these practices and their expected outcomes. However, their underlining meaning remains the same. The Harvard model noted that by properly managing stakeholders' interests and other situational factors, organisations could adopt practices such as encouraging employee influence, human resource flow, reward systems, and work systems. The expected outcomes of adopting these practices include commitment, congruence, and cost-effectiveness (Beer et al., 1984). In their matching model, Fombrun et al. (1984) recognised a cyclic approach to workforce management practices such as selection, performance appraisal, reward systems and continuous development. The sole outcome of adopting these practices is improved organisational performance, which is an extension of the improvement in the employees' performance. Like the Harvard model, the Warwick model recognises the importance of workforce management content such as human resource flows, work systems, rewards systems, and employee relations. The effective deployment of these practices will see the attainment of the organisation's business strategy context and significant human resource outputs (Hendry & Pettigrew, 1990). Guest (1997), in the Guest model, stated that practices such as selection, training, appraisal, rewards, job design, employee involvement, status, and security would eventually lead to outcomes such as commitment, quality, and flexibility. Based on these outcomes, the Guest model can best be described as a soft workforce management model that considers the commitment aspect rather than the control of workers. From the model, the outcomes eventually lead to momentous performance of the organisation in areas such as high productivity, quality, and innovation, as well as low levels of absenteeism of the workforce, low labour turnover, low levels of conflict on the job and few customer complaints.

According to McLagan and Bedrick (1982), the American Society for Training and Development (ASTD) commissioned research on producing the true meaning of excellence in training and development. Undertaken by Patricia McLagan and her team, this research saw the development of the human resource wheel, which identified nine critical practices that influence the development of workers. These practices are training and development, organisation development, organisation/job design, human resource planning, selection and staffing, personnel research and information systems, compensation and benefits, employee assistance, and union/labour relations. It is believed that properly adopting these practices will lead to improved quality of work–life, increased productivity, worker satisfaction, improved worker development, and improved readiness for change. Over time, the ASTD workforce management wheel has become a popular reference for studies on workforce management practices.

Pfeffer (1994), in the study of attaining competitive advantage through human effort, recognised sixteen important practices. These 16 initial practices are employment security, selectivity in recruiting, high wages, incentive pay, employee ownership, information sharing, participation and empowerment, teams and job-redesign, training and skills development, cross-utilisation and cross-training, symbolic egalitarianism, wage compression, promotion from within, long-term perspective, measurement of practices, and overarching philosophy (Pfeffer, 1994). However, these 16 practices were further reduced to seven major practices in assessing organisation success by Pfeffer (1998). The new practices advocated were employment security, selective hiring, decentralised decision-making compensation based on organisational performance, extensive training, minimal status distinction and barriers, and sharing financial and performance information.

Table 4.1 shows the summary of the different workforce management practices that have been adopted over time and that are crucial to the development of a conceptual construction workforce management model in this study. Extant literature has revealed that to attain the very best from the soft workforce management approach, practices such as recruitment and selection, compensation and benefits, performance management and appraisal, employee involvement and empowerment, and training and development as essential for organisations to adopt (Aladwan et al., 2015; Dessler, 2011; Har et al., 2010; Marescaux et al., 2013; Ojo & Raman, 2019). Further scrutiny of the practices in Table 4.1 also shows that these five workforce management practices are the most reoccurring practices within the body of knowledge. Thus, these five management practices form the foundations for this book's proposed construction workforce management model.

## Summary

This chapter sheds light on the concept of motivation in general and the construction industry. The chapter also reviewed existing workforce management-related theories and models, revealing the best-fit approach towards attaining an effective workforce management model within a construction organisation. The review further suggested the need for strategic workforce management with a classical view using a soft workforce management approach that embraces employees' empowerment and development through trust. Ultimately, this book identified five major practices that best suit the soft workforce management approach as critical constructs in the proposed construction workforce management model. However, considering the uniqueness of the construction industry, wherein high importance is placed on human capital because organisations operate in a competitive environment, workforce management must consider the emotions of the workers and ascertain the influence of the environment on the workforce management strategy being adopted. Although these two constructs (emotion and environment) were not explored in the reviewed models, they were considered as gaps in existing workforce management models that need to be considered. These two constructs are discussed in Chapter 5 of this book.

# References

Aboramadan, M., Albashiti, B., Alharazin, H., & Dahleez, K. A. (2020). Human resources management practices and organisational commitment in higher education: The mediating role of work engagement. *International Journal of Educational Management, 34*(1), 154–174.

Abu Keir, M. Y. (2016). *Staff perceptions of how human resource management practices influence organisational performance: Mediating roles of organisational culture, employees' commitment and employee retention in Bahrain Private Universities.* Thesis submitted to the Cardiff School of Management in partial fulfilment of the requirements for the degree of Doctor of Philosophy. Cardiff Metropolitan University, Western Avenue, Cardiff, UK.

Abuazoom, M. M. I., Hanafi, H., & Ahmad, Z. (2017). Influence of HRM practices on project performance: Conceptual framework. *International Journal of Academic Research in Business and Social Sciences, 7*(3), 47–54.

Ackroyd, S., Kirkpatrick, I., & Walker, R. (2007). Public management reform in the UK and its consequences for professional organisation: A comparative analysis. *Public Administration, 85*(1), 9–26.

Adams, J. S. (1965). Inequity in social exchange. In L. Berkowitz (Ed.), *Advances in experimental social psychology* (Vol. 2). Academic Press.

African Organisation of English-speaking Supreme Audit Institutions (AFROSAI – E). (2018). *Human resource management (HRM) framework and handbook for SAIs* (1st ed.). AFROSAI – E. https://afrosai-e.org.za/wp-content/uploads/2019/07/HR-Management-Handbook-for-SAIs-2019.pdf

Agyepong, S. A., Fugar, F. D. K., & Tuuli, M. M. (2010). The applicability of the Harvard and Warwick models in the development of human resource management policies of large construction companies in Ghana. In S. Laryea, R. Leiringer, & W. Hughes (Eds.), *Proceedings of The West Africa Built Environment Researchers Conference and Workshop (WABER)*, Accra, Ghana, 27–28 July, 525 – 534.

Aina, O. O. (2000). *The effect of incentive schemes on construction productivity in Nigeria.* [M.Sc. thesis]. Obafemi Awolowo University, Ile-Ife, Nigeria.

Aina, O. O. (2014). Application of motivation theories in the construction industry. *IOSR Journal of Business and Management, 16*(7), 1–6.

Aladwan, K., Bhanugopan, R., & D'Netto, B. (2015). The effects of human resource management practices on employees' organisational commitment. *International Journal of Organizational Analysis, 23*(3), 472–492.

Alderfer, C. (1989). Theories reflecting my personal experience and life dent. *The Journal of Applied Behavioral Science, 25*(4), 351–351.

Al-Emadi, A. A. Q., & Schwabenland, C. (2015). An investigation into the SHRM perspectives effectiveness: A comparative study. *International Journal of Management and Business Studies, 5*(3), 180–188.

Amit R., & Schoemaker, P. J. H. (1993). Strategic assets and organizational rent. *Strategic Management Journal, 14*(1), 33–46.

Appelbaum, E., Bailey, T., Berg, P., & Kallegert, A. (2000). *Manufacturing advantage: Why high-performance work systems pay off.* ILR Press.

Armstrong, M. (2003). *A handbook of human resource management practice* (9th ed.). Kogan Page.

Armstrong, M., & Taylor, S. (2014). *Amstrong's handbook of human resource management practice* (13th ed.). Kogan Page.

Barney, J. B. (1995). Looking inside for competitive advantage. *Academy of Management Executive, 9*(4), 49–61.

Beer, M., Spector, B., Lawrence, P., Quinn Mills, D., & Walton, R. (1984). *Managing human assets.* The Free Press.

Benson, J. D. (2008). Motivation, productivity and change management. *Research Starters Business: Motivation, Productivity and Change Management, 1*, 1–12.

Borcherding, J. D., & Laufer, A. (1981). Financial incentive to raise productivity. *Journal of Construction Division, 107*(9), 745–756.

Bos-Nehles, A. C., Van Riemsdijk, M. J., & Looise, J. (2013). Employee perceptions of line management performance: Applying the AMO theory to explain the effectiveness of line managers' HRM implementation. *Human Resource Management, 52*(6), 861–877.

Bowey, A. M. (1976). *The sociology of organisations*. Hodder and Stoughton.

Boxall, P. F. (1992). Strategic HRM: A beginning, a new theoretical direction. *Human Resource Management Journal, 2*(3), 61–79.

Boxall, P. F., & Purcell, J. (2003). *Strategy and human resource management*. Palgrave Macmillan.

Brunetto, Y., Farr-Wharton, R., & Shacklock, K. (2011). Using the Harvard HRM model to conceptualise the impact of changes to supervision upon HRM outcomes for different types of Australian public sector employees. *The International Journal of Human Resource Management, 22*(3), 553–573.

Burns, T., & Stalker, G. M. (1966). *The management of innovation* (2nd ed.). Tavistock.

Busienei, J. R., K'Obonyo, P., & Ogutu, M. (2013). Effect of universalistic perspective of human resource strategic orientation on performance of large private manufacturing firms in Kenya. In *AIBUMA Conference*, Nairobi, Kenya.

Carrell, M. R., & Dittrich, J. E. (1978). Equity theory: The recent literature, methodological considerations, and new directions. *Academy of Management Review, 3*, 202–210.

Cascio, W., & Bailey, E. (1995). International human resource management: The state of research and practice. In O. Shenkar (Ed.), *Global perspectives of human resource management*. Prentice Hall.

Chang, W. A., & Huang, T. C. (2005). Relationship between strategic human resource management and firm performance: A contingency perspective. *International Journal of Manpower, 26*(5), 434–449.

Child, J. (1977). *Organisations, a guide to problems and practices*. Harper and Row.

Cropanzano, R. (1993). *Justice in the workplace: Approaching fairness in human resource management*. Academic Press, Inc.

Das, T. K., & Teng, B. S. (2001). Trust, control and risk in strategic alliances: An integrated framework. *Organization Studies, 22*(4), 253–285.

Delery, J., & Doty, D. (1996). Modes of theorising in strategic human resource management: Tests of universalistic, contingency and configurational performance predictions. *Academy of Management Journal, 39*(4), 802–835.

Delery, J. E. (1998). Issues of fit in strategic human resource management: Implications for research, *Human Resource Management Review, 8*(3), 289–309.

Dessler, G. (2011). *Human resource management* (12th ed.). Pearson.

Doty, D. H., Glick, W. H., & Huber, G. P. (1993). Fit, equifinality, and organisational effectiveness: A test of two configurational theories. *Academy of Management Journal, 36*, 1196–1250.

Druker, J., White, G., Hegewisch, A., & Mayne, L. (1996). Between hard and soft HRM: Human resource management in the construction industry. *Construction Management and Economics, 14*(5), 405–416.

Duke, K., & Udono, E. N. (2012). A new paradigm in traditional human resource management practices. *Journal of Management and Sustainability, 2*(2), 158–162.

Edgar, F., & Geare, A. (2005). HRM practice and employee attitudes: Different measures – different results. *Personnel Review, 34*(5), 534–549.

Eisenhardt, K. M., & Martin, J. A. (2000). Dynamic capabilities: What are they? *Strategic Management Journal, 21*(10/11), 1105–1121.

Elger, A. J. (1975). Industrial organisations. In J. B. McKinlay (Ed.), *Processing People, Cases in Organisational behaviour*. Holt, Rinehart and Winston.

Fiss, P. C., Marx, A., & Cambre, B. (2013). Configurational theory and methods in organisational research. *Research in the Sociology of Organizations, 38*, 1–22.

Fombrun, C. J., Tichy, N. M., & Devanna, M. A. (1984). *Strategic human resource management*. Wiley.

Gibson, J. L., Ivancevich, J. M., & Donnelly, J. H. (1979). *Organisations: Behaviour, structure, processes*. Business Publications.

Gould-Williams, J., & Davies, F. (2005). Using social exchange theory to predict the effects of HRM practice on employee outcomes. *Public Management Review*, (1), 1–24.

Greenberg, E. R. (1991). Downsizing: AMA survey results. *Compensation and Benefits Review*, 23, 33–38.

Guest, D. E. (1987). Human resource management and industrial relations. *Journal of Management Studies*, *14*(5), 503–521.

Guest, D. E. (1997). Human resource management and performance: A review of the research agenda. *The International Journal of Human Resource Management*, *8*(3), 263–276.

Guest, D. E. (1999). Human resource management: the workers' verdict. *Human Resource Management Journal*, 9(2), 5–25.

Hancock, D. J. (2006). What value does money play in the motivation of 'knowledge workers' such as project managers? In *Proceedings of the IEEE international engineering management conference engineering management: The human technology interface*, Bahia, Brazil, September 2006, pp. 127–131.

Har, W. C., Tan, B. I., Loke, S., & Hsien, L. V. (2010). The impact of HRM practices on KM: A conceptual model. *Australian Journal of Basic and Applied Sciences*, *4*(12), 5281–6291.

Harney, B. (2016). Contingency theory. In S. Johnstone & A. Wilkinson (Eds.), *An Encyclopedia of human resource management*. Edward Elgar.

Haseltine, C. S. (1976). Motivation of construction workers. *Journal of Construction Division*, *102*, 497–509.

Hendry, C., & Pettigrew, A. M. (1990). Human resource management: An agenda for the 1990s'. *International Journal of Human Resource Management*, *1*(1), 17–43.

Herzberg, F. (1959). *The motivation to work* (2nd ed.). John Wiley and Sons, Inc.

Hope, V. (1994). *HRM and corporate cultural control: The limits to commitment* [Paper presentation]. Annual Conference of the British Academy of Management, Lancaster University, UK.

Huczynski, A. A., & Buchanan, D. (2001). *Organisational behaviour: An introductory text* (4th ed.). Pearson.

Huselid, M. A. (1995). The impact of human resource management practices on turnover, productivity, and corporate financial performance. *Academy of Management Journal*, *38*, 635–672.

Innes, P., & Wiesner, R. (2012). Beyond HRM intensity: Exploring intra-function HRM clusters in SMEs. *Small Enterprise Research*, *19*(1), 32–51.

Ivancevich, J., Konopaske, R., & Matteson, M. T. (2008). *Organisational behaviour and management* (8th ed.). McGraw-Hill Higher Education.

Kandula, S. R. (2003). *Human resource management in practice with 300 models: Techniques and tools*. Sage.

Ketchen, D. J., Thomas, J. B., & Snow, C. C. (1993). Organisational configurations and performance: A comparison of theoretical approaches. *Academy of Management Journal*, *36*, 1278–1313.

Khawaja, K., Azhar, S., & Arshad, A. (2014). Examining strategic human resource management and organisational effectiveness in Pakistani organisations. *International Journal of Human Resource Studies*, *4*(3), 214–227.

Kochan, T. A., Katz, H., & McKersie, R. (1986). *The transformation of American industrial relations*. Basic Books.

Kreitner, R., & Kinicki, A. (2008). *Organisational behaviour* (8th ed.). McGraw-Hill.

Kumar, R. S., & Murthy, T. P. R. (2013). A conceptual framework of international human resource management practices. *International Journal of Management and Business Studies*, *3*(2), 33–39.

Legge, K. (1978). *Power, innovation and problem solving in personnel management*. McGraw-Hill.

Legge, K. (1989). Human resource management: A critical analysis. In J. Storey (Ed.), *New perspectives in human resource management* (pp. 21–36). Routledge.

Legge, K. (1998). The morality of HRM. In C. Mabey, D. Skinner, & T. Clark (Eds.), *Experiencing human resource management*. Sage.

Locke, E. A. (1968). Towards a theory of task motivation and incentives. *Organisational Behaviour and Human Performance, 3*(2), 157–189.

Locke, E. A., & Latham, G. P. (1990). *A theory of goal setting and task performance*. Prentice-Hall.

Loosemore, M., Dainty, A. R. J., & Lingard, H. (2003). *Human resource management in construction projects – Strategic and operational approaches*. Taylor and Francis.

Lunenburg, F. C. (2011). Expectancy theory of motivation: Motivating by altering expectations. International Journal of Management, Business, and Administration, *15*(1), 1–6.

MacDuffie, J. P. (1995). Human resource bundles and manufacturing performance: Organisational logic and flexible production systems in the world auto industry. *Industrial and Labour Relations Review, 2*(48), 197–221.

Mahoney, J. T., & Pandian, J. R. (1992). The resource-based view within the conversation of strategic management. *Strategic Management Journal, 13*(5), 363–380.

Maloney, W. F., & McFillen, J. M. (1983). Research needs in construction worker performance. *Journal of Construction Engineering and Management, 109*(2), 245–254.

Marescaux, E., De Winne, S., & Sels, L. (2013). HR practices and HRM outcomes: The role of basic need satisfaction. *Personnel Review, 42*(1), 4–27.

Marsden, A. (2002). *Handle with care. CIMA Insider*, pp. 20–21.

Martin-Alcazar, F., Romero-Fernandez, P., & Sanchez-Gardey, G. (2005). Strategic human resource management: Integrating the universalistic, contingent, configurational and contextual perspectives. *Journal of Human Resource Management, 16*(5), 633–659.

Maslow, A. H. (1943). A theory of human motivation. *Psychological Review, 50*(4), 370–396.

Mckenzie, K. I., & Harris, F. (1984). Money: The only motivator. *Building Technology Management, 22*, 25–29.

McLagan, P. A., & Bedrick, D. (1982). *Models for excellence: The results of the ASTD training and development competency study*. American Society for Training and Development.

Mintzberg, H. (1983). *Structures in fives: Designing effective organisations*. Prentice-Hall.

Mondy, R. W., & Noe, R. M. (1996). *Human resource management* (6th ed.). Prentice Hall.

Naidu, S., & Chand, A. (2014). A comparative analysis of best human resource management practices in the hotel sector of Samoa and Tonga. *Personnel Review, 43*(5), 798–815.

Ngwenya, L. M., Aigbavboa, C., & Thwala, W. (2018). *Assessing employee motivation in a South African construction company*. Proceedings of the International Conference on Industrial Engineering and Operations Management., Washington DC, USA, September 27–29, pp. 1101–1109.

Ojo, A. O., & Raman, M. (2019). Role of green HRM practices in employees' pro-environmental it practices. In Á. Rocha et al. (Eds.), *WorldCIST'19, AISC 930*, pp. 678–688.

Osterman, P. (1994). How common is workplace transformation and who adopts it? *Industrial and Labour Relations Review, 47*, 173–188.

Paauwe, J. (2004). *HRM and performance: Achieving long-term viability*. University Press.

Paauwe, J., & Boon, C. (2009). Strategic HRM. *Critical Review*, 38–52.

Pfeffer, J. (1998). Seven practices of successful organisation. *California Management Review, 40*(2), 96–124.

Pfeffer, J. (1994). *Competitive advantage through People – Unleashing the power of the workforce*. Harvard Business School Press.

Schrader, C. R. (1972). Boosting construction workers productivity. *Journal of Civil Engineering, 42*, 61–63.

Schmidt, D. R., & Marwell, G. (1972). Withdrawal and reward reallocation as responses to inequity. *Journal of Experimental Social Psychology*, *8*, 207–21.

Schwartz, S. H. (1999). A theory of cultural values and some implications for work. *Applied Psychology*, *48*(1), 23–47.

Shrader, C. R. (1972). Boosting construction worker productivity. *Journal of Engineering*, *42*, 61–63.

Silverman, D. (1970). *The theory of organisations*. Heinemann.

Smriti, C. (2009). *Human resource management functions: Managerial, operative and advisory function*. http://www.yourarticlelibrary.com/hrm/human-resource-management-functions-managerial-operative-and-advisory-function/27995/

Stoner, J. A. F., Freeman, R. E., & Gilbert, D. R. (1999). *Management* (6th ed.). Prentice-Hall.

Storey, J. (1995). *Human resource management: A critical text*. Routledge.

Teece, D. J., Pisano, G., & Shuen, A. (1997). Dynamic capabilities and strategic management. *Strategic Management Journal*, *18*(7), 509–533.

Teece, D. J., & Pisano, G. (1994). *The dynamic capabilities of firms: An introduction*. Working Paper for the International Institute for Applied Systems Analysis, pp. 1–34.

Truss, C., Gratton, L., Hope-Valley, V., McGovern, P., & Stiles, P. (1997). Soft and hard models of human resource management: A reappraisal. *Journal of Management Studies*, *34*(1), 53–73.

Tsui, A. S., Pearce, J. L., Porter, L. W., & Tripoli, A. M. (1997). Alternative approaches to the employee-organisation relationship: Does investment in employees pay off? *Academy of Management Journal*, *40*(5), 1089–1121.

Vroom, V. H. (1964). *Work and motivation*. Jossey-Bass.

Walton, R. E. (1985a). From control to commitment in the workplace. *Harvard Business Review*, *63*(2), 77–84.

Walton, R. E. (1985b). Towards a strategy of eliciting employee commitment based on policies of mutuality. In R. E. Walton & P. R. Lawrence (Eds.), *HRM trends and challenges*. Harvard Business School Press.

Wanous, J., & Zwany, A. (1977). A cross sectional test of need hierarchy theory. *Organizational Behavior and Human Decision Processes*, *18*(1), 78–78.

Whitener, E. M. (2001). Do 'high commitment' human resource practices affect employee commitment. *Journal of Management*, *27*, 515–535.

Whittington, R. (1993). *What is strategy, and does it matter?* Routledge.

Wilson, D. J. (1979). *Need importance and need satisfaction for construction operatives*. M.Sc. Project Report, Loughborough University of Technology, UK.

Wood, S. (1979). A reappraisal of the contingency approach to organisation. *The Journal of Management Studies*, *16*, 234–254.

Wood, S. (1996). High commitment management and unionisation in the UK. *International Journal of Human Resource Management*, *7*(1), 41–58.

Wright, P. M., & Snell, S. A. (1991). Toward an integrative view of strategic human resource management. *Human Resource Management Review*, 1, 203–225.

Wright, P. M., & McMahan, G. C. (1992). Theoretical perspectives for strategic human resource management. *Journal of Management*, *18*(2), 295–320.

Yang, L. R., Chen, J. H., Wu, K. S., Huang, D. M., & Cheng, C. H. (2014). A framework for evaluating relationship among HRM practices, project success and organisational benefit. *Qual Quant*, *49*, 1039–1061.

Yap, G. H. (1992). *Herzberg and the motivation of labour only subcontractors* [Unpublished M.Sc. Thesis]. University of Bath, England.

Zhai, X., Liu, A. M. M., & Fellows, R. (2014). Role of human resource practices in enhancing organisational learning in Chinese construction organisation. *Journal of Management in Engineering*, *30*(2), 194–220.

Zheng, C., Rolfe, J., Lee, D., & Bretherton, P. (2007). Strategic people management of coal mining firms in Central Queensland. *Management Research News*, *30*(9), 689–704.

Chapter 5

# Gaps in Construction Workforce Management Research

### Abstract

The importance of humans to the successful delivery of construction projects has led to the emergence of research attention on construction workforce management. As such, this chapter uncovers emotional intelligence (EI) and the external environment as critical aspects of workforce management practices that have not gained substantial attention in past workforce management studies. While some theories and models (existing outside the construction domain) have considered the external environment, none of these models is specific to the construction industry. Furthermore, EI has received less attention within existing workforce management models. Through a review of related studies and theories, this chapter noted that the EI of construction workers and their senior management is crucial to the performance of these workers and the ultimate performance of their organisations. In the same vein, since construction organisations do not operate in silos, the external environment significantly influences the operations of organisations in the construction industry. The environment exact pressures that can influence workforce management practices and technological innovations construction organisations adopt.

*Keywords*: Construction workers; emotional intelligence; emotional competency; external environment; institutional theory; workforce management.

## Introduction

This chapter discusses the gaps in the reviewed theories and models relating to workforce management in chapter four. Past studies have revealed the absence of a workforce management model in construction. Therefore, to make the generic workforce management model befitting to the construction industry, the gaps in these existing

Construction Workforce Management in the Fourth Industrial Revolution Era, 103–125
Copyright © 2024 by Lerato Aghimien, Clinton Ohis Aigbavboa and Douglas Aghimien
Published under exclusive licence by Emerald Publishing Limited
doi:10.1108/978-1-83797-018-620241005

models were identified and filled in the proposed model. Although these gaps might have been mentioned in some of the past models, they were, in most cases, mentioned as variables with less focus on how they can affect the whole workforce management process. The identified gaps discussed in this chapter are emotional intelligence (EI) and the external environment in relation to workforce management practices in construction organisations. At the end of the chapter, the lessons learnt from the assessment of these constructs are summarised, and the conclusion is drawn.

## Gaps in Construction Workforce Management Research

The review of existing studies shows a paucity of construction workforce management models. Furthermore, chapter four's review of existing theories, models, and practices uncovered many workforce management practices. Some of these practices were modified within several studies, and sometimes changes in their naming were evident. With over 20 workforce management practices uncovered, it was apparent that the most reoccurring and standard practices which embrace the soft workforce management approach are:

(1) recruitment and selection;
(2) compensation and benefits;
(3) performance management and appraisal;
(4) employee involvement and empowerment; and
(5) training and development.

These five practices are germane to developing a suitable workforce management model for the construction industry. However, the construction industry has been described as unique and dynamic. A tailor-made management model is needed to suit the industry's characteristics best. To this end, further assessment of the existing models shows less emphasis has been given to two key issues: EI and environment. In construction, where workers play a crucial role in the success of projects, their EI and those of their senior management are important to both the success of projects and the organisations. In the same vein, construction organisations operate in a complex environment shaped by legislation, regulations, policies, stakeholders, competitors, and pervasive digital technologies. This environment will impact the management of workers in the industry and is worth exploring. To this end, these two aspects of workforce management are explored in this chapter.

## Emotional Intelligence

There is no gainsaying that the construction industry globally relies heavily on human resources to deliver its products (Oke et al., 2017b; Schmidt & Hunter, 1998). Carefully managing, nurturing, and improving the performance of these workers using the right sets of workforce management practices have also been reiterated in past studies (Chang & Teng, 2017). By employing the right practices, organisations can have more creative employees who are innovative and ingenious thinkers. This set of employees can create a substantial competitive advantage for the organisation through their ability to provide fast and helpful responses to problems (Jafri et al., 2016). For this to be achieved, workforce management departments, as well as practitioners, are saddled with the responsibility of examining diverse psychological approaches such as EI which is currently gaining recognition in both the mainstream culture and business community since its reintroduction by Goleman in 1995 (Di Fabio & Kenny, 2019; Mattingly & Kraiger, 2019; Meyer et al., 2004; Vakola et al., 2004). From the viewpoint of Joseph et al. (2015, p. 298), EI '…is currently considered a widely accepted practitioner tool for hiring, training, leadership development, and team building by the business community'. Unfortunately, this beneficial tool is missing in past workforce management models earlier reviewed.

Previous studies have noted that EI has gained attention because intelligence quotient (IQ), which has been the major means of evaluating cognitive intelligence in the past, is not enough to determine project performance and success. However, if IQ can be combined with EI, projects' performance can be improved, and project success can be attained (Cherry, 2014; Erkutlu & Chafra, 2012). Porter (2015) submitted that the study of EI is evolving, and it can examine human behaviour, which is believed to be identified through achievement, fulfilment, passion, and modification. Goleman (1998), who reintroduced this concept, described EI as the limit for perceiving our feelings and those of others, motivating ourselves, and overseeing feelings in ourselves and our relationships. Drawing from this description, Oke et al. (2017a) concluded that EI is concerned with individuals' behavioural and personal attitudes, enabling them to conform to acceptable organisational performance standards.

Notwithstanding the importance of EI to the improvement of performance within organisations, as noted by Love et al. (2011), there is a scarcity of studies that have focussed on the role of EI in workforce management within organisations (Ngwenya et al., 2019). In the view of Darvishmotevali et al. (2018), while there is an urgent need to understand the relationship between employee creativity and EI, there is a scarcity of research in this area. In the same vein, there is a paucity of information on EI in relation to workforce management activities in the quest for better construction organisations' performance (Cao & Fu, 2011; Ngwenya et al., 2019). Ngwenya et al. (2019) submitted that the handful of available studies on EI in construction studied fringe issues such as the role of EI in construction (Cao & Fu, 2011; Lindebaum & Cassell, 2012; Love et al., 2011; Mo & Andrew, 2007), the challenges facing EI in construction (Oke et al., 2017b), as well as the benefits of EI within the construction industry (Oke et al., 2017a). Others went further to study the EI of construction students (Mo & Andrew, 2007). This reveals a huge knowledge gap in terms of the key understanding of EI in construction, especially in the context of workforce management.

## Understanding the Concept of Emotional Intelligence

### *Intelligence*

'Intelligence' is one of psychology's most studied fields, yet there is no consensus on how it should be defined or measured (Ogurlu, 2015; Stein, 2009). Despite the long history of research on this complex phenomenon, the lingering belief that it is possible to describe intelligence approximately, but not fully, abounds. While several theories have been propounded to give a clear view of what intelligence is, a consensus exists that the definition of intelligence by one theory negates the submissions of others. However, while there is no single standard definition, there are strong similarities between the various definitions offered over time (Legg & Hutter, 2006). Carter (2005) described intelligence as the capacity to gain knowledge and understanding and use these in various contexts. Legg and Hutter (2006) defined intelligence as a person's ability to realise set goals, no matter the environment. These descriptions of intelligence are supported by Hultin's (2011) suggestion that two elements prove to be evident in the various definitions of intelligence. The first is that intelligence has to do with the ability to learn from experience, and the second is the ability to adapt to one's environment.

Neisser et al. (1996) noted that everyone is different, likewise, their ability to comprehend, adapt to different environments, learn from experience, and their capacity to reason. While these individual variations can be significant, they are never completely consistent. This means that the intellectual performance of any given person will vary as judged by different criteria on different occasions and in different domains. Also, this intelligence can either be cognitive or non-cognitive. According to Stein (2009), cognitive intelligence is the most common form of intelligence known to man. This form of intelligence emphasises the abilities of a person to carry out deep rational thinking, relate effectively with the environment and act purposefully.

Furthermore, cognitive intelligence is an expression of thoughts controlled by the brain and is mostly measured using IQ. Non-cognitive intelligence involves the non-intellectual use of the human brain. One such situation is EI, which relates to individuals' emotions and not their intellect.

### *Emotion*

Just like intelligence, the definition of emotion has also been challenging. Das (2017) described emotion as an explicit feeling or sensation in the mind that is a driving force to other dimensions, such as memory, intelligence, and physical activities, to fulfil their actions to pursue a set goal. Kleinginna and Kleinginna (1981) also noted that emotion points to how individuals feel. In Stein's (2009) view, emotions are a crucial source of information that helps individuals make sense of their social environment. Schacter et al. (2011) described emotions as positive or negative experiences that produce different physiological, behavioural, and cognitive changes. Emotion has been described as the most important dimension of the human mind. As such, Cabanac (2002) and Ogungbile et al. (2019) described emotion as a conscious experience that is depicted by rigorous mental actions that result in some measure of satisfaction or dissatisfaction. According to Panksepp (2005), while it may seem as if individuals acting based on their emotions are not thinking, on the contrary, a rigorous mental process is required to interpret events and act accordingly. Also, in most cases, these emotions are entangled with issues such as disposition, behaviour, and motivation (Barrett & Russell, 2015). Hakkak et al. (2015) concluded that emotions entail critically examining the negative and positive sides of a situation to proffer the most suitable solutions to a complicated problem. As such, it becomes important for individuals to decipher intelligently what they feel and how they act in a way that will not affect them or others negatively.

## *Emotional Intelligence*

The genesis of EI dates to the early '90s. As early as the 1900s, Charles Darwin identified the importance of emotional expression for survival. In the 1920s, psychologist Edward Thorndike described the concept of 'social intelligence' as managing and understanding others (Thorndike & Stein, 1937). In the 1940s, Wechsler (1943) suggested that various effective components of intelligence can play an important role in the success of an individual's life. Around the 1950s, in an era known as humanistic psychology, scholars such as Abraham Maslow focused on how people can build emotional strength. Also, in the mid-1970s, the notion of multiple intelligences emerged in the development of EI. The concept was propounded by Howard Gardner, who introduced the idea that intelligence was more than just a single, general capability (Gardner, 1975). Additionally, in 1983, Gardner introduced the theory of multiple intelligences in his book *Frames of Mind*. Gardner (1983) suggested that individuals possessed more than one type of intelligence that was cognitive. His theory focused on intrapersonal intelligence, which is the ability to comprehend one's feelings, motivation and fears, and interpersonal intelligence, which is the ability to comprehend the desires, motivations and intentions of others (Gardner, 1983). In 1985, Wayne Payne's doctoral dissertation, 'A Study of Emotion: Developing Emotional Intelligence; Self-Integration; Relating to Fear, Pain and Desire,' introduced the term 'emotional intelligence' (Payne, 1985, p. 1). In 1987, Keith Beasley used the term 'emotional quotient' in an article published in Mensa Magazine (Beasley, 1987). However, Reuven Bar-On claims to have used the term in an unpublished version of a graduate thesis. In 1990, after the publication of a landmark article titled 'Emotional Intelligence' in the journal of *Imagination, Cognition, and Personality* by psychologists Peter Salovey and John Mayer, EI became a widely recognised term in the discourse of scholars (Salovey & Mayer, 1990). Subsequently, in 1995, the concept of EI was popularised by Daniel Goleman's book *Emotional Intelligence: Why It Can Matter More than IQ* (Goleman, 1995, p. 1).

Butler and Chinowsky (2006) opined that EI had garnered vast credibility in the psychological, sociological, and medical fields globally over time. Hamarta et al. (2009) further corroborate this assertion by stating that the American Dialect Society noted that EI was the most important new word in the late 1990s. In emphasising the importance of EI, Burgess (2005) asserts that while human beings cannot be modelled to behave in one particular way because occasionally, they behave erratically, EI still offers clarity and a language that enables quicker choices and makes them more effective as a group. In the view of Stein (2009), EI focusses on one's ability to be aware of, understand and manage both one's own and other people's emotions to adapt to life's demands and pressures. This makes the field of EI potent, with different studies exploring it.

Different definitions of EI complement each other in seeking to understand one's and the other's emotions (Emmerling & Goleman, 2003). Historically, EI was defined as a subset of social intelligence, which includes the ability to monitor one's and others' feelings and emotions, differentiate between them, and use this knowledge to guide one's thoughts and behaviour (Salovey & Mayer, 1990). Mayer and Salovey (1997) later revised the definition and compartmented it into four proposed abilities that are distinctive yet related. These are perceiving, using, understanding, and managing emotion. According to Gayathri and Meenakshi (2013), most researchers adopt Mayer and Salovey's definition of EI. Goleman (1995) defined EI as a skill that comprises self-control, zeal, persistence, and the ability to motivate oneself. Subsequently, Goleman et al. (2000) redefined EI as the capacity to recognise one's feelings and those of others, motivating oneself and managing emotions effectively in self and others. Additionally, Bar-On (1997) described EI as a variety of non-cognitive abilities and competencies that influence one's ability to cope with environmental demands and pressures.

According to Riggio and Reichard (2008), EI was initially meant to understand how people deal with their emotions. With time, this transcended from understanding how people deal with their own emotions to how they perceive others' emotions and react to them. This is evident in Salovey and Mayer's (1990) earlier description of EI. To simplify the understanding of EI, Mayer and Salovey (1997) described it as an individual's ability to understand their own and others' emotions, be able to use emotions to simplify cognitive issues, perceive emotional information, and control their own and others' emotions. In the submission of Wong and Law (2002), EI includes the ability to self-evaluate one's emotions, evaluate the emotion of others, adjust one's emotions, and at the same time, use one's emotions effectively. In simpler terms, EI is the ability to notice and express emotions and views in the exact way they occur. Ngwenya et al. (2019), therefore, concluded that EI is the awareness of an individual's emotions and those of others, the ability to control the diverse emotions one feels, and simultaneously express compassion for others.

Overall, intelligence is considered one of the most desirable traits for one to have, while emotions are part of every individual's daily life. These emotions are evident in an individual's actions, decisions, and judgements. Emotionally intelligent people recognise this and use their reasoning instead of emotions. Therefore, the concept of EI ties together the fields of intelligence and emotions (Mayer et al., 2004; Salovey & Grewal, 2005). Increasingly, EI has become an eminent indicator of an individual's knowledge, skills and abilities in the workplace, school and personal life. Moreover, EI is vital to job performance, decision-making, motivation, and leadership (Naz, 2016).

## Theories of Emotional Intelligence

In understanding the theory underpinning EI in this current study, the popular EI models that have been embraced over time were reviewed. Zhang (2013) submitted that several theories and models have been designed around the concept since its introduction. However, only three models have become popular. These are the mixed model developed by Goleman in 1995, the Bar-On EI competencies model and the ability model developed by Mayer, Salovey, and Caruso in 2004. While the ability and Bar-On models have become popular in understanding EI, this book draws from Goleman's mixed model owing to its versatility and popularity among most EI studies, as observed by Zhang (2013).

Moreover, the other two models have come under serious scrutiny in past studies. For example, Zhang (2013) submitted that some past studies had challenged the ability model as it was perceived as less practical and involved a process similar to testing or measuring general cognitive intelligence. It was further criticised as lacking predictive validity in certain workplaces. However, Goleman's mixed model emphasises EI as an extensive collection of skills and competencies that drive leadership performance.

### *Ability Model*

The ability model emphasises an individual's ability to process emotional information and coordinate its usage in navigating the social environment (Zhang, 2013). It was posited that the abilities of individuals in processing emotional information are expressed in four adaptive behaviours, which were explained by the four branches of the ability model. These four branches are perceiving, using, understanding, and managing emotions (Mayer et al., 2001):

(1) The first branch, perceiving emotions, reflects the most fundamental aspect of EI, making processing all other emotional information possible.
(2) The second branch, using emotions, is the ability to use emotions to stimulate different cognitive activities, such as thinking and solving problems.
(3) The third branch, understanding emotions, involves understanding emotional language and appreciating complex relationships among emotions.
(4) The fourth branch manages emotions and entails regulating one's feelings and the feelings of others.

### *Bar-on Emotional Intelligence Competencies Model*

The Bar-on model is inclined towards personality than emotional information, as seen in the ability model. The model opined that EI is a combination of different non-cognitive skills, competencies, and abilities that can influence an individual's chances of excelling in an environment that requires more than usual – an environment that increases pressure on individuals (Opengart, 2005). The Bar-on model sees EI as a construct that should not be separated from social competencies (Bar-On, 2006). Based on this submission, Bar-On (2006, p. 14) defined EI in the social context as 'a cross-section of interrelated emotional and social competencies, skills, and facilitators that determine how effectively we understand and express ourselves, understand others, communicate with them, and cope with daily demands'. These competencies were theorised into five components: intrapersonal traits, interpersonal traits, adaptability, stress management, and general mood EI (Bar-On, 1997, 2006).

### *Goleman's Mixed Model of Emotional Intelligence*

According to Goleman (1995), in explaining EI, consideration must be given to its linkage with the social abilities of an individual that complement their abilities to process personal emotions and the emotions of others. Therefore, EI is a mixture of social and emotional competence, hence the name 'mixed model' (O'Boyle et al., 2011). Goleman (1998) further stressed that this mixed model was designed to emphasise EI as an extensive collection of skills and competencies crucial to leadership performance. The early model, which was later revised, is a five-construct model geared towards understanding EI. These constructs are:

(1) Self-awareness.
(2) Self-regulation/management.
(3) Motivation.
(4) Empathy.
(5) Social skills.

While the self-awareness, self-regulation/management, and motivation aspects are personal skills (how individuals manage themselves), empathy and social skills are seen as social skills that relate to how individuals manage their relationships with others. Goleman (1998) included a set of emotional competencies (25), which are learned capabilities (not inborn talents) which can be improved on and developed to achieve great performance. These emotional competencies can be regarded as learned capabilities based on EI, resulting in outstanding performance at work. They determine an individual's potential for learning practical skills based on the five elements of EI (self-awareness, motivation, self-regulation, empathy, and social skills).

*1. Self-awareness*

According to Hamarta et al. (2009), self-awareness is a state of self-consciousness through a vivid understanding of an individual's internal state, resources, intuitions, and preferences. Goleman (1998) described it as a state of in-depth understanding of emotional feelings, needs, weaknesses, drives, and strengths. It was also noted that individuals with good self-awareness tend to have a better knowledge of the exact way they feel in any situation (Goleman, 1995). In the view of Temaismithi (2013), people who are perceived, to be honest with themselves and others are strong regarding self-awareness because they express their emotions freely and accurately. They generally have a sense of how they are affected by their feelings, how these affect those around them and ultimately, their performance. Goleman (1998) contends that individuals with good levels of self-awareness are never carried away by their emotions to the point of overreacting in any situation; rather, in stressful situations, they tend to maintain self-reflectiveness. The plus side of this set of individuals is that they get jobs done faster and better than most of their counterparts, owing to their self-awareness.

In the view of Mayer and Salovey (1997), self-awareness can be in three distinct forms: self-aware, engulfed, and accepting. Individuals who fall within the category of self-awareness are instantaneously aware of their moods as they emerge. However, they always strive to have a balanced outlook on life as they are never overwhelmed by their emotional state. These individuals are never obsessed, nor do they ponder on bad moods (Goleman, 1995). In most cases, individuals in the engulfed state of self-awareness are swamped by their negative emotional state, and as such, shaking it off becomes a daunting task. Once they are aware of their emotions, they become overwhelmed and often lack perspective (Goleman, 1995). Lastly, the individuals in the *accepting* state of self-awareness have the clearest understanding of their emotions but are lackadaisical in changing their current state of mind (Temaismithi, 2013). In Goleman's (1995) view, this set of individuals often exhibits laissez-faire attitudes, a pattern found in distressed people.

## 2. Self-regulation/management

Self-regulation/management is the management of self-awareness regarding impulses and resources (Goleman, 1998; Hamarta et al., 2009). While different descriptions such as 'managing emotions', 'self-regulation', and 'self-management' have been used over time to describe this construct (Goleman, 1995, 1998; Temaismithi, 2013), they all point to the fact that this component of EI gives a sense of being emotionally free. Temaismithi (2013) noted that people with good self-management skills are always in control of their impulses and feelings because of their ability to think and create a fair and trust-enabled environment. This type of environment gives rise to better productivity and reduces hostility. In the view of Goleman (1995), having poor self-management might lead to an individual suffering depression, while a good sense of it is most likely to lead to a quick bounce-back from upsets and life's setbacks. Goleman (1998) noted important self-management variables such as:

(1) self-control which has to do with keeping disruptive emotions and impulses in check;
(2) trustworthiness which involves maintaining standards of harmony and integrity;
(3) conscientiousness which involves taking responsibility for personal performance;
(4) adaptability which has to do with flexibility in handling change; and
(5) innovation which involves being comfortable with novel ideas, approaches, and information.

## 3. Motivation

Motivation is the emotional tendencies that shape or propel an individual's goal attainment (Goleman, 1998). Aremu (2005) further described it as the eagerness of an individual to satisfy needs. This construct induces a particular human behaviour. It directs that behaviour, explaining how certain forms of behaviour can be maintained or preserved (Aremu, 2005). In Goleman's (1995) view, every accomplishment has its underlying factors that include the ability of an individual to delay gratification, self-controlling of emotions, stifling impulsiveness, and staying motivated. This involves properly ordering emotions to be goal-focussed through self-motivation and mastery and paying more attention to detail. It is a conscious attempt by people who are very competent in social awareness to always stay motivated.

Goleman (1995) noted that a cognitive mental capacity creeps in when emotions overpower concentration in an individual's thoughts. This mental state of mind is termed 'working memory', which controls all other cognitive activities from talking, thinking, and even solving arithmetic logic or life problems because it is an executive function par excellence in a person's mental life. Working memory, however, could be easy to deal with or even complicated, depending on the individual's social awareness level. Thus, the importance of self-motivation to an individual's performance cannot be overemphasised (Aremu, 2005; Burgess, 2005; Temaismithi, 2013). Goleman (1995) posited that success is the persistence and eagerness shown in the face of setbacks, which are mainly dependent on emotional traits and self-motivation. People with high levels of self-motivation are most likely to be highly effective and productive in whatever they do. It is a drive that makes people desire more achievement, even greater than they naturally could (Goleman, 1995). Goleman (1998) submitted that self-motivation involves a drive for achievement which involves striving to improve or meet a standard of excellence; a commitment which involves aligning with the goals of an organisation; an initiative which is the readiness to act on opportunities; and optimism which is the persistence of pursuing goals despite obstacles and setbacks.

*4. Empathy*

Empathy is the awareness of others' feelings, needs, and concerns (Goleman, 1998). This construct is also known as social awareness, and it builds on the concept of self-awareness since it is only when an individual is aware of their feelings, needs, and concerns that they can consider the feelings of others. Besides, the extent to which an individual is open to emotions determines their ability to read feelings in others. In essence, empathy builds on self-awareness (Goleman, 1995). However, it is possible to be completely detached from the feelings of others, and this, over time, has been recognised as one of the major shortfalls of EI of most individuals (Stein, 2009; Temaismithi, 2013). It has been noted that people with good empathy levels are easily accepted by others (Burgess, 2005). Empathy, in most cases, can be traced to the infant stage of an individual, as even at a tender stage, infants tend to feel sympathy for others without understanding what they are feeling. However, this feeling needs to be trained for the individual to be emotionally intelligent about others' feelings (Goleman, 1995).

Understandably, Temaismithi (2013) pointed out that empathy is crucial for leaders in organisations to retain their talents. This is because they need to maintain these talents through understanding and recognising their feelings and relating with them on such a level of understanding. The danger in not having this EI ability lies in losing crucial knowledge such talents possess. Goleman (1998) noted that empathy requires understanding others, developing others, being service-oriented, leveraging diversity, and being politically aware.

*5. Social skills*

Social skills involve adeptness and inducing desirable responses in others (Goleman, 1998). In the view of Temaismithi (2013), this is the ability to canvass others to do one's bidding. While this ability is manipulative in most cases (Devonish & Greenidge, 2010), social skills are supposed to be an organised ability to involve others in succeeding to get things done (Goleman, 1998). According to Aremu (2005), this EI ability is a pointer to the extent to which a person can perceive emotions, understand others' emotions, and motivate them by facilitating their thoughts to achieve a common goal. Therefore, a common agreement in past studies is that people with good social skills can develop a great working network within the shortest possible time (Aremu, 2005; Goleman, 1995; Temaismithi, 2013). Goleman (1998) submitted that social skills involve a skill set such as:

(1) influence which involves being able to persuade others;
(2) communication through proper listening and sending convincing messages;
(3) conflict management;
(4) leadership;
(5) being a catalyst of change;
(6) nurturing relationships;
(7) collaboration and cooperation; and
(8) creating group synergy in the pursuit of a common goal.

It is important to note that the revised mixed model eliminated and merged some constructs and emotional competencies. This reduced these emotional competencies from twenty-five to twenty core EI competencies (Goleman et al., 2000). The new mixed model is a four-construct model which includes the following:

(1) Self-awareness – emotional self-awareness, accurate self-assessment, and self-confidence.
(2) Self-management – self-control, trustworthiness, conscientiousness, adaptability, achievement drive, and initiative.
(3) Social awareness – empathy, service orientation, and organisational awareness.
(4) Relationship management – developing others, influencing, communication, conflict management, leadership, being a change catalyst, building bonds, and teamwork/collaboration.

Based on the above, it is necessary for workforce management practitioners in construction organisations to improve the EI of their workers and themselves. Through the development of the EI of construction workers, the self-awareness and relationship with others can improve among these workers, leading to improved performance, as noted in past studies (Love et al., 2011; Opengart, 2005; Vratskikh et al., 2016). In the same vein, improving the EI of workforce management personnel will facilitate more conscious interaction with the workers through understanding their feelings and concerns. As such, addressing workers' issues based on proper understanding will ensure employees' commitment to the organisation.

## Emotional Intelligence in Construction Workforce Management

According to Mattingly and Kraiger (2019), practitioners involved in organisations' workforce management are increasingly becoming more aware of the need to employ, train and develop employees with higher levels of EI. This is a result of the inherent benefits EI proposes for organisations. According to Wong and Law (2002), EI can, to a large extent, help predict work performance outcomes. Vratskikh et al. (2016) established that some job-related attitudes, such as job satisfaction, safety behaviour, readiness to identify with the organisation, and diverse workplace attitudes exhibited by workers emanate from their EI. In the same vein, work-related outcomes such as profitability, organisational performance, innovations, and creativity of workers have been observed to be influenced by EI (Darvishmotevali et al., 2018; Kim et al., 2012; Vratskikh et al., 2016). The study of Darvishmotevali et al. (2018) in North Cyprus examined EI's effect on frontline employees' creativity using a quantitative approach. It was found that an employee's creativity is positively affected by EI. In Iran, Hakkak et al. (2015) investigated EI's influence on the social-mental factors of workers' productivity using the Bar-On model with some identified social-mental factors. It was concluded that a positive effect of EI on social-mental factors of workers' productivity exists. The study of Rahimi and Rostami (2018) also revealed that EI positively influences job engagement and organisational performance. Also, Adigüzel and Kuloğl (2019, p. 26) submitted that '...EI has a positive and significant effect on employees' organisational identity, the goal-oriented performance, and emotional commitment between individuals and in the organisation in general'. Erkutlu and Chafra (2012) noted that if EI is given proper consideration, organisations stand the chance of improving their workforce's communication, leadership, and thinking skills.

In construction, Dulaimi and Langford (1999) noted that every organisation's target is continuously improving performance, which is achievable through properly understanding the industry's workforce. However, it has been observed that human interaction is filled with emotional content. If these emotions are not properly considered, they might pose serious problems for construction organisations (Ashkanasy & Cooper, 2008; Lindebaum & Cassell, 2012; Lundberg & Young, 2001). It is therefore left to the workforce management department in construction organisations to give attention to the EI of their workforce to achieve better individual and organisational performance. This is also important, as past studies have noted that construction workers have been known to lack empathy due to the nature of the job (Aliu et al., 2021). As a result, it has been noted that the survival of construction workers and their continuous growth in the industry requires building and nurturing their EI (Aliu et al., 2022). However, as earlier noted, studies on EI in construction have been scant (Ngwenya et al., 2019), and this begs the need for a construction workforce management model that incorporates the concept of EI. Available studies from the construction space have pinpointed some advantages of considering EI in managing construction workers. By developing the EI of construction workers, self-awareness and relationship with others can improve and lead to improved performance (Love et al., 2011; Vratskikh et al., 2016). Hobbs and Smyth (2012) examined the working relationship on a large construction project and discovered that EI helped the collaborative working strategy in a project, leading to better overall project delivery. Kukah et al. (2022) noted that EI of construction workers offers better employee and project performance, inspired leadership, effective stress management, better communication and increased confidence among construction practitioners. Saini and Soni (2016) also assert that EI impacts construction employees' performance. Oke et al. (2017b) noted that EI offers direction for the attainment of effective overall project performance and, at the same time, will aid communication between construction clients and project teams, building workers' confidence. More so, Acheampong et al. (2021) submitted that effectively managing the EI of the construction workforce will lead to an increase in overall project performance.

## External Environment

It is interesting to note that the workforce management practices uncovered in Chapter 4 exist within the context of a construction organisation's internal environment. For instance, recruitment and selection are a function of the need within an organisation. Also, compensation, benefits, training, and development, aside from other factors, are primarily functions of the culture within many organisations. Similarly, performance management and employee involvement depend on the decisions and the operation of management within the organisation. EI, discussed earlier as a gap in existing workforce management studies, is also a function of individuals and management decisions. Therefore, it becomes crucial to understand the role of the external environment wherein organisations properly manage the construction workforce, especially since construction organisations do not function in silos. The activities of construction organisations are influenced by external factors that could affect the effectiveness of their workforce management and the organisation's overall performance.

Dewettinck and Remue (2011) submitted that the difference between workable workforce management practices and those that are less effective is evident in the differences in the internal and external environmental factors present in different geographical areas. It was highlighted that the external environment factors such as culture, politics, legislation, economy, and societal norms vary from one country to another. These factors play an important role in the success of the workforce management practices being adopted. From the perspective of Lengnick-Hall and Beck (2009), five important external factors can be considered in developing the best workforce management practices for an organisation. These are political factors, social and legal factors, the labour market, the nature of the industry, and the culture of the country.

Examining the Harvard model by Beer et al. (1984), some of these external factors noted above are embedded under the stakeholder interests and situational factors. For example, government and unions are part of the stakeholders' interest construct, while labour market, laws and societal values are embedded in the situational factors. Similarly, the matching model by Fombrun et al. (1984) revealed that there is a tight fit between strategy, organisational structure and policies, which occurs in the presence of economic, political, and cultural forces. These three forces can be seen as external forces. However, the model focusses on what happens within the organisational environment (internal environment). The Warwick model by Hendry and Pettigrew (1990) acknowledges the importance of the influence of the outer context, also known as the macro-environmental factors, on the inner context of workforce management. Agyepong et al. (2010) observed that by design, the Warwick model allows the impact of external factors on internal operations to be analysed. The outer context of the model deals with socio-economic, technical, political-legal and competitive issues. The Guest model, however, did not consider the external environment's influence.

Although most of the past studies and models that considered the external environment have it as factors embedded within other constructs (Beer et al., 1984) or as 'standalone' constructs influencing other internal constructs (Fombrun et al., 1984; Hendry and Pettigrew, 1990), none looked at the handling of the pressure from these external factors as a crucial workforce management practice that could affect the overall performance of organisations. While politics, social, legal, economic, and labour markets can help shape organisations' workforce management practices, external environmental pressure is also a driving force for the proper adoption or non-adoption of different concepts. Past studies averred that organisations that are cautious of their external business environment and are prompt in responding to the associated pressure tend to survive better than those that failed to pay attention to these issues (Moysés et al., 2010; Zhang et al., 2011). In the view of McGee and Sawyerr (2003), this external environment refers to the physical and social factors that can impact an organisation's decision-making but exist outside the confines of the organisation.

In deciphering the concept of pressure from the external business environment and its associated variables, this study focuses on the institutional theory, which over time has been described as the most suitable theory for assessing the pressure of the environment on an organisation (Gutierrez et al., 2015; Hsu et al., 2006; Quinton et al., 2018; Roberts & Greenwood, 1997; Teo et al., 2003). Furthermore, the institutional theory showcases the influence of external environment pressure on adopting technology and innovation within organisations. The influence of the external environment on the adoption of innovative workforce management approaches within the current fourth industrial revolution era is worthy of exploration.

## Institutional Theory

In the view of DiMaggio and Powell (1983), the institutional theory emanated based on the realisation that organisations are always in a strict competitive environment. These organisations compete for power, social fitness, good economic standing, and recognition within the institution to which they belong. As these organisations compete for these desires mentioned above, they tend to be under severe pressure to conform to what exists within their institution. Failure to conform to the existing norms within their institutions might lead to questioning their legitimacy. This failure to conform results in the organisation's inability to secure resources and social support (DiMaggio & Powell, 1983; Teo et al., 2003; Tolbert, 1985). Herein lies the concept of institutional theory.

The institutional theory is most popular in the area of innovation adoption (Liu et al., 2010; Rogers et al., 2007; Teo et al., 2003) as it is believed that the pressure exerted by the external environment can affect the adoption or non-adoption of innovative ideas within an organisation (Liu et al., 2010; Roberts & Greenwood, 1997). DiMaggio and Powell (1983) submitted that the institutional environment dictates the rules of social expectations and norms necessary for organisations to have the right structure and behaviour and the right operations and practices. Therefore, before considering whether to adopt an innovation, proper consideration must first be given to the expectations and norms within the institution. In considering the expectations of the industry (construction in the case of this current study), the inherent benefits of adopting such innovation are considered and based on the result of the evaluation, the decision on whether to adopt or not is taken (DiMaggio & Powell, 1983; Scott, 1995).

In the context of workforce management practices, the construction industry has specific expectations in terms of project delivery and the use of human resources. Similarly, the cultural context plays a significant role in the effective use of labour. For instance, many developing countries have policies regarding the use of a substantial amount of labour in the delivery of construction projects. This is the government's way of improving employment (Aghimien et al., 2021). There is no denying that such policies will invariably influence construction organisations' recruitment and selection process and their adoption of any technology that will limit the number of workers employed. Therefore, construction organisations, like every other organisation, are under severe pressure to conform to their institutional environment (Aghimien et al., 2022; Teo et al., 2003). DiMaggio and Powell (1983) identified three major types of isomorphic pressures that emanate from the institutional environment. This pressure can either be coercive, normative, or mimetic.

*1. Coercive pressure*

This type of pressure emanates from political influences and the problem of legitimacy. DiMaggio and Powell (1983) submitted that this type of pressure is most likely to result from formal and informal pressures experienced by organisations from other organisations on which they depend. It can also stem from the cultural expectations in society. In some cases, these pressures come from bodies with higher levels of authority and higher resource power (Hsu et al., 2006; Teo et al., 2003). A typical example is when government promotes the use of a high amount of labour to deliver public infrastructure to promote employment. In such a case, to conform to their environment's expectations, construction organisations will be under considerable pressure to employ more workers.

Similarly, Brender and Markov (2013), Gupta et al. (2013), Low et al. (2011) as well as Quinton et al. (2018) all submitted that coercive pressure might come from the organisation's customers, suppliers or trading partners. This is because these individuals, either formally or informally, exert the same pressure on the organisation to adopt certain innovative solutions. In construction, organisations might be influenced to use a certain type of labour owing to the demand from their clients. Similarly, complicated or specialised materials and equipment supply might lead to specialised labour demand. This invariably will influence the job function of workforce management departments in acquiring these specialised labourers.

Furthermore, Hsu et al. (2006) and King et al. (1994) also noted that government pressure is crucial to innovation adoption as they tend to create strict requirements for organisations doing business with them or provide some incentives for such organisations. Therefore, through strategic legislation, the government may pressure organisations to adopt certain innovations in the delivery of construction projects in the country. This type of pressure is common in the construction industry, as the government is believed to be the industry's biggest client, and its decisions significantly affect the industry, either positively or negatively (Oke et al., 2018; Ogbu, 2017).

## 2. Normative pressure

DiMaggio and Powell (1983) noted that normative pressure arises from professionalisation. According to Quinton et al. (2018), the expectation comes from being part of a profession. This type of pressure can come from existing rules and regulations that an organisation needs to comply with to remain in business within an industry or to have social legitimisation. Hsu et al. (2006) averred that trade associations or the wider regulatory environment mostly drive these rules and regulations. In the context of this book, these rules are driven by different construction regulatory and professional bodies. Alshamaila et al. (2013) noted that the industry market scope is a key aspect to assess in understanding normative pressure on innovation adoption. This is crucial as every profession has its boundaries. The market boundary within which an organisation exists is bound to play an important role in the type and extent of innovation adoption of such an organisation. According to Awa *et al.* (2017), normative pressure can be measured using variables such as regulations on technical assistance and partnership, safety provision and staff insurance, environmental impact compliance and policies.

## 3. Mimetic pressure

Mimetic pressure results from a standard response to uncertainty. According to DiMaggio and Powell (1983), most organisations tend to copy what their counterparts in the industry are doing. This is because, in most cases, these organisations are uncertain of the expected outcome of the innovation they intend to adopt or how to develop new ideas (DiMaggio and Powell, 1983; Quinton et al., 2018). Teo et al. (2003) opined that an organisation would want to emulate the footsteps of other organisations that share the same goals, produce the same commodity, have similar suppliers and customers, and face similar challenges as they do. It is not unlikely that the volatile nature of most business environments will make many organisations consciously monitor their counterparts and somehow mimic their activities to remain competitive. This type of pressure leads to a retaliatory and endless vicious circle. When organisations mimic their counterparts, those they are mimicking tend to do something else to stay ahead of the competition, so this circle continues (Awa et al., 2017).

In mimicking others, organisations will always pick only positive, innovative traits of their successful competitors (Oliveira & Martins, 2011; Pang & Jang, 2008). According to Quinton et al. (2018), uncertainty within the business environment can also make organisations feel pressured to imitate their competitors, especially in the area of technology, rather than creating their own. Mimetic pressure can also be described as competitive pressure. In fact, this type of pressure can be a strong incentive and adoption driver for most organisations (Gutierrez et al., 2015; Hsu et al., 2006). Awa et al. (2017) measured this type of pressure using operational necessity, strategic necessity, vendor or third-party pressure, and adoption by competitors. Past studies have also noted that as competition increases, innovative technology usage increases (Hsu et al., 2006; Rai & Bajwa, 1997). This pressure can prove remarkable for organisations to stay competitive by using technologies to improve workforce management. Workforce management departments in construction organisations can learn from other organisations by mimicking their adoption of human resource information systems or data-driven workforce management that can help effectively manage the organisations' workforce.

## External Environment Influence on Construction Workforce Management

So far, it is evident that coercive pressure will play a crucial part in shaping the adopted workforce management practices within construction organisations. For instance, government legislation promoting local labour to deliver public infrastructure can help shape how construction organisations recruit and select their workers. These legislations might also influence the use of relevant fourth industrial revolution technologies to improve project delivery and reduce physical human effort. Similarly, construction clients and suppliers might influence how labour is used for their projects and handling specialised materials. Besides, professional bodies' regulations can shape construction organisations' workforce management practices regarding the laid-down rules and regulations to which these organisations must conform. Also, the construction industry's culture in terms of some workforce management practices might largely influence the practices being adopted. For instance, the recruitment, selection, compensation and benefits of workers within the industry might be influenced by the common law within the industry. What is obtainable within the industry will extensively influence what organisations will employ. In the same vein, technologies that are common or popular within the industry, like BIM and IoT, can be adopted by organisations based on their popularity and the need to conform with happenings in the industry. Also, since normative pressure centres around pressure to ensure security and safety for personnel (Awa et al., 2017), construction organisations might be under pressure to ensure a safe and healthy working environment for their employees. This will also entail using technologies like robotics in dangerous situations to keep humans away from harmful activities. However, mimetic pressure must be handled carefully to adopt positive culture, innovations or ideas from other counterparts in the industry. The competitive pressure from competitors can be mimicked to develop the organisation's workforce better or can be seen as a motivation to employ better workforce management practices that will further improve the organisation's workforce performance and overall organisational performance.

## Summary

This chapter has identified the gaps in existing workforce management models to provide a more integrated perspective on construction workforce management. The chapter revealed the need for workforce management practitioners and departments in the construction industry to inculcate the practice of improving workers' EI. Similarly, the influence of the external environment on the workforce management practices to be adopted was also highlighted. These external environments are believed to exert pressure on the workforce management practitioners and departments in organisations to either adopt or not adopt the right practices and innovation. Thus, it is concluded that to have a holistic construction workforce management model that will help improve the performance of employees and the overall performance of construction organisations, practices such as recruitment and selection, compensation and benefits, training and development, performance management and appraisal, employee involvement and empowerment as well as EI and external environment must be considered.

## References

Acheampong, A., Owusu-Manu, D., Kissi, E., & Tetteh, P. T. (2021). Assessing the influence of emotional intelligence (EI) on project performance in developing countries: The case of Ghana. *International Journal of Construction Management*, Ahead-of-print. https://doi.org/10.1080/15623599.2021.1958279

Adigüzel, Z., & Kuloğl, E. (2019). Examination of the effects of emotional intelligence and authentic leadership on the employees in the organisations. *International Journal of Organizational Leadership, 8*, 13–30.

Aghimien, D. O, Aigbavboa, C. O, Meno, T., & Ikuabe, M. (2021). Unravelling the risks of digitalisation in the construction industry of developing countries. *Construction Innovation, 21*(3), 456–475.

Aghimien, D. O, Aigbavboa, C. O, Oke, A. E., & Aghimien, L. M. (2022). Latent institutional environment factors influencing construction digitalisation. *International Journal of Construction Education and Research, 18*(2), 142–158.

Agyepong, S. A, Fugar, F. D. K., & Tuuli, M. M. (2010). The applicability of the Harvard and Warwick models in the development of human resource management policies of large construction companies in Ghana. In S. Laryea, R. Leiringer, & W. Hughes (Eds.), *Proceedings of The West Africa Built Environment Researchers Conference and Workshop (WABER)*, Accra, Ghana, 27–28 July, pp. 525–534.

Aliu, J., Aigbavboa, C., & Thwala, W. (2021). *A 21st Century Employability Skills Improvement Framework for the Construction Industry.* Routledge, UK.

Aliu, J., Aghimien, D., Aigbavboa, C., Ebekozien, A., Oke, A. E., Adekunle, S. A., Akinradewo, O., & Akinshipe, O. (2022). Developing emotionally competent engineers for the ever-changing built environment. *Engineering, Construction and Architectural Management*, ahead-of-print. https://doi.org/10.1108/ECAM-08-2022-0806

Alshamaila, Y., Papagiannidis, S., & Li, F. (2013). Cloud computing adoption by SMEs in the north east of England: A multi-perspective framework. *Journal of Enterprise Information Management, 26*(3), 250–275.

Aremu, A. O. (2005). A confluence of credentialing, career experience, self-efficacy, emotional intelligence, and motivation on the career commitment of young police in Ibadan, Nigeria. *Policing: An International Journal of Police Strategies & Management, 28*(4), 609–618.

Ashkanasy, N. M., & Cooper, C. L. (2008). Introduction. In N. M. Ashkanasy & C. L. Cooper (Eds.), *Research companion to emotions in organizations.* Edward Elgar.

Awa, H. O., Ojiabo, O. O., & Orokor, L. E. (2017). Integrated technology-organisation-environment (T-O-E) taxonomies for technology adoption. *Journal of Enterprise Information Management, 30*(6), 893–921.

Bar-On, R. (1997). *Development of the BarOn EQ-i: A measure of emotional and social intelligence* [Paper presentation]. The 105th Annual Convention of the American Psychological Association, American Psychological Association, Chicago.

Bar-On, R. (2006). The Bar-On model of emotional-social intelligence (ESI). *Psicothema, 18*(Suppl.), 13–25.

Barrett, L., & Russell, J. (2015). *The psychological construction of emotion.* Guilford Press.

Beasley, K. (1987). The emotional quotient. *Mensa Magazine – United Kingdom Edition.*

Beer, M., Spector, B., Lawrence, P., Quinn Mills, D., & Walton, R. (1984). *Managing human assets.* The Free Press.

Brender, N., & Markov, I. (2013). Risk perception and risk management in cloud computing: Results from a case study of Swiss companies. *International Journal of Information Management, 33*(5), 726–733.

Burgess, R. C. (2005). A model for enhancing individual and organisational learning of 'emotional intelligence': The drama and winner's triangles. *Social Work Education, 24*(1), 97–112.

Butler, C. J., & Chinowsky, P. S. (2006). Emotional intelligence and leadership behaviour in construction executives. *Journal of Management in Engineering, 22*(3), 119–125.

Cabanac, M. (2002). What is emotion? *Behavioural Processes, 60*(2), 69–83.

Cao, J., & Fu, Y. (2011). A survey on the role of emotional intelligence in construction project. *Advances in Information Sciences and Service Sciences, 3*(9), 107–113.

Carter, P. (2005). *The complete book of intelligence tests.* John Wiley & Sons Ltd.

Chang, J., & Teng, C. (2017). Intrinsic or extrinsic motivations for hospitality employees' creativity: The moderating role of organisation-level regulatory focus. *International Journal of Hospitality Management, 60,* 133–141.

Cherry, K. (2014). *IQ or EQ: Which one is more important.* http://www.psychology.about.com/od/intelligence/fl/IQ-or-EQ-Which-One-Is-More-Important.html

Darvishmotevali, M., Altinay, L., & De Vita, G. (2018). Emotional intelligence and creative performance: Looking through the lens of environmental uncertainty and cultural intelligence. *International Journal of Hospitality Management, 73,* 44–54.

Das, K. K. (2017). A theoretical approach to define and analyse emotions. *International Journal of Emergency Mental Health and Human Resilience, 19*(4), 1–14.

Devonish, D., & Greenidge, D. (2010). The effect of organisational justice on contextual performance, counterproductive work behaviours, and task performance: Investigating the moderating role of ability-based emotional intelligence. *International Journal of Selection and Assessment, 18*(1), 75–86.

Dewettinck, K., & Remue, J. (2011). Contextualising HRM in comparative research: The role of the Cranet network. *Human Resource Management Review, 21*(1), 37–49.

Di Fabio, A., & Kenny, M. E. (2019). Resources for enhancing employee and organisational well-being beyond personality traits: The promise of emotional intelligence and positive relational management. *Personality and Individual Differences, 151*(1), 1–11.

DiMaggio, P., & Powell, W. (1983). The iron cage revisited: institutional isomorphism and collective rationality in organisational fields. *American Sociological Review, 48*(2), 147–160.

Dulaimi, M. F., & Langford, D. (1999). Job behaviour of construction project managers: Determinants and assessment. *Journal of Construction Engineering and Management, 125*, 256–264.

Emmerling, R. J., & Goleman, D. (2003). EI: Issues and common misunderstandings. http://www.eiconsortium.org/research/ei_issues_and_common_misunderstandings.htmc

Erkutlu, H., & Chafra, J. (2012). The impact of team empowerment on proactivity: The moderating roles of leader's emotional intelligence and proactive personality. *Journal of Health Organization and Management, 26*(5), 560–577.

Fombrun, C. J., Tichy, N. M., & Devanna, M. A. (1984). *Strategic human resource management.* Wiley.

Gardner, H. (1975). *The shattered mind.* Knopf.

Gardner, H. (1983). *Frames of mind.* Basic Books.

Gayathri, N., & Meenakshi, K. (2013). A literature review of emotional intelligence. *International Journal of Humanities and Social Science Invention, 2*(3), 45–44.

Goleman, D. (1995). *Emotional intelligence.* Bantam Books.

Goleman, D. (1998). *Working with emotional intelligence.* Refereed Articles.

Goleman, D., Boyatiz, R. E., & Rhee, K. S. (2000). Clustering competence in emotional intelligence: Insights from the emotional competence inventory. In R. Bar-On & J. D. A. Parker (Ed.), *Handbook of emotional intelligence.* Jossey-Bass.

Gupta, P., Seetharaman, A., & Raj, J. (2013). The usage and adoption of cloud computing by small and medium businesses. *International Journal of Information Management, 3*(5), 861–874.

Gutierrez, A., Boukrami, A., & Lumsden, R. (2015). Technological, organisational and environmental factors influencing managers' decision to adopt cloud computing in the UK. *Journal of Enterprise Information Management, 28*(6), 788–807.

Hakkak, M., Nazarpoori, A., Mousavi, S. N., & Ghodsi, M. (2015). Investigating the effects of emotional intelligence on social-mental factors of human resource productivity. *Journal of Work and Organizational Psychology, 31*, 129–134.

Hamarta, E., Deniz, M. E., & Saltal, N. (2009). Attachment styles as a predictor of emotional intelligence. *Educational Sciences: Theory and Practice, 9*(1), 213–229.

Hendry, C., & Pettigrew, A. M. (1990). Human resource management: An agenda for the 1990s'. *International Journal of Human Resource Management, 1*(1), 17–43.

Hobbs, S., & Smyth, H. (2012). Emotional intelligence in engineering project teams. The Joint CIB International Symposium of W055, W065, W089, W118, TG76, TG78, TG81648, and TG84, Cape town, South Africa, 23–25 January, pp. 648–660.

Hsu, P. F., Kraemer, K. L., & Dunkle, D. (2006). Determinants of e-business use in US firms. *International Journal of Electronic Commerce, 10*, 9–45.

Hultin, M. (2011). *Emotional intelligence: The three major theories in the field.* Submitted to the University of Skövde, Sweden.

Jafri, M. H., Dem, C., & Choden, S. (2016). Emotional intelligence and employee creativity: Moderating role of proactive personality and organisational climate. *Business Perspectives and Research. 4*(1), 54–66.

Joseph, D. L., Jin, J., Newman, D. A., & O'Boyle, E. H. (2015). Why does self-reported emotional intelligence predict job performance? A meta-analytic investigation of mixed EI. *Journal of Applied Psychology, 100,* 298–342.

Kim, T., Yoo, J., Lee, G., & Kim, J. (2012). Emotional intelligence and emotional labour acting strategies among frontline hotel employees. *International Journal of Contemporary Hospitality Management, 24*(7), 1029–1046.

King, J. L., Gurbaxani, V., Kraemer, K., McFarlan, F. W., Raman, K. S., & Yap, C. S. (1994). The institutional factors in information technology innovation. *Information Systems Research, 5*(2), 139–168.

Kleinginna, P. R., & Kleinginna, A. M. (1981). A categorised list of emotion definitions, with suggestions for a consensual definition. *Motivation and Emotion, 5*(4), 345–379.

Kukah, A. S. K., Owusu-Manu, D. G., & Edwards, D. (2022). Critical review of emotional intelligence research studies in the construction industry. *Journal of Engineering Design and Technology,* Ahead-of-print. https://doi.org/10.1108/JEDT-08-2021-0432

Legg, S., & Hutter, M. (2006). A collection of definitions of intelligence. *Frontiers in Artificial Intelligence and Applications, 157,* 17–24.

Lengnick-Hall, C. A., & Beck, T. E. (2009). Resilience capacity and strategic agility: Prerequisites for thriving in a dynamic environment. In C. Nemeth, E. Hollnagel, & S. Dekker (Eds.), *Resilience engineering perspectives* (Vol. 2). Ashgate Publishing.

Lindebaum, D., & Cassell, C. (2012). A contradiction in terms? Making sense of emotional intelligence in a construction management environment. *British Journal of Management, 23,* 65–79.

Liu, H., Ke, W., Wei, K. K., Gu, J., & Chen, H. (2010). The role of institutional pressures and organisational culture in the firm's intention to adopt internet-enabled supply chain management systems. *Journal of Operations Management, 28,* 372–384.

Love, P., Edwards, D., & Wood, E. (2011). Loosening the Gordian knot: The role of emotional intelligence in construction. *Engineering, Construction and Architectural Management, 18*(1), 50–65.

Low, C., Chen, Y., & Wu, M. (2011). Understanding the determinants of cloud computing adoption. *Industrial Management and Data Systems, 111*(7), 1006–1023.

Lundberg, C. C., & Young, C. A. (2001). A note on emotions and consultancy. *Journal of Organizational Change Management, 14,* 530–538.

Mattingly, V., & Kraiger, K. (2019). Can emotional intelligence be trained? A meta-analytical investigation. *Human Resource Management Review, 29,* 140–155.

Mayer, J. D., & Salovey, P. (1997). What is emotional intelligence? In P. Salovey & D. Sluyter (Ed.), *Emotional development and emotional intelligence: Educational implications.* Basic Books.

Mayer, J. D., Salovey, P., & Caruso, D. (2004). Models of emotional intelligence. In J. R. Sternburg (Ed.), *Handbook of intelligence.* Cambridge University Press.

Mayer, J. D., Salovey, P., Caruso, D. R., & Sitarenios, G. (2001). Emotional intelligence as a standard intelligence. *Emotion, 1,* 232–242.

McGee, J. E., & Sawyerr, O. O. (2003). Uncertainty and information search activities: A study of owner–managers of small high-technology manufacturing firms. *Journal of Small Business Management, 41,* 385–401.

Meyer, B. B., Fletcher, T. B., & Parker, S. J. (2004). Enhancing emotional intelligence in the health care environment: An exploratory study. *The Health Care Manager, 23*(3), 225–234.

Mo, Y. Y., & Andrew, R. J. (2007). Measuring and enhancing the emotional intelligence of construction management students: An empirical investigation. *Journal for Education in the Built Environment, 2*(1), 110–129.

Moysés, J. F., Kestelman, H. N., Beecker, L. C., Jr., & Torres, M. C. S. (2010). *Strategic planning and management in healthcare organisations.* Publishing Company FGV.

Naz, S. (2016). Emotional intelligence of physically challenged and normal secondary school students: A comparative study. *International Journal of Advanced Research and Development, 1*(10), 58–65.

Neisser, U., Boodoo, G., Bouchard, T. J., Boykin, A. W., Brody, N., & Ceci, S. J., Hal, P., Loehin, J. C., Perloff, R., Sternberg, R. J., & Urbina, S. (1996). Intelligence: Knowns and unknowns. *American Psychologist, 51*, 77–101.

Ngwenya, L., Aigbavboa, C., & Thwala, W. (2019). Mapping out research focus for emotional intelligence in human resource management in the construction industry. *IOP Conference Series: Materials Science and Engineering, 640*, 1–10.

O'Boyle, E. H., Humphrey, R. H., Pollack, J. M., Hawver, T. H., & Story, P. A. (2011). The relation between emotional intelligence and job performance: A meta-analysis. *Journal of Organisational Behaviour, 32*(5), 788–818.

Ogbu, C. P. (2017). Survival practices of indigenous construction firms in Nigeria. *International Journal of Construction Management, 18*(1), 78–91.

Ogungbile, A. J., Awodele, O. A., & Oke, A. E. (2019). Appraisal of the factors affecting emotional intelligence of construction professionals in Nigeria. Nigerian Institute of Quantity Surveyors (NIQS), 4th Research Conference – NIQS RECON4, 10–12 September, Enugu, Nigeria.

Ogurlu, U. (2015). Relationship between cognitive intelligence, emotional intelligence and humor styles. *International Online Journal of Educational Sciences, 7*(2), 15–25.

Oke, A., Aigbavboa, C., & Sepuru, M. (2017a). Benefits of emotional intelligence to construction industry: A case of Gauteng region, South Africa. *Proceedings of Environmental Design and Management International Conference (EDMIC)*, held between 22–24 May, at the Obafemi Awolowo University, Ile-Ife, Nigeria, pp. 523–531.

Oke, A. E, Aghimien, D. O., & Adedoyin, A. A. (2018). SWOT analysis of indigenous and foreign contractors in a developing economy. *International Journal of Quality and Reliability Management, 35*(6), 1289–1304.

Oke, A., Aigbavboa, C., Ngcobo, N., & Sepuru, M. (2017b). Challenges of emotional intelligence among construction stakeholders. In *International Conference on Construction and Real Estate Management*, Guangzhou, China, pp. 33–40.

Oliveira, T., & Martins, M. (2011). Literature review of information technology adoption models at firm level. *The Electronic Journal Information Systems Evaluation, 14*(1), 110–121.

Opengart, R. (2005). Emotional intelligence & emotion work: Examining constructs from an interdisciplinary framework. *Human Resource Development Review, 4*(1), 49–62.

Pang, M., & Jang, W. (2008). Determinants of the adoption of ERP within the T-O-E framework: Taiwan's communications industry. *Journal of Computer Information Systems, 48*(3), 94–102.

Panksepp, J. (2005). *Affective neuroscience: The foundations of human and animal emotions.* Oxford University Press.

Payne, W. (1985). *A study of emotion: Developing emotional intelligence; self-integration; relating to fear, pain and desire* [PhD Dissertation]. The Union for Experimenting Colleges and Universities, USA.

Porter, M. (2015). *Emotional intelligence and transformational leadership in the ZZ and UK construction industry* (pp. 57–78.). Pamerston North, New Zealand: Massey University.

Quinton, S., Canhoto, A., Molinillo, S., Pera, R., & Budhathoki, T. (2018). Conceptualising a digital orientation: Antecedents of supporting SME performance in the digital economy. *Journal of Strategic Marketing, 26*(50), 427–439.

Rahimi, M., & Rostami, A. (2018). The effect of emotional intelligence on job engagement and organizational performance. *Revista ECORFAN, 9*(20), 1–14.

Rai, A., & Bajwa, D. S. (1997). An empirical investigation into factors relating to the adoption of executive information systems: An analysis of EIS for collaboration and decision support. *Decision Science, 28*(4), 939–974.

Riggio, R. E., & Reichard, R. J. (2008). The emotional and social intelligences of effective leadership: An emotional and social skill approach. *Journal of Managerial Psychology, 23*(2), 169–185.

Roberts, P. W., & Greenwood, R. (1997). Integrating transaction cost and institutional theories: Toward a constrained-efficiency framework. *Academy of Management Journal, 22*(2), 346–373.

Rogers, K. W., Purdy, L., Safayeni, F., & Duimering, P. R. (2007). A supplier development program: Rational process or institutional image construction? *Journal of Operations Management, 25*(2), 556–572.

Saini, A., & Soni, N. (2016). Role of emotional intelligence in construction industry: A review. *International Journal of Civil Engineering and Technology, 7*(4), 339–344.

Salovey, P., & Grewal, D. (2005). The science of emotional intelligence. *American Psychological Society, 14*(6), 281–285.

Salovey, P., & Mayer, J. D. (1990). Emotional intelligence. *Imagination, Cognition and Personality, 9*(3), 185–211.

Schacter, D. L., Gilbert, D. T., Wegner, D. M., & Hood, B. M. (2011). *Psychology (European ed.)*. Palgrave Macmillan.

Schmidt, F. L., & Hunter, J. E. (1998). The validity and utility of selection methods in personnel psychology: Practical and theoretical implications of 85 years of research findings. *Psychological Bulletin, 124*, 262–274.

Scott, R. W. (1995). *Institutions and organisations*. Sage.

Stein, S. J. (2009). *Emotional intelligence for dummies*. John Wiley and Sons.

Temaismithi, V. (2013). The effect of emotional intelligence on leadership performance. In *7th International Academic Conference proceedings*, International Institute of Social and Economic Sciences, Prague, Czech Republic, pp. 670–674.

Teo, H. H., Wei, K. K., & Benbasat, I. (2003). Predicting intention to adopt interorganizational linkages: An institutional perspective. *MIS Quarterly, 27*(1), 19–49.

Thorndike, R. L., & Stein, S. (1937). An evaluation of the attempts to measure social intelligence. *Psychological Bulletin, 34*, 275–284.

Tolbert, P. S. (1985). Institutional environments and resource dependence: Sources of administrative structure in institutions of higher education. *Administrative Science Quarterly, 30*(1), 1–13.

Vakola, M., Tsaousis, I., & Nikolaou, I. (2004). The role of emotional intelligence and personality variables on attitudes toward organisational change. *Journal of Managerial Psychology, 19*(2), 88–110.

Vratskikh, I., Masa'deh, R., Al-Lozi, M., & Maqableh, M. (2016). The impact of emotional intelligence on job performance via the mediating role of job satisfaction. *International Journal of Business and Management, 11*(2), 69–91.

Wechsler, D. (1943). Non intellective factors in general intelligence. *Psychological Bulletin, 37*, 444–445.

Wong, C. S, & Law, K. S. (2002). The effects of leader and follower emotional intelligence on performance and attitude: An exploratory study. *The Leadership Quarterly, 13*(3), 243–274.

Zhang, L. (2013). Improving performance of construction projects: A project manager's emotional intelligence approach. *Engineering, Construction and Architectural Management, 20*(2), 195–207.

Zhang, X., Majid, S., & Foo, S. (2011). The contribution of environmental scanning to organisational performance. *Singapore Journal of Library and Information Management, 40*, 65–88.

# Chapter 6

# Conceptualising Construction Workforce Management

## Abstract

This book aimed to conceptualise a construction workforce management model suitable for effectively managing workers in construction organisations. To this end, this chapter presents the conceptualised model, which consists of seven workforce management practices with their respective measurement variables. Drawing from existing theories, models, and practices, the chapter concludes that a construction organisation that will attain its strategic objectives in the current fourth industrial revolution era must be willing to promote effective recruitment and selection, compensation and benefits, performance management and appraisal, employee involvement and empowerment, training and development, as well as improving workers emotional intelligence and handling external environment pressure. These practices can promote proactiveness, participation, and improved skills and can lead to effective commitment, better quality, and flexibility within the organisation.

*Keywords*: Conceptual model; human resource management; personnel management; motivation; workforce; workforce management

## Introduction

This chapter presents a conceptualised construction workforce management model developed based on the extensive review of existing studies, as seen in Chapters 4 and 5. The chapter discusses the different workforce management practices that form the proposed model's latent constructs and the variables identified to measure them. Practices such as recruitment and selection, compensation and benefits, training and development, performance management, employee involvement, emotional intelligence (EI), and external environment were discussed as the main constructs of the proposed construction workforce management model.

Construction Workforce Management in the Fourth Industrial Revolution Era, 127–157
Copyright © 2024 by Lerato Aghimien, Clinton Ohis Aigbavboa and Douglas Aghimien
Published under exclusive licence by Emerald Publishing Limited
doi:10.1108/978-1-83797-018-620241006

These constructs and measurement variables were identified from existing models, theories, and related workforce management studies. Furthermore, the chapter uncovers some expected outcomes of successfully implementing the proposed workforce management practices within the construction industry.

## Variable Selection for Construction Workforce Management

This study was designed to develop a workforce management model that construction organisations can adopt. This chapter conceptualised a seven-construct model based on the review of existing theories, models, and related workforce management studies. These constructs and their attributed measurement variables are discussed accordingly.

## Recruitment and Selection

Recruitment and selection have been termed an important workforce management practice designed to maximise the number of workers to fulfil an employer's strategic objectives and goals. By description, this construct refers to the process of recruiting, screening, shortlisting, and selecting the right candidates to fill vacant positions within an organisation (Gusdorf, 2008). Castello (2006) describes recruitment and selection as a set of functions and processes of choosing the right person at the right time for the right position to fulfil the resource requirements of a company. Likewise, Aaker (1989) earlier identified recruitment and selection as being related to an organisation's understanding of the workforce needed to maintain a competitive advantage over their competitors. According to Gamage (2014), the quality of the employees within the firm is heavily dependent on the efficiency of these two functions. As a result, Sangeetha (2010) noted that the phases in the recruitment and selection process require careful consideration and time. This is because recruiting and selecting the wrong candidates with the wrong capabilities will have negative implications in future (Gamage, 2014; Henderson, 2011).

On the one hand, recruitment is characterised as finding and attracting individuals with eligible qualifications on a timely basis and encouraging them to apply for job vacancies within an organisation (Opatha, 2010). There are two primary phases of this process. The first is strategic planning which defines the objectives and goals of the organisation. The second is workforce planning which is necessary to determine whether there is a shortage or surplus of employees or just enough staff to fulfil the organisational objectives. The objective of recruitment is to obtain the number and quality of workers and aid in creating a pool of eligible candidates for the right job in the company (Heery & Noon, 2001; Ofori & Aryeetey, 2011). Primarily, companies try to attract and retain the interest of suitable candidates in the recruitment process while simultaneously trying to present potential applicants with a positive image. This recruitment process is dynamic because people are constantly retiring or being replaced, promoted or sometimes dismissed within organisations. The construction industry is no different as the ageing population has continued to be a problem, with youths not readily willing to venture into the industry due to its risk-averse nature. Similarly, changes in technology, processes and markets can all mean that positions are re-configured and made available to the new labour force, thereby activating the recruitment process.

In this light, organisations would undertake a job analysis wherein job seekers are aligned with a job opening (Delaney & Huselid, 1996). Armstrong (2003, p. 327) describes job analysis as '...the process of collecting, evaluating and setting up job content to provide the basis for job description and gather information on recruitment, training, job evaluation and performance management'. In addition, job analysis is termed as the method of determining the skills, roles or expertise required for executing job tasks for the success of an organisation (Swanepoel et al., 2000). Marchington and Wilkinson (2005) suggested that conducting a job analysis may not be necessary each time a vacancy opens, especially in organisations with high labour turnover, like in the case of construction. However, it was noted that job evaluation makes it possible to analyse whether existing job requirements and individual specifications and competency profiles are suitable for future needs. According to Nel and Werner (2017), the recruitment of employees can be influenced by some factors, which, if not properly managed, can affect the success of the whole process. These factors include internal factors such as organisational policy, organisational culture, pay and working conditions, external factors such as government or trade union restrictions, labour market conditions, and the image of the company; and demographic factors such as age, gender, race, pregnancy, marital status, ethnicity, colour, sexual orientation, disability, religion, conscience, belief, culture, and language.

On the other hand, selection is the method of selecting the most appropriate candidate for a specified position in an organisation from a pool of applicants (Mondy & Noe, 1996). The crucial objective for selection is to hire the candidate best suited to the organisation's job duties and culture. According to Gamage (2014), selection practices will determine who is hired and when the selection process is properly designed, qualified applicants will be identified and matched to the job accurately. Moreover, it is necessary to use the appropriate selection methods suitable for the job and implement them effectively. The methods may comprise application forms, interviews, references, evaluation centres, and formal tests. Based on the nature of the job, it is imperative that these methods remain consistent (Chanda et al., 2010). A huge amount of money is spent on recruiting the right candidate for a job, so the company must follow a well-defined and consistent selection process. If the wrong employee is selected, the cost to induct and train the wrong candidate will be a huge loss to the employer in terms of money, effort, and time (Heery & Noon, 2001). According to Nel and Werner (2017), the selection process in most organisations is influenced by external environmental factors such as legislation, the community, the nature of the labour market, cultural background and related political issues, and internal environment factors such as the size of organisation, motivation and interest, job environment, organisational culture, type of organisation, organisation objectives, speed of decision making, application pool, and selection methods.

From a general perspective, an organisation seeking to recruit can achieve this either from within existing staff in the organisation or externally by recruiting new ones. No matter the number of quality staff within an organisation, introducing new faces occasionally into the mix is important for organisational development. This recruitment can be done through advertisements which over time have become the most popular recruitment source. With technological advancement proposed by the fourth industrial revolution, e-recruitment using existing web-based tools such as organisations' intranet or the internet has also gained traction in most organisations (Allen et al., 2007). This e-recruitment process covers all recruitment practices performed using different electronic means and the Internet (Brandão et al., 2019). It allows organisations to attract many applicants at a low cost. More so, with various preliminary online procedures, applicants that do not match the vacant position criteria are excluded (Brandão et al., 2019; Faliagka et al., 2012). Also, organisations can recruit using employment agencies, also known as labour brokers, for an agreed fee.

Organisations are also open to the option of labour offices, employee referrals, and institutes of higher institutions (Akuamoa et al., 2016; Keshav, 2013). According to Akuamoa et al. (2016), the selection process can entail an initial or preliminary interview to separate the unqualified candidates from those qualified for the job. Careful assessment of the application pool and confirmation from submitted references about the candidates can also be conducted. Confirmation can be done before the candidate is invited for an interview to confirm the character and behaviour of the candidate under assessment. Some organisations, particularly large ones with adequate funding, can adopt a phycological test in their selection process. Then the interview process is conducted. This process is largely subjective as it relies on the subjective view of the expert panel in selecting a successful candidate. After the interview, the particulars of successful candidates are submitted to the supervisor for approval, and then a physical examination of the selected candidate is done if the job function requires such.

It is imperative to note that past studies have adopted and modified Edgar and Geare (2005) five recruitment and selection variables to determine the best practices for recruiting and selecting candidates. These variables include an impartial recruitment and selection process, a recruitment and selection process void of favouritism, the use of interview panels, appointments based on merit, and no need for further attention to be placed on the recruitment method within the organisation. Naidu and Chand (2014) suggested that past literature on best workforce management practices has noted that in terms of attaining effective recruitment and selection, organisations must be open to the option of recruiting internally or externally. They can adopt the norms of internal promotion of staff to vacant positions, adopt an employment test in their selection process, create fair and equal employment opportunities for all candidates, ensure that terms and conditions of employment are agreed upon on a collaborative basis, adopt a recruitment system that is based on merit, talent and experience, ensure the job previews are realistic, adopt seasonal recruitment and also ensure behavioural profiling during the recruitment and selection process.

In construction, Abu-Darkoh (2014) assessed issues surrounding recruitment and selection and identified 16 recruitment and selection methods within the industry. Prominent among these methods is the use of advertisements in newspapers, internal recruitment, the use of a labour office, employee referrals, radio adverts and Internet recruitment. It was further noted that these methods have some level of influence on the performance of employees. However, the extent to which these methods influence performance is unknown. Thus, recruitment within construction organisations in this current era of fourth industrial revolution can be done through internal selection from staff within the organisation by promotions, transfers, internal advertisements, or the recall of former employees, or externally through the placement of adverts (Abu-Darkoh, 2014; Akuamoa et al., 2016), e-recruitment (Akuamoa et al., 2016), a labour office (Keshav, 2013), use of preliminary online procedures to match candidates with vacant positions (Faliagka et al., 2012; Brandão et al., 2019), employment agencies, employee referrals recruitment directly from professional bodies or institutes of higher learning (Nel & Werner, 2017). Selection, on the other hand, involves careful screening of candidates for eligibility (Nel & Werner, 2017), conducting a reasonable selection test to ascertain the psychological fitness of candidates (Akuamoa et al., 2016), thorough reference and background checks of candidates (Abu-Darkoh, 2014), unbiased interview sessions (Gomez-Mejia et al., 2004; Tansley et al., 2001; Redman & Wilkinson, 2001), physical examinations of the candidates (Akuamoa et al., 2016; Mathis & Jackson, 2006), and making job offers to successful candidates (Abu-Darkoh, 2014). Including line managers in this recruitment and selection process has been noted to be crucial to the success of the process and the eventual performance or underperformance of the selected candidate (Dess & Shaw, 2001).

Albeit the recruitment and selection processes being crucial to organisational performance, certain factors affect its success. Otoo et al. (2018) investigated issues such as feedback delay after an interview, difficulty identifying available vacancies due to poor publicity, nepotism and favouritism, high cost of the whole process, impersonation and misrepresentation of candidates, and poor workforce planning. Kaplan and Norton (2004) observed poor workforce planning as a major hindrance to successful recruitment and selection. When a planning system fails, there is the likelihood of a failed recruitment and selection process, which negatively affects the organisation's business strategy. Past studies have also revealed issues surrounding the ability to conduct a thorough job analysis and get the right talent for the right job within the organisation, which has been an issue facing most recruitment and selection processes over time. Creating a balance between potential employees and the job function for which they are being hired is crucial to employee performance, job satisfaction, and commitment (Djabatey, 2012; Rohini & Keerthika, 2018). Failure to include line managers in the recruitment and selection process has also been noted as a problem facing the process in most organisations (Dess & Shaw, 2001). Rohini and Keerthika (2018) also highlighted issues such as the ability to attract the right talent, competition among candidates, the narrow focus of the workforce management department, misalignment of candidates with job function as well as the duration of the process.

Recruitment and selection in the context of this book is conceptualised *as the careful process of attracting, selecting, and retaining the right construction workforce for a specified job function that has been carefully designed to attain the organisation's specific objectives.* To assist construction organisations in overcoming some of the challenges mentioned above regarding successful recruitment and selection, some measurement variables have been identified and outlined below:

(1) Adopt competency and experience-based recruitment (AFROSAI-E, 2018; Naidu & Chand, 2014).
(2) Advertise vacancies using electronic platforms (Brandão et al., 2019; Reshetnikova et al., 2019).

(3) Allow collaborative decisions on conditions of employment (Naidu & Chand, 2014).
(4) Analyse the long-term resource requirement of the organisation (Cornelius et al., 2001).
(5) Base appointments on merit (Edgar & Geare, 2005; Naidu & Chand, 2014).
(6) Conduct induction to instil a strong sense of vision and values (AFROSAI-E, 2018).
(7) Conduct reference and background checks (Naidu & Chand, 2014).
(8) Conduct seasonal recruitment (Naidu & Chand, 2014).
(9) Create realistic job previews/descriptions (Naidu & Chand, 2014).
(10) Determine an appropriate reward system that will attract talent (Cornelius et al., 2001).
(11) Employ an external recruitment system (Naidu & Chand, 2014).
(12) Employ an internal recruitment system (Naidu & Chand, 2014).
(13) Include the line manager in the recruitment and selection process (Dess & Shaw, 2001).
(14) Profile behaviour of selected candidates (Naidu & Chand, 2014).
(15) Promote internship and learnership programmes (Naidu & Chand, 2014).
(16) Provide applicants with information about the organisation for an easy decision on offer acceptance (Castello, 2006).
(17) Recruit and select impartially in the absence of favouritism (Aladwan et al., 2015; Edgar & Geare, 2005; Naidu & Chand, 2014).
(18) Use electronic platforms to screen and evaluate selected candidates carefully (Faliagka et al., 2012).
(19) Use of head-hunting process.
(20) Use of preliminary online measures to match candidates with vacant positions (Brandão et al., 2019).
(21) Use of unbiased interview panels (Aladwan et al., 2015; Edgar & Geare, 2005).

## Compensation and Benefits

Compensation is an important function of workforce management and forms an important part of the cash outflow of a company. It often equals up to 50% of organisations' cash outflows and is even higher for some service organisations (Gomez-Mejia et al., 2012). Williams et al. (2008) noted that the compensation of employees within an organisation forms the largest part of the expenses incurred by most business organisations. It has often been referred to as all types of remuneration and benefits provided by a company to workers as a result of their employment contract (Dessler, 2011; Griffin, 2012). Mondy (2010, pp. 268–269) submitted that compensation could be defined as '…the total of all rewards provided to employees in return for their service, the overall purposes of which are to attract, retain and motivate employees'. In the view of Ivancevich et al. (2008), compensation systems are designed to attract, retain and empower workers towards more effective performance while complying with all labour laws. Therefore, developing a good employee compensation system is essential for any organisation and its employees

(Dessler, 2011). This is based on the premise that improperly designed compensation schemes can result in a wage rate that is too high and unnecessary or paying less, which can guarantee a lower quality of employment and a high turnover of employees (Dessler, 2011). Likewise, internally inequitable salary scales reduce the morale and productivity of workers and result in employee dissatisfaction. Where workers are unhappy with the form of compensation, their contribution towards achieving organisational goals tends to be lower. In severe cases, dissatisfaction due to inadequate compensation may decrease efficiency, trigger strikes, increase grievances and lead to forms of physical or psychological withdrawal ranging from absenteeism and employee turnover to poor mental health (Werther & Davis, 1996).

Compensation packages can be considered a total rewards system containing direct (monetary) and indirect (non-monetary) rewards. Direct compensation refers to the monetary benefits employees receive in return for their services rendered to the organisation (Armstrong, 2003). The monetary benefits include a basic salary, house rent allowance, leave travel allowance, medical aid, special allowances, bonuses, and provident funds. They are given at regular intervals and at a definite time. On the other hand, indirect compensation is mostly related to the work being carried out, and it does not directly involve money. This can be seen in training employees, opportunities for career development, recognition for jobs being done, autonomy and even the scope of work itself (Armstrong, 2003; Adeoye & Ziska Fields, 2014). Naidu and Chand (2014) assessed employee compensation in terms of merit-based pay, objective performance appraisal, staff being informed about the economic situation within the organisation, giving financial incentives and bonuses for good performance, and showing appreciation and recognising good performance.

Past studies have noted the importance of creating a compensation and benefits package or system with which employees will be satisfied, as this, over time has influenced employees' attitudes within organisations (Williams et al., 2008). Similarly, Bustamam et al. (2014) and Greene (2014) agreed that effective management of employees' compensation could be a useful tool for positive organisational behaviour and employee productivity. In the view of Patnaik and Suar (2019), compensation is a means of attracting, retaining and motivating employees. This is because employees tend to utilise their skills and put in significant effort in return for an expected compensation that reflects their effort. When these employees are dissatisfied with this expected compensation, there is every possibility that their input might be severely affected (Adeoye & Ziska Fields, 2014; Danish & Usman, 2010). According to Williams et al. (2008), employees' satisfaction with their compensation and benefits packages can be seen in terms of their reaction to their pay equity or the difference between what they receive and what they perceive is due to them for the job done. Heneman and Schwab (1985) noted that this satisfaction of employees with their compensation and benefits can be viewed from the perspective of employees' satisfaction with their level of pay, satisfaction with the payment structure in the organisation, satisfaction with their pay increases, satisfaction with the administration of payment in the organisation, and satisfaction with the benefits they receive. However, Miceli and Lane (1991) opined that this employee satisfaction can be measured by the satisfaction they derive from their pay level, satisfaction with the system of payment between different jobs in the organisations, satisfaction with the system of payment within their current jobs in the organisations, satisfaction with the level and system of benefit they receive. In merging these two frameworks for measuring compensation and benefits satisfaction (i.e. Heneman & Schwab, 1985; Miceli & Lane, 1991), Williams et al. (2008) concluded that ideal compensation satisfaction should be measured based on the satisfaction with the level of pay, satisfaction with the structure of payment, satisfaction with the pay increases, satisfaction with the variable pay such as bonuses, commissions and incentives, satisfaction with the mode of administering the payment, satisfaction with the level of benefit received, satisfaction with the system of determining the benefit due to an employee, and satisfaction with the mode of administering the benefits.

According to Hancher et al. (1997), the construction industry has a reoccurring problem in the area of compensation. The reason for this problem is said to be the industry's unsafe nature, which has seen the constant request for compensation commensurate to the unsafe work being done within the industry. In the same vein, attractive compensation and benefits such as offering employees market-competitive salaries, quality health care cover, tailoring benefits according to employees' unique needs, and providing savings and retirement plans are viable means of retaining employees within construction organisations. In the current fourth industrial revolution era, the use of information technology tools in the compensation process often allows managers in construction organisations to monitor and change employee compensation where needed (Tripathi & Singh, 2017). Moreover, digital platforms promote flexible benefits and compensation packages that allow workers to change their benefits packages as their needs change (Gueutal & Falbe, 2005). This will go a long way in ensuring construction workers are involved in deciding how their benefits are administered.

Based on the reviewed studies and for this current work, the compensation and benefit construct are conceptualised *as carefully designed monetary and non-monetary reward packages given to workers by construction organisations in return for their services and with the sole aim of attracting, retaining, and empowering them towards more effective performance.* In achieving successful compensation and benefits processes within construction organisations, the needed variables are highlighted below:

(1) Design compensation and benefit in accordance with labour law (Ivancevich et al., 2008).

(2) Ensure employees' satisfaction with benefits received (Heneman & Schwab, 1985; Miceli & Lane, 1991; Williams et al., 2008).

(3) Ensure employees' satisfaction with direct wages/salary (Heneman & Schwab, 1985; Miceli & Lane, 1991; Williams et al., 2008).

(4) Ensure employees' satisfaction with the pay structure within the organisation (Heneman & Schwab, 1985; Miceli & Lane, 1991; Williams et al., 2008).

(5) Ensure employees' satisfaction with the policies and procedures of pay administration (Heneman & Schwab, 1985; Williams et al., 2008).

(6) Ensure employees' satisfaction with the policies and procedures of benefits administration (Miceli & Lane, 1991; Williams et al., 2008).

(7) Ensure employees' satisfaction with the procedure for benefits determination (Williams et al., 2008).

(8)  Ensure employees' satisfaction with their pay raise (Heneman & Schwab, 1985; Miceli & Lane, 1991; Williams et al., 2008).

(9)  Ensure employees' satisfaction with variable pay procedures (bonuses, commissions, incentives) (Naidu & Chand, 2014; Williams et al., 2008).

(10)  Ensure equity in salary scale (Werther & Davis, 1996).

(11)  Show appreciation and recognition for good performance (Naidu & Chand, 2014).

(12)  Use of information technology tools in the compensation process (Tripathi & Singh, 2017).

## Performance Appraisal and Management

Performance management and appraisal have been a topical issue among many scholars and practitioners. While these two aspects of workforce management are related, they are not identical. On the one hand, performance appraisal refers to a formal process that occurs within specified periods wherein employees are evaluated by their superiors (in most cases, their line managers) based on a set of dimensions. They are scored using predefined measurement metrics and are given feedback on the evaluation ratings. Performance appraisal is a process whereby standards for job promotion are created, and employees are coached and trained, and feedback on improving employees' performance is given based on an evaluation of their performance (Snell & Bohlander, 2012).

On the other hand, performance management refers to the array of activities, policies, procedures, and interventions put in place by the management of an organisation to assist employees in advancing their performance (DeNisi & Murphy, 2017). Performance management, according to Turner (2017), is important in improving both employee and organisational performance, attaining the strategic objectives of the organisation, and at the same time, promoting some form of personal development. AFROSAI-E (2018, p. 31) have earlier described performance management as '...a process by which managers and staff work together to plan, monitor and review staff's work objectives and overall contribution to the organisation'. Kaviya and Hema (2015, p. 2093) described it as '...a continuous process of identifying, measuring and developing performance in organisations by linking each individual's performance and objectives to the organisation's overall mission and goals'. Unlike the annual review of the performance of employees, the management of employees' performance involves continuous setting of objectives, evaluating the progress made, and using such evaluation to provide reasonable feedback and on-going coaching to ensure that the set objectives are met (AFROSAI-E, 2008).

Nel and Werner (2017) noted that ideally, performance management within any organisation should follow the stages of performance planning, coaching and mentoring, measurement and evaluation, and feedback and documentation. In the same vein, Marawar (2013) gave the steps for good performance management and appraisal, including planning, performing the appraisal, evaluating the employees, and finalising the results. In the view of Poovitha et al. (2018), issues around:

(1)  performance factors;

(2)  behavioural factors;

(3)  social factors;
(4)  personal effectiveness; and
(5)  grading systems need to be given thorough consideration in the management of employees' performance.

Performance factors such as attendance and punctuality, the accuracy of work done, the knowledge of the job being done, and the ability to improve in performance as well as the management skills of the employees, are worth assessing. In terms of their behavioural factors, past incidents need to be evaluated; the ability to take the initiative, solve problems and make decisions, promote cultural diversity, the sense of responsibility, level of dependability and productivity are worth assessing. Employees' customer focus, customer relations, social conduct, employer-employee relationships, and adaptability are all assessed under the social factors. The employees' personal effectiveness includes assessing their ability to relate with others and perform well in a team, employees' creativeness, work etiquette, self-motivation, and ability to handle stress. The grading system is viewed from the perspective of the employees' educational qualifications, years of experience within the organisation, set targets that have been met by the employees, documented process, and result evaluation.

Tang and Sarsfield-Baldwin (1996) assessed the distributive and procedural justice of performance appraisal in relation to the satisfaction and commitment of employees. Six principal factors were identified, namely fairness, distributive justice, two-way communication, trust, clarity, and understanding. It is pertinent to note that past studies have strongly related performance appraisal with fairness. This is because fair and transparent performance appraisal within any organisation tends to positively impact workers' attitudes (Aboramadan et al., 2020). Looking at Tang and Sarsfield-Baldwin (1996) assessment, fairness was assessed in terms of how the employees felt about the rating of their last performance evaluation vis-à-vis their perceived performance. It also assessed how fair the employees perceived their last performance appraisal to be, the accuracy of their last performance appraisal, how justified the employees perceived their supervisors to be in evaluating their performance, the employees' perception of the freeness of bias in the performance appraisal, and employee's perception of the disparity between their own self-rating and that of their supervisors in the last performance appraisal.

Similarly, Whiting et al. (2008) assessed the relationship between employees' perceived ideal performance appraisal and their actual appraisal. This was done with a view to determine the relationship between the perceived and actual performance appraisal from employees' perspectives and their satisfaction, usefulness and fairness and organisational attitudes. In doing this, the study assessed the employees' satisfaction with their performance appraisal, the perceived usefulness of the performance appraisal, and the fairness of the process. It has earlier been noted that employees are most likely to be satisfied with their performance appraisal when they trust their supervisor and when they get support from these supervisors. Also, satisfaction may be derived when there is reasonable feedback on the performance appraisal in terms of how to develop their skills further, get paid for their performance, and advance in their career. This satisfaction can also come when they feel their perspectives on their performance are considered. In the same vein, the perception of the usefulness of the performance appraisal system is influenced by the supervisor's relations with the employee, the relevance of the different aspects of the performance appraisal, the feedback received, the setting of goals and measures put in place to help employees develop, as well as the intended purpose of the performance appraisal (Dipboye & de Pontbriand, 1981). Similarly, it has been noted that employees will consider the performance appraisal system fair if they can influence the outcome of the process or are listened to without affecting the outcome of the assessment (Gabris & Ihrke, 2001; Korsgaard & Roberson, 1995).

It has been noted that effective performance management and appraisal can lead to positive organisational commitment among employees. Also, it can be used to predict employees' job satisfaction, commitment to work, and performance level (Behery & Paton, 2008; Shahnawaz & Juyal, 2006). According to McMahon (2013), some of the pitfalls of performance management in most organisations include the hostility between managers and employees, conflicting objectives and short-term objectives, poor interpersonal and interview skills of managers, lack of interview follow-up, failure to review the performance evaluation system in place, and the complexity of the performance system.

In the current fourth industrial revolution era, construction organisations can adopt some of the identified approaches for effective performance appraisal and management of the construction workforce. Furthermore, organisations can use automated, self-service, and electronic workforce management systems to promote their performance management process. This is done to achieve the ultimate objective of influencing employee behaviour to enhance performance (Rondeau, 2018). Managers within these construction organisations can easily assess employees' performance, collect and write performance reports, and provide comprehensive feedback to workers through digital systems (Cardy & Miller, 2005). Moreover, organisations with automated performance appraisal and management use various assessment tools, such as workforce performance management suite systems and talent management tools, to evaluate goals and interpret outcomes and other employee data. This helps to reduce the paperwork and lessens the time and cost burden on organisations. Additionally, human resource analytic systems make it easier to collect, record, and retrieve performance data from different sources and provide managers with better knowledge required to identify and resolve employee performance problems in terms of behaviour and results (Jayabalan et al., 2021).

For this study, the construct performance management and appraisal are conceptualised as *a continuous process whereby construction organisational performance is measured and developed through evaluating and improving set employees' objectives in the organisation*. In achieving a successful performance management and appraisal process within construction organisations, variables that need to be in place have been identified and outlined below:

- Clearly communicate set objectives to the employee (Nel & Werner, 2017).
- Constantly review individual and group performance (Nel & Werner, 2017).
- Constantly review set organisational objectives (Nel & Werner, 2017).
- Develop an action plan to correct deviations in performance (Nel & Werner, 2017; Whiting et al., 2008).

- Ensure a bias-free performance rating (Aboramadan et al., 2019; Tang & Sarsfield-Baldwin, 1996).
- Ensure accurate performance appraisal using appropriate digital tools (Tang & Sarsfield-Baldwin, 1996).
- Ensure fair performance appraisal (Tang & Sarsfield-Baldwin, 1996).
- Ensure individual goals align with organisational goals (Nel & Werner, 2017).
- Evaluate employees' progress using digital assessment tools (AFROSAI-E, 2018; Nel & Werner, 2017; Marawar, 2013).
- Practise fairness in the evaluation process (Tang & Sarsfield-Baldwin, 1996; Whiting et al., 2008).
- Provide coaching and mentoring (Nel & Werner, 2017).
- Provide quality performance feedback (AFROSAI-E, 2018; Nel & Werner, 2017).
- Set achievable organisational objectives for employees (AFROSAI-E, 2018; Nel & Werner, 2017).

## Training and Development

Training and development are essential to the successful enhancement of the proficiency of people in the workplace. It has implications for efficiency, occupational health and safety, and personnel development (Goldstein & Ford, 2002). Devi and Shaik (2012) stated that training is designed for the present, concentrating on the employees' current jobs and improving their specific skills and the ability to perform their jobs. On the other hand, the development of workers has a holistic view that focusses on changing attitudes, enhancing performance and the future jobs within the company. According to Noe (2010), training refers to a company's planned initiative to enhance employees' job-related competencies. These competencies consist of behaviours, knowledge, or skills that are of paramount importance to the high performance of an organisation. Moreover, the mandate for training is for workers to acquire knowledge, improve skills and behaviours presented in training programs and apply them to their daily work activities (Noe, 2010). Training enables companies to compete and face the ever-changing demands of their business environment (Warnich et al., 2014).

Robust training and development systems are vital because they increase an organisation's competitive advantage over rivals and help workers perform their jobs better (Ngwenya et al., 2019). An organisation needs more than basic skills development to maintain a competitive advantage. It needs to view training and development broadly as an avenue to create intellectual capital. Intellectual capital consists of basic skills (skills needed to perform one's job), advanced skills (knowledge-sharing using technology), comprehension of the customer or industrial system, and self-motivated creativity (Noe, 2010). Ohabunwa (1999) noted that when companies train their staff, managers and supervisors would have the confidence to delegate authority to their subordinates. However, if subordinates are not properly trained, it would be difficult for their superiors to delegate authority to them. However, training and development are the basic responsibility of management. Managers must be actively involved in these practices to meet organisational goals. The supervisor should be responsible for training employees for effective job performance, improving their careers and promoting their self-development (Noe, 2010). It is without doubt that training is the foundation of sound management, making employees more efficient and productive. According to AFROSAI-E (2018), employees must acquire new skills through training provided by the organisations, apply these new skills to their job functions, and share them with other employees to ensure knowledge retention. On the other hand, managers must identify the training needs of their employees, ensure that they are trained in these identified areas and employ the knowledge gained in the discharge of their activities in the organisation.

Behnam (2014) remarked that effective training and development can promote positive job satisfaction within an organisation, change the culture within the organisation, improve workplace performance and the number of technical skills within the organisation, and enhance revenue generation. Botha and Du Plessis (2017) noted that through training and development, organisations stand a chance to enjoy benefits such as improved job knowledge and skills, employees' identification with the organisation, a climate of openness and trust, improved vertical and horizontal relationships, improved productivity, effective decision making and problem-solving, development for promotion, enhanced overall performance of an organisation, and helping employees adjust to change. Aladwan et al. (2015) also submitted that effective training and development have a linear significant relationship with employees' commitment to their organisation, performance, and work value. Similarly, Albrecht et al. (2015) opined that through effective training and development, improved job satisfaction, employee engagement, and overall employee and organisational performance can be attained. From the perspective of the human capital theory, effective training and development offer organisations improved productivity as well as the value of organisations' human resources (Welbourne & Andrews, 1996). Furthermore, effective training and development within organisations have been strongly linked with organisational commitment (Aboramadan et al., 2019; Aladwan et al., 2015). This further reinforces the assertion that employees' training and development are crucial for construction organisations adopting the soft workforce management approach to improve organisational commitment, flexibility and quality of their workforce.

Botha and Du Plessis (2017) argued that training of employees can either be off-the-job or on-the-job training. While off-the-job training is conducted outside the job vicinity in the form of workshops and seminars, on-the-job training involves coaching (one-on-one instruction), job rotation (job transfer training), junior boards (assignments-based training), job instruction training (rigid and standard learning), understudying, mentoring, learner-controlled instruction, behaviour modelling (observation learning), learnership training (learnership or apprenticeship), and vestibule training (learning is simulated environment). Similarly, Naidu and Chand (2014) measured training and development with organisations using the training needs analysis, induction, on-the-job training, and off-the-job training. Snell and Dean (1992) mentioned that the on-the-job approach to training and development is the most widely adopted form within most organisations. This is because the approach offers a low cost of training, reduced use of valuable company time, and immediate productivity. However, Nel and Werner (2017) warned that the induction of employees into an organisation should not override or eliminate the necessity to train and develop employees as both serve different functions, and it is the right of the employee to be trained and developed for better performance in the organisation. Training can also be in the form of remedial skill training conducted to fill the skill gaps of an employee or a group of employees, especially in this current fourth industrial revolution era, where rapid technological advancement is evident. Training employees to acquire the necessary skills to adopt and use these technologies can form part of an organisation's training and development target. More so, training can be specific to a firm or transferable. In other words, training can be conducted to improve an employee's functioning in specific activities peculiar to their current organisations alone. It can also be generic, whereby experience gained can be used in other organisations.

Behnam (2014) noted that in most organisations, management adopted employees' development from the aspect of planned workforce development, whereby employees are developed to foster and secure the needed workforce for organisations' set objectives. Also, development can be skill development targeted at developing specific individual or group skills or career development. Edgar and Geare (2005) adopted a four-item scale to measure organisational training and development. They assessed the organisations' provision of training opportunities needed in improving employees' skills, creating avenues for employees to discuss their training and development requirements with the management of the organisation, payment for all training and development of employees as well as the commitment of organisations to the training and development of their employees. These assessment scales were also adopted by Aladwan et al. (2015) in assessing the effect of workforce management practices on organisational commitment and by Bhanugopan et al. (2013) in measuring workforce management practices in Jordan.

The construction industry has been described as a complex industry which relies heavily on human capital (Druker et al., 1996; Loosemore et al., 2003). Unfortunately, the industry's slow response to workers' training and development has also been noted (Druker et al., 1996; Ojambati et al., 2012). This leads to the need for a more effective approach towards improving the training and development of the industry's workers to ensure adequate and continuous delivery of the industry's services. The current fourth industrial revolution era offers construction more opportunities to train and develop their workforce more efficiently. This is because digital tools also offer improved training, as online meeting platforms allow a more technical approach to training that enhances the experience of new workers. In addition, implementing technology allows for more effective training of new employees while allowing workers to access onboarding and training programs anywhere (Neeraj, 2018). For instance, with cloud computing and storage, employees can access recordings of training sessions anywhere. Also, digital classrooms allow workforce management practitioners to quickly train many employees and assess their progress through computerised testing programmes (Neeraj, 2018).

For this study, training and development construct is conceptualised as a process of changing workers' attitudes, enhancing performance and creating future jobs within an organisation through improving *employees' skills and ability to perform their current jobs using on-site or off-site training approaches*. In achieving a successful training and development process within construction organisations, the variables required were identified and outlined below:

(1)  Conduct training need assessment (AFROSAI-E, 2018; Behnam, 2014; Naidu & Chand, 2014).
(2)  Create avenues for employees to discuss their training and development requirements (Edgar & Geare, 2005).
(3)  Ensure future competence development (Naidu & Chand, 2014).
(4)  Ensure newly acquired skills are applied on the job (AFROSAI-E, 2018).
(5)  Ensure newly acquired skills are shared with other employees (AFROSAI-E, 2018).
(6)  Invest in digital technologies and training needs (Edgar & Geare, 2005; Snell & Dean, 1992).
(7)  Promote acting capacity (Botha & Du Plessis, 2017; Ojambati et al., 2012).
(8)  Promote career development (Behnam, 2014).
(9)  Promote leadership development (Bradley & Karl, 2011; Ojambati et al., 2012).
(10) Promote skills development (Behnam, 2014; Coyle-Shapiro et al., 2016; Edgar & Geare, 2005).
(11) Top management commitment to training and development (Edgar & Geare, 2005; Snell & Dean, 1992).
(12) Use coaching/supervisor training (Botha & Du Plessis, 2017; Ojambati et al., 2012).
(13) Use formal training process extensively (Snell & Dean, 1992).
(14) Use of apprenticeships (Botha & Du Plessis, 2017; Bradley & Karl, 2011; Ojambati et al., 2012).
(15) Use of emerging technologies in training (Bradley & Karl, 2011; Ojambati et al., 2012).
(16) Use of induction and orientation (Aboramadan et al., 2019; Bradley & Karl, 2011; Coyle-Shapiro et al., 2016; Naidu & Chand, 2014; Ojambati et al., 2012).
(17) Use of job rotation (Bradley & Karl, 2011; Ojambati et al., 2012)
(18) Use off-the-job training method (Botha & Du Plessis, 2017; Naidu & Chand, 2014).
(19) Use on-the-job training method (Botha & Du Plessis, 2017; Naidu & Chand, 2014).
(20) Use understudy and mentoring (Botha & Du Plessis, 2017).

## Employee Involvement and Empowerment

Geroy et al. (1998) described employee empowerment as the process whereby the culture within an organisation gives room for employees to make decisions within the working environment. These employees are held accountable for their decisions and are responsible for their outcomes within acceptable parameters. Hand (1993) noted that empowering employees is simply the process of encouraging employees to make decisions and initiate actions with little or no input or directives from management. In a more concise definition, Nesan and Holt (1999) defined empowerment of employees as '…the process of giving employees the authority to take decisions, relating to their work processes and functions, and within the limits provided by management, but requiring them to assume full responsibility and risk for their actions'. Price et al. (2004) regard this empowerment as an economically and socially acceptable job enrichment process promoting employees' motivation and commitment to work.

On the other hand, employee involvement has been described as '…a participative process to use the entire capacity of workers, designated to encourage employee commitment to organisational success' (Lawler & Mohrman, 1989, pp. 26–31). This concept has been closely linked with employee empowerment. It is easily understood by employees and managers because it is usually uniformly implemented within organisations, unlike employee empowerment, which is challenging to implement uniformly (Halvorsen, 2005). According to Hammuda and Dulaimi (1997), employee involvement entails providing employees with the necessary information, influence and incentives. Leana (1987) noted that employee involvement could be participative, where employees have partial control in the decision-making process with their supervisor, or it can be delegative, wherein the employee has complete control of the decision-making. Marescaux et al. (2013) described this practice as employees' participation which is a periodic and structured consultation between the management of an organisation and its employees regarding the job and job conditions of the employees. In the same vein, Heery and Noon (2001) described this participation of employees as a system whereby employees can participate in management decision-making. Apostolou (2000) concluded that employee involvement implies that every employee is considered a unique asset to the organisation and is encouraged to contribute to meeting organisational goals. However, employee empowerment implies that management recognises employees' ability to solve organisational issues. As such, they are willing to provide these employees with the necessary tools and authority to solve these issues and ensure continuous performance.

According to Holt et al. (2000), employee empowerment is not an act or a physical incident but a perception that employees are in control of what happens within their working environment and can handle those processes effectively and efficiently. Unfortunately, the construction industry, in its nature, tends to reduce feelings of self-efficacy and a sense of belonging among its workforce. This, therefore, begs the need for a well-thought-out plan to ensure employee involvement and empowerment to achieve increased employee commitment and, by extension, better overall performance. Apostolou (2000) noted that employee involvement and empowerment can only be possible when factors such as giving employees responsibility, training employees to accept responsibility, communicating and giving feedback, and giving rewards and recognition are in place. Holt et al. (2000, p. 49) identified nine major characteristics of empowerment in construction organisations. These are:

(1) leadership which involves establishing new goals for the organisation that can be clearly disaggregated (devolved) and encouraged at all levels;
(2) empowerment implementation system that acts as an enabler to leadership;
(3) resources that are built into the system to enable realisation of the new goals, with emphasis on continual training;
(4) embracing all within an organisation to become enthusiastic about making the new system work;

(5) continuous training for the entire organisation as an integral feature;
(6) encouraging teamwork with various teams at all levels implement the goals defined under leadership and within the parameters of the system and resources;
(7) ensuring process improvement in order to align individuals' strengths with the goals of empowerment and making every employee a process owner;
(8) making continual performance measurement the cornerstones of monitoring an empowered organisation;
(9) adopting recognition as a motivator by placating the aspirations of individuals and rewarding enthusiasm for change and improved performance'.

Naidu and Chand (2014, p. 804) viewed this workforce management practice from the perspective of employee consultation and cooperation. The study measured this construct by '...collaboratively setting the goals and objectives of the organisation; right staff at the right place of service; employee involvement in quality control circles; using attitudes survey to control quality; and team briefing'. Despite the importance of involving and empowering employees, several challenges within the construction industry have made this practice impossible within the industry. Holt et al. (2000) noted some challenges facing effective employee empowerment within the construction industry. These challenges exist in the form of poor commitment from management within construction organisations, underrating the extent to which empowerment can influence employees' performance, resistance to changes in behaviour, excess bureaucracy, poor adoption or failure to adopt continuous learning and poor communication.

Within the current fourth industrial revolution era with ubiquitous digital technologies, construction organisations must ensure the involvement and empowerment of their workforce to get optimum productivity, commitment, and overall performance. Aside from adopting the measures mentioned above, using digital technologies can prove very helpful. The workforce management practitioners or departments within construction organisations can get recommendations, reactions, and viewpoints on employee- and employee-centric aspects faster using online surveys and reviews (Galgali, 2017). Furthermore, introducing digital platforms in an organisation will allow workers to use technology-based self-service software that encourages employee participation (Venterink, 2017). This creates a significant shift from the traditional workforce management strategies and activities adopted within organisations to a more digitalised approach.

For this study, employee involvement and empowerment are conceptualised *as the process whereby management within a construction organisation provides workers with tools and authority to solve issues within the organisation and each worker is encouraged to participate in meeting the set objectives of the organisation.* In achieving a successful employee involvement and empowerment process within construction organisations, the variables required were identified and outlined below:

(1) Align individual strength with empowerment goals (Holt et al., 2000; Nesan, 1997).
(2) Allow collaborative setting of organisational goals and objectives (Naidu & Chand, 2014).

(3) Brief teams, communicate and give feedback using digital tools (Apostolou, 2000; Naidu & Chand, 2014).
(4) Create systems that promote empowerment and involvement (Holt et al., 2000; Nesan, 1997).
(5) Ensure continuous measurement of performance (Holt et al., 2000; Nesan, 1997).
(6) Ensure employee involvement in quality control circles (Naidu & Chand, 2014).
(7) Ensure enthusiastic participation in the attainment of the company's goals (Apostolou, 2000; Holt et al., 2000; Nesan, 1997).
(8) Ensure the right staff at the right place of service (Naidu & Chand, 2014).
(9) Make resources available for continuous training (Apostolou, 2000; Holt et al., 2000; Nesan, 1997).
(10) Promote leadership (AFROSAI-E, 2018; Holt et al., 2000; Nesan, 1997).
(11) Promote reward and recognition (Apostolou, 2000; Holt et al., 2000; Nesan, 1997).
(12) Promote teamwork (Holt et al., 2000; Nesan, 1997).
(13) Use self-service digital platforms to promote participation (Venterink, 2017).

## Emotional Intelligence

EI, which is concerned with individuals' behavioural and personal attitudes that enable them to conform to acceptable performance standards within an organisation (Oke et al., 2017), is gradually becoming a widely accepted tool in hiring and managing employees (Joseph et al., 2015). Goleman (1998) has described it as the point at which individuals recognise their feelings and those of others to motivate and oversee feelings in themselves and their relationship with others. In assessing EI, several theories have been postulated and models developed. As noted in Chapter 5, this study draws from Goleman's mixed model owing to its versatility and popularity among most EI studies (Zhang, 2013). Goleman's model identified 20 EI variables grouped under four distinct categories, namely:

(1) self-awareness (emotional self-awareness, accurate self-assessment, and self-confidence);
(2) self-management (self-control, trustworthiness, conscientiousness, adaptability, achievement drive, and initiative);
(3) social awareness (empathy, service orientation and organisational awareness); and
(4) relationship management (developing others, influencing others, communication, conflict management, leadership, change catalyst, building bonds, and teamwork/collaboration).

The first two relate (i.e. self-awareness and self-management) to personal skills, while the last two (i.e. social awareness and relationship management) relate to social skills (Goleman et al., 2000).

It is necessary for workforce management practitioners and construction organisations' departments to improve the EI of their workers and themselves. Through the development of the EI of construction workers, their self-awareness and relationship with others can improve, leading to improved performance (Love et al.,

2011; Vratskikh et al., 2016). In the same vein, improving workforce management practitioners' EI, more conscious interaction with the workforce, understanding their feelings and concerns and addressing these issues based on this understanding will go a long way in ensuring employees' commitment to the organisation.

For this study, EI is conceptualised as *promoting positive employees' reactions to their emotions and to those of others in the optimum discharge of their job functions*. These variables measuring EI were adapted from Goleman's mixed model (Goleman et al., 2000) and are outlined below. The concept of EI and its benefits have been extensively discussed in chapter five of this book:

(1) Be a change catalyst.
(2) Create an environment that promotes initiative.
(3) Empathy.
(4) Ensure adaptability.
(5) Ensure organisational awareness among employee.
(6) Influence.
(7) Practise conflict management.
(8) Promote accurate self-awareness.
(9) Promote achievement drive.
(10) Promote building bonds.
(11) Promote conscientiousness (care and diligence in carrying out tasks).
(12) Promote effective communication.
(13) Promote emotional self-awareness.
(14) Promote employee-to-employee mentoring (developing others).
(15) Promote leadership among employees.
(16) Promote self-confidence.
(17) Promote self-control.
(18) Promote service orientation.
(19) Promote teamwork.
(20) Promote trustworthiness.

## External Environment

Assessing the role of the external environment in achieving effective construction workforce management in the era of the fourth industrial revolution is crucial, especially since construction organisations do not function alone. Past studies have noted the importance of assessing the external environment. However, most have embedded external environmental factors within order constructs, and none have assessed this from the perspective of handling the pressure from this external environment as a crucial practice that could affect the overall performance of organisations. To clearly understand how the external environment can exact pressure on the workforce management practices of construction organisations, the institutional theory was adopted (please refer to Chapter 5). This theory views pressure from three dimensions which are coercive, mimetic and normative pressure. While coercive pressure emanates from political influences and the problem of legitimacy, normative pressure arises from professionalisation, and mimetic pressure results from a standard response to uncertainty (Aghimien et al., 2022; DiMaggio & Powell, 1983).

In construction, the environment plays a crucial role in how projects are delivered and using technologies to deliver projects and improve workforce management effectively. For instance, the industry has been characterised as dangerous for workers (Akinlolu et al., 2020; Cai et al., 2018; Chan & Aghimien, 2022). This necessitates the need for effective occupational health and safety within the industry. Digital technologies offer significant benefits in ensuring the safety of construction workers. These technologies include; robotics and automation, warning systems, UAVs, sensors, laser scanners, building information modelling (BIM), wearable sensing devices, RFID, and quick response codes. These technologies can be integrated into the project from the design stage to reduce potential construction hazards and facilitate workplace safety (Akinlolu et al., 2020; Bahrin et al., 2016; Karakhan & Alsaffar, 2019). For instance, BIM has an integrated safety management framework, which detects possible hazards before work starts and recommends risk reduction steps (Zhang et al., 2013). In addition, it allows construction site workers to record near-hits, allowing managers and supervisors to identify and minimise possible occupational hazards (Shen & Marks, 2015). Smart wearables help managers monitor employees' job activities and health and take significant action as necessary (Manning, 2017). The availability and use of these technologies by competitors will spur construction organisations to equally adopt these technologies to remain competitive and relevant and attain legitimacy within the industry. Herein lies the concept of institutional pressure.

For this study, the external environment construct is conceptualised as *workforce management practitioners or departments' ability to handle the pressure from the external environment and convert it into a positive drive to achieve better employee performance.* The variables measuring this construct are outlined below. This dimension has also been extensively discussed in chapter five:

(1) Clients' demand for personnel and technologies (Alshamaila et al., 2013; Awa et al., 2017; Quinton et al., 2018).
(2) Competitive pressure (Awa et al., 2017).
(3) Construction industry's regulations (Alshamaila et al., 2013; Teo et al., 2003).
(4) Culture and values in the construction industry (Dewettinck & Remue, 2011).
(5) Evolving nature of the construction industry (Lengnick-Hall & Beck, 2009).
(6) Government policies and legislations (Dewettinck & Remue, 2011; Lengnick-Hall & Beck, 2009; Quinton et al., 2018).
(7) Industry's regulation on the use of digital technologies (Awa et al., 2017; Aghimien et al., 2022).
(8) Nature of the labour market (Lengnick-Hall & Beck, 2009).
(9) Political climate (Dewettinck & Remue, 2011; Lengnick-Hall & Beck, 2009).
(10) Regulations on the extent of partnership (Awa et al., 2017).
(11) Scope of the market of the organisation (Specific boundaries of the organisation's activities) (Alshamaila et al., 2013; Hsu et al., 2006).
(12) Socio-economic climate (Dewettinck & Remue, 2011; Lengnick-Hall & Beck, 2009).
(13) Suppliers and subcontractors demand personnel and technologies (Alshamaila et al., 2013; Awa et al., 2017; Quinton et al., 2018).
(14) Use of technologies to provide safety and security for workers (Awa et al., 2017).

# Expected Outcomes of Effective Construction Workforce Management

Adopting the aforementioned workforce management practices promises significant outcomes for construction organisations, their employees, and the construction industry. Oosthuizen and Nienaber (2010) mentioned that a better competitive advantage could be derived from effective management of organisations' workforce. With the right employees with the right expertise, construction organisations stand to be more competitive as fast and efficient solutions can be derived from the right talents. Furthermore, the organisations stand to benefit from increased profit. Guest (1997) opined that one of the major outcomes of adopting the right workforce management practices is financial outcomes in the form of profits for the organisation.

Several studies have also noted the aspect of maximum productivity and increased performance. Ngwenya and Aigbavboa (2017) submitted that adopting the right workforce management practices will largely influence the performance and productivity of employees, their knowledge of the job, and their competencies to ensure better productivity. From a technology adoption perspective, some organisations also adopt digital technologies to improve employees' productivity. This is because these technologies allow organisations' workforce to grow their skills, resulting in increased employee productivity (Bissola & Imperatori, 2013; Panos & Bellou, 2016). Adopting digital technologies will improve productivity by automating and substituting low-value administrative work with high-value-added tasks (Marler & Parry, 2016). More so, the diffusion of digital tools into workforce management offers a faster and more informed decision-making mechanism. This is because it allows the proper storage, retrieval and upgrading of existing data relating to the skills and competencies of employees. With digital tools like big data analytics, stored data can be analysed to provide a quicker and more informed decision-making mechanism (Garcia-Arroyo & Osca, 2019).

Regarding compensation, Dessler (2011) mentioned that employees tend to be less productive when they are dissatisfied with the equity in their salary. Therefore, adopting the right practices relating to compensation and benefits might help ensure equity in remuneration and subsequent satisfied and productive employees. This submission is affirmed by past studies that have noted that effective management of employees' compensation can be a useful tool needed for positive organisational behaviour and productivity among employees (Bustamam et al., 2014; Greene, 2014). The organisation also stands to gain better organisational performance with the implementation of proper workforce management practices (Albrecht et al., 2015).

Better overall construction performance can also be a result of organisations adopting the right practices. In construction, where organisations are expected to deliver projects within well-defined project criteria such as cost, time, quality, health and safety, among others, having the right digital tools and employees with the right expertise to help deliver these projects is essential. Also, the industry stands to gain better quality and innovative construction through effective workforce management practices (Guest, 1997). Several workforce management practices, such as compensation, training and development and employee involvement, have been linked to job satisfaction, commitment, less employee turnover, culture change within an organisation, improved workplace performance and the number of technical skills within the organisation (Albrecht et al.,2015; Behnam, 2014; Behery & Paton, 2008; Shahnawaz & Juyal, 2006). Below is the summary of these expected outcomes of effective construction workforce management in the fourth industrial revolution era:

(1) Better organisational profit.
(2) Better overall construction performance.
(3) Better quality and innovative construction output.
(4) Better work flexibility.
(5) Change in organisational culture.
(6) Competitive advantage.
(7) Cost-effective construction service delivery.
(8) Effective knowledge management through digital tools.
(9) Ensuring the right employee is on the right project.
(10) Harmony in the work environment.
(11) Improved client satisfaction.
(12) Improved employee and organisational productivity
(13) Improved work experience and confidence of employees
(14) Increased employee performance
(15) Increased employees' affective commitment
(16) Increased job satisfaction
(17) Increased organisational performance
(18) Low labour turnover
(19) Organisational citizenship.

## Theorising the Conceptualised Workforce Management Model

Considering the need for better delivery of services in the construction industry through the effective use of construction organisations' resources, particularly human capital and technology, and the absence of a holistic workforce management model in the industry, this study set out to explore the concept of workforce management in construction and propose a conceptual workforce management model that can be adopted and modified to suit situations within diverse construction organisations. The study draws from the strength of the strategic theory, which believes in aligning workforce activities to organisations' goals and objectives. Through this alignment, increased performance within the organisation can be achieved (Guest, 1997). In developing the proposed model, the review of extant studies suggested the need for strategic workforce management with a classical view using a soft workforce management approach that embraces employees' empowerment and development through trust. This perspective was adopted to counter the popular view of the construction workforce as just resources required for project delivery. While drawing from the classical approach of maximising the workforce's potential within an organisation, the study viewed these workforces as the key element whose behavioural commitment to organisational objectives can help achieve the strategic goals set by the organisation.

Based on the forementioned, the study theorises that a construction organisation that will attain its strategic objectives in the current fourth industrial revolution era must be willing to promote:

(1) recruitment and selection;
(2) compensation and benefits;
(3) performance management and appraisal;
(4) employee involvement and empowerment;
(5) training and development;
(6) emotional intelligence; and
(7) external environment, as core workforce management practices within the organisation.

These practices can promote proactiveness, participation, and improved skills and can lead to effective commitment, better quality and flexibility among others within the organisation. Fig. 6.1 gives a conceptualised construction workforce management model. Also, Fig. 6.2 gives a full view of the conceptualised model, including the practices and their measuring variables. Construction organisations seeking to strategically improve the management of their workforce can adopt the variables suitable to the conditions within their organisations. The proposed model is designed to serve as a base for further assessment within construction organisations.

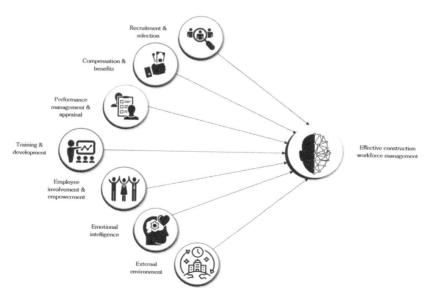

Fig. 6.1.    Conceptualised Construction Workforce Management Model.
*Source*: Author's compilation (2023).

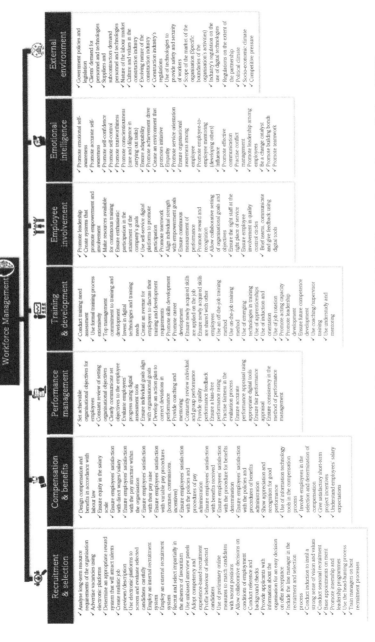

Fig. 6.2.  Proposed Conceptual Construction Workforce Management Model. *Source:* Author's compilation (2023).

## Summary

This chapter discussed the workforce management practices and their sub-attributes required for effective construction workforce management. Drawing from past theories, models and related workforce management-studies, this chapter conceptualised a seven-construct model that construction organisations can adopt to improve their workforce management. The next chapter uses experts' opinion to explore the suitability and applicability of the conceptualised construction workforce management model.

## References

Aaker, D. A. (1989). Managing assets and skills: The key to a sustainable competitive advantage. *California Management Review*, *31*, 91–106.

Aboramadan, M., Albashiti B., Alharazin, H., & Dahleez, K. A. (2019). Human resources management practices and organizational commitment in higher education: The mediating role of work engagement. *International Journal of Educational Management*.

Aboramadan, M., Albashiti, B., Alharazin, H., & Dahleez, K. A. (2020). Human resources management practices and organisational commitment in higher education: The mediating role of work engagement. *International Journal of Educational Management*, *34*(1), 154–174.

Abu-Darkoh, M. (2014). *Employee recruitment and selection practices in the construction industry in Ashanti region.* Thesis submitted to the Department of Managerial Science, Kwame Nkrumah University of Science and Technology, Ghana.

Adeoye, A. O., & Ziska Fields, Z. (2014). Compensation management and employee job satisfaction: A case of Nigeria. *Journal of Social Sciences*, *41*(3), 345–352.

African Organisation of English-speaking Supreme Audit Institutions (AFROSAI – E). (2018). *Human resource management (HRM) framework and handbook for SAIs* (1st ed.). AFROSAI – E https://afrosai-e.org.za/wp-content/uploads/2019/07/HR-Management-Handbook-for-SAIs-2019.pdf

Aghimien, D. O., Aigbavboa, C. O., Oke, A. E., & Aghimien, L. M. (2022). Latent institutional environment factors influencing construction digitalisation. *International Journal of Construction Education and Research*, *18*(2), 142–158.

Akinlolu, M., Haupt, T. C., Edwards, D. J., & Simpeh, F. (2020). A bibliometric review of the status and emerging research trends in construction safety management technologies. *International Journal of Construction Management*, *22*(14), 2699–2711.

Akuamoa, W. S., Amedagbui, K., Buabasah, D. Y., & Letsa – Agbozojoseph, K. (2016). The impact of effective recruitment and selection practice on organisational performance (a case study at University of Ghana). *Global Journal of Management and Business Research: Administration and Management*, *16*(11), 1–10.

Aladwan, K., Bhanugopan, R., & D'Netto, B. (2015). The effects of human resource management practices on employees' organisational commitment. *International Journal of Organizational Analysis*, *23*(3), 472–492.

Albrecht, S. L., Bakker, A. B., Gruman, J. A., Macey, W. H., & Saks, A. M. (2015). Employee engagement, human resource management practices and competitive advantage: An integrated approach. *Journal of Organizational Effectiveness: People and Performance*, *2*(1), 7–35.

Allen, D. G., Mahto, R. V., & Otondo, R. F. (2007). Web-based recruitment: Effects of information, organisational brand, and attitudes toward a web site on applicant attraction. *The Journal of Applied Psychology*, *92*(6), 1696–1708.

Alshamaila, Y., Papagiannidis, S., & Li, F. (2013). Cloud computing adoption by SMEs in the north east of England: A multi-perspective framework. *Journal of Enterprise Information Management, 26*(3), 250–275.

Apostolou, A. (2000). *Employee Involvement.* Report produced for the EC funded project. https://www.urenio.org/tools/en/employee_involvement.pdf

Armstrong, M. (2003). *A handbook of human resource management practice* (9th ed.). Kogan Page.

Awa, H. O., Ojiabo, O. O., & Orokor, L. E. (2017). Integrated technology-organisation-environment (T-O-E) taxonomies for technology adoption. *Journal of Enterprise Information Management, 30*(6), 893–921.

Bahrin, M. A. K., Othman, M. F., Nor, N. H., & Azli, M. F. T. (2016). Industry 4.0: A review on industrial automation and robotic. *Jurnal Teknologi (Sciences and Engineering), 78*(6–13), 137–143.

Behery, M. H., & Paton, R. A. (2008). Performance appraisal-cultural fit: Organisational outcomes within the UAE. *Education, Business and Society: Contemporary Middle Eastern Issues, 1*(1), 34–49.

Behnam, N. (2014). *Human resource development in construction industry.* UC.

Bhanugopan, R., Aladwan, K., & Fish, A. (2013). A structural equation model for measuring human resource management practices in the Jordanian organisations. *International Journal of Organizational Analysis, 21*(4), 565–587.

Bissola, R., & Imperatori, B. (2013). Facing e-HRM: The consequences on employee attitude towards the organisation and the HR department in Italian SMEs. *European Journal of International Management, 7*(4), 450–468.

Botha, C., & Du Plessis, M. (2017). Employee development and career management. In Nel & Werner (Eds.), *Human resource management* (10th ed.). Oxford University Press.

Bradley, T. B., & Karl, H. (2011). Training and development. *Encyclopedia of Business* (2nd ed.). https://www.encyclopedia.com/social-sciences-and-law/economics-business-and-labor/businesses-and-occupations/training-and-development

Brandão, C., Silva, R., & dos Santos, J. V. (2019). Online recruitment in Portugal: Theories and candidate profiles. *Journal of Business Research, 94*, 273–279.

Bustamam, F. L., Teng, S. S., & Abdullah, F. Z. (2014). Reward management and job satisfaction among frontline employees in hotel industry in Malaysia. *Procedia – Social and Behavioural Sciences, 144*, 392–402.

Cai, S., Ma, Z., Skibniewski, M., Guo, J., & Yun, L. (2018). *Application of automation and robotics technology in High-Rise building construction: An overview.* In Proceedings of the 35th International Symposium on Automation and Robotics in Construction, Berlin, Germany, 20–25 July.

Cardy, R. L., & Miller, J. S. (2005). eHR and performance management: A consideration of positive potential and the dark side. In H. G. Gueutaland & D. L. Stone (Eds.), *The brave new world of eHR: Human resource management in the digital age.* Jossey-Bass.

Castello, D. (2006). Leveraging the employee life cycle, *CRM Margazine, 10*(12), 48–58.

Chan, W. W. M., & Aghimien, D. O. (2022). Safe working cycle: Is it a panacea to combat construction site safety accidents in Hong Kong? *Sustainability, 14*(2), 1–17.

Chanda, A., Bansal, T., & Chanda, R. (2010). Strategic integration of recruitment practices and its impact on performance on Indian enterprises. *Research and Practice in Human Resource Management, 18*(1), 1–15.

Cornelius, N., Gooch, L., & Todd, S. (2001). Managing difference fairly: An integrated 'partnership' approach. In M. Noon & E. Ogbonna (Eds.), *Equality, diversity and disadvantage in employment.* Palgrave Macmillan.

Coyle-Shapiro, J. A.-M., Diehl, M.-R., & Chang, C. (2016). The employee–organisation relationship and organisational citizenship behaviour. In P. M. Podsakoff, S. B. Mackenzie, & N. P. Podsakoff (Eds.), *The Oxford handbook of organizational citizenship behaviour.* Oxford University Press.

Danish, R. Q., & Usman, A. (2010). Impact of reward and recognition on job satisfaction and motivation: An empirical study from Pakistan. *International Journal of Business and Management, 5*(2), 159–167.

Delaney, J. T., & Huselid, M. A. (1996). The impact of human resource management practices perceptions of organisational performance. *The Academy of Management Journal, 39*(4), 949–69.

DeNisi, A. S., & Murphy, K. R. (2017). Performance appraisal and performance management: 100 years of progress? *Journal of Applied Psychology, 102*(3), 421–433.

Dess, G. G., & Shaw, J. D. (2001). Voluntary turnover, social capital, and organizational performance. *The Academy of Management Review, 26*(3), 446–456.

Dessler, G. (2011). *Human resource management* (12th ed.). Pearson.

Devi, V., & Shaik, N. (2012). Evaluating training and development effectiveness-A measurement model. *Asian Journal of Management Research, 2*(1), 722–735.

Dewettinck, K., & Remue, J. (2011). Contextualising HRM in comparative research: The role of the Cranet network. *Human Resource Management Review, 21*(1), 37–49.

DiMaggio, P., & Powell, W. (1983). The iron cage revisited: Institutional isomorphism and collective rationality in organisational fields. *American Sociological Review, 48*(2), 147–160.

Dipboye, R. L., & de Pontbriand, R. (1981). Correlates of employee reactions to performance appraisals and appraisal systems. *Journal of Applied Psychology, 73*, 551–558.

Djabatey, E. N. (2012). *Recruitment and selection practices of organisation.* A case study of HFC bank (GH) Ltd. Thesis submitted to the Institute of Distance Learning, Kwame Nkrumah University of Science and Technology, Ghana.

Druker, J., White, G., Hegewisch, A., & Mayne, L. (1996). Between hard and soft HRM: Human resource management in the construction industry. *Construction Management and Economics, 14*(5), 405–416.

Edgar, F., & Geare, A. (2005). HRM practice and employee attitudes: Different measures – Different results. *Personnel Review, 34*(5), 534–549.

Faliagka, E., Tsakalidis, A., & Tzimas, G. (2012). An integrated e-recruitment system for automated personality mining and applicant ranking. *Internet Research, 22*(5), 551–568.

Gabris, G. T., & Ihrke, D. M. (2001). Does performance appraisal contribute to heightened levels of employee burnout? The results of one study. *Public Personnel Management, 30*(2), 157–172.

Galgali, P. (2017). Digital transformation and its impact on organisations' human resource management. *IOR and Stakeholder Management,* MCM, School of Communication and Information, Rutgers University, USA.

Gamage, A. S. (2014). Recruitment and selection practices in manufacturing SMEs in Japan: An analysis of the link with business performance. *Ruhuna Journal of Management and Finance, 1*(1), 37–52.

Garcia-Arroyo, J., & Osca, A. (2019). Big data contributions to human resource management: A systematic review. *The International Journal of Human Resource Management, 32*(10), 1–27.

Geroy, G. D., Wright, P. C., & Anderson, J. (1998). Strategic performance empowerment model. *Empowerment in Organisations, 6*(2), 57–65.

Goldstein, I. L., & Ford, K. (2002). *Training in organisations: Needs assessment, development and evaluation* (4th ed.). Wadsworth.

Goleman, D. (1998). *Working with emotional intelligence.* Refereed Articles.

Goleman, D., Boyatiz, R. E., & Rhee, K. S. (2000). Clustering competence in emotional intelligence: Insights from the emotional competence inventory. In R. Bar-On & J. D. A. Parker (Eds.), *Handbook of emotional intelligence.* Jossey-Bass.

Gomez-Mejia, L. R., Balkin, D. B., & Cardy, L. R. (2012). *Managing human resources.* Pearson.

Griffin, R.W. (2012). *Fundamentals of management.* Masson, Ohio. South-Western Cengage Learning.

Greene, R. J. (2014). The role of employee ownership in the total rewards strategy. *Compensation and Benefits Review, 46*(1), 6–9.

Guest, D. E. (1997). Human resource management and performance: A review of the research agenda. *The International Journal of Human Resource Management, 8*(3), 263–276.

Gueutal, H. G., & Falbe, D. L. (2005). HR: Trends in delivery methods. In H. G. Gueutal & D. L. Stone (Eds.), *The brave new world of eHR* (pp. 190–225). Jossey-Bass.

Gusdorf, M. L. (2008). *Recruitment and selection: Hiring the right person*. Staffing Management Instructor Notes and Activities. https://www.shrm.org/certification/educators/Documents/09-0152%20Gusdorf_Instructor_Notes.pdf

Halvorsen, D. L. (2005). AAn Investigation of Employee Satisfaction and Employee Empowerment Specific to On-Site Supervisors in the Residential Construction Industry. A thesis summited to Brigham Young University, USA.

Hammuda, I., & Dulaimi, M. F. (1997). The theory and application of empowerment in construction: A comparative study of the different approaches to empowerment in construction, service and manufacturing industries. *International Journal of Project Management, 15*, 289–296.

Hancher, D. E., de la Garza, J. M., & Eckere, G. K. (1997). Improving workers' compensation management in construction. *Journal of Construction Engineering and Management, 123*(3), 285–291.

Hand, M. (1993). Freeing the victims. *Total Quality Management, 5*(3), 1–11.

Heery, E., & Noon, M. (2001). *A dictionary of human resource management*. Oxford University Press.

Henderson, I. (2011). *Human resource management for MBA Students* (2nd ed.). CIPD.

Heneman, H. G., & Schwab, D. P. (1985). Pay satisfaction: Its multidimensional nature and measurement. *International Journal of Psychology, 20*(1), 129–141.

Holt, G. D., Love, P. E. D., & Nesan, L. J. (2000). Employee empowerment in construction: An implementation model for process improvement. *Team Performance Management: An International Journal, 6*(3/4), 47–51.

Hsu, P. F., Kraemer, K. L., & Dunkle, D. (2006). Determinants of e-business use in US firms. *International Journal of Electronic Commerce, 10*, 9–45.

Ivancevich, J., Konopaske, R., & Matteson, M. T. (2008). *Organizational Behaviour and Management* (8th Ed.), New York: McGraw-Hill Higher Education.

Jayabalan, N., Makhbul, Z. K. M., Senggaravellu, S. N., Subramaniam, M., & Ramly, N. A. B. (2021). The impact of digitalisation on human resource management practices in the automotive manufacturing industry. *Journal of Southwest Jiaotong University, 56*(5), 524–537.

Joseph, D. L., Jin, J., Newman, D. A., & O'Boyle, E. H. (2015). Why does self-reported emotional intelligence predict job performance? A meta-analytic investigation of mixed EI. *Journal of Applied Psychology, 100*, 298–342.

Kaplan, R. S., & Norton, D. P. (2004). *Strategy maps: Converting intangible assets into tangible outcomes*. Harvard Business School Press.

Karakhan, A., & Alsaffar, O. (2019). Technology's role in safety management. *Professional Safety Journal, 64*(1), 43–45.

Kaviya, B., & Hema, C. (2015). Performance management in construction. *International Journal of Innovative Research in Science, Engineering and Technology, 4*(4), 2093–2100.

Keshav, P. (2013). Internal sources and methods of recruitment. *Academy of Management Journal, 38*, 635–672.

Korsgaard, M. A., & Roberson, L. (1995). Procedural justice in performance evaluation: The role of instrumental and non-instrumental voice in performance appraisal discussions. *Journal of Management, 21*(4), 657–669.

Lawler, E. E., & Mohrman, S. A. (1989). High involvement management. *Personnel, 66*, 26–31.

Leana, C. R. (1987). Power relinquishment versus power sharing: Theoretical clarification and empirical comparison of delegation and participation. *Journal of Applied Psychology, 72*, 228–233.

Lengnick-Hall, C. A., & Beck, T. E. (2009). Resilience capacity and strategic agility: Prerequisites for thriving in a dynamic environment. In C. Nemeth, E. Hollnagel, & S. Dekker (Eds.), *Resilience engineering perspectives* (Vol. 2). Ashgate Publishing.

Loosemore, M., Dainty, A. R. J., & Lingard, H. (2003). *Human resource management in construction projects – Strategic and operational approaches.* Taylor and Francis.

Love, P., Edwards, D., & Wood, E. (2011). Loosening the Gordian knot: the role of emotional intelligence in construction. *Engineering, Construction and Architectural Management, 18*(1), 50–65.

Manning, E. (2017). *Six questions exploring the direction of wearable safety technology on the jobsite.* https://www.constructionbusinessowner.com/technology/iot-wearables-construction-industry

Marawar, S. (2013). Performance appraisal system to improve construction productivity. *International Journal of Scientific and Research Publications, 3*(11), 1–8.

Marchington, M., & Wilkinson, A. (2005). *Human resource management at work: People management and development* (3rd ed.). Chartered Institute of Personnel and Development.

Marescaux, E., De Winne, S., & Sels, L. (2013). HR practices and HRM outcomes: The role of basic need satisfaction. *Personnel Review, 42*(1), 4–27.

Marler, J., & Parry, E. (2016). Human resource management, strategic involvement and e-HRM technology. *The International Journal of Human Resource Management, 27*(19), 2233–2253.

Mathis, R. L., & Jackson, J. H. (2006). *Human resource management* (11th ed.). Thomson/South-Western.

McMahon, G. (2013). Performance management: Chapter 7 in human resource management. In R. Carbery & C. Cross (Eds.), *Performance management in human resource management.* Palgrave Macmillan.

Miceli, M. P., & Lane, M. P. (1991). Antecedents of pay satisfaction: A review and extension. In K. M. Rowland & G. R. Ferris (Eds.), *Research in personnel and human resources management* (Vol. 9). JAI Press.

Mondy, R. W. (2010). *Human resource management* (11th ed.). Prentice Hall.

Mondy, R. W., & Noe, R. M. (1996). *Human resource management* (6th ed.). Prentice Hall.

Naidu, S., & Chand, A. (2014). A comparative analysis of best human resource management practices in the hotel sector of Samoa and Tonga. *Personnel Review, 43*(5), 798–815.

Neeraj. (2018). Role of digitalisation in human resource management. *International Journal of Emerging Technologies and Innovative Research, 5*(1), 284–288.

Nel, P. S., & Werner, A. (2017). *Human resource management* (10th ed.). Oxford Press.

Nesan, L. J. (1997). *A generic model for effective implementation of empowerment in construction contractor organisations* [PhD thesis]. Built Environment Research Unit, University of Wolverhampton, Wolverhampton.

Nesan, L. J., & Holt, G. D. (1999). *Empowerment in construction: The way forward for performance improvement.* Research Studies Press.

Ngwenya, L. M., & Aigbavboa, C. (2017). Improvement of productivity and employee performance through an efficient human resource management practice. *Advances in Intelligent Systems and Computing, 498*, 727–737.

Ngwenya, L. M., Aigbavboa, C., & Thwala, W. (2019). Effects of training and development on employee performance in a South African construction company. In *14th International Organization, Technology and Management in Construction Conference*, Zagreb, Croatia, 4–7 September, pp. 845–852.

Noe, R. A. (2010). *Employee training and development* (5th ed.). McGraw-Hill/Irwin.

Ofori, D., & Aryeetey, M. (2011). Recruitment and selection practices in small and medium enterprises. *International Journal of Business Administration, 2*(3), 45–60.

Ohabunwa, S. (1999). *Nigeria business environment in the new millennium* [Paper presentation]. HRDB UNILAG on Renovating our corporate management practices for the New Millemium, Lagos, Nigeria, 19 May.

Ojambati, T. S., Akinbile, B. F., & Abiola-Falemu, J. O. (2012). Personnel training and development: A vital tool for construction workers performance. *Journal of Emerging Trends in Engineering and Applied Sciences, 3*(6), 996–1004.

Oke, A., Aigbavboa, C., Ngcobo, N., & Sepuru, M. (2017). Challenges of emotional intelligence among construction stakeholders. In *International Conference on Construction and Real Estate Management* (pp. 33–40), Guangzhou, China.

Oke, A., Aigbavboa, C., & Sepuru, M. (2017). Benefits of emotional intelligence to construction industry: A case of Gauteng region, South Africa. *Proceedings of Environmental Design and Management International Conference (EDMIC)*, held between 22–24 May, at the Obafemi Awolowo University, Ile-Ife, Nigeria, pp. 523–531.

Oosthuizen, P., & Nienaber, H. (2010). The status of talent management in the South African consulting civil engineering industry in 2008: A survey. *Journal of the South African Institution of Civil Engineering, 8*(1), 107–118.

Opatha, H. H. D. N. P. (2010). *Human resource management*. Sharp Graphic House (Pvt) Ltd.

Otoo, I. C., Assumin, J., & Agyei, P. M. (2018). Effectiveness of recruitment and selection practices in public sector higher education institutions: Evidence from Ghana. *European Scientific Journal, 14*(13), 199–214.

Panos, S., & Bellou, V. (2016). Maximising e-HRM outcomes: A moderated mediation path. *Management Decision, 54*(5), 1088–1109.

Patnaik, P., & Suar, D. (2019). Analyses of publications on compensation management from 2004 to 2017. *Compensation & Benefits Review, 51*(2), 55–76.

Poovitha, R., Ambik, D., & Lavanya, B. (2018). A Review on performance management and Appraisal. *International Research Journal of Engineering and Technology, 5*(1), 1012–1015.

Price, A. D. F., Bryman, A., & Dainty, A. R. J. (2004). Empowerment as a strategy for improving construction performance. *Leadership and Management in Engineering, 4*(1), 27–37.

Quinton, S., Canhoto, A., Molinillo, S., Pera, R., & Budhathoki, T. (2018). Conceptualising a digital orientation: Antecedents of supporting SME performance in the digital economy. *Journal of Strategic Marketing, 26*(50), 427–439.

Redman, T., & Wilkinson, A. (2001). *Contemporary human resource management*. Pearson Education.

Reshetnikova, I., Zotkina, N., & Gusarova, M. (2019). Selection of recruitment methods in construction organisations. *MATEC Web of Conferences, 265*, 1–6.

Rohini, I., & Keerthika, V. (2018). Recruitment process in a construction firm-A case study. *International Journal of Engineering Science Invention, 7*(1), 22–36.

Rondeau, K. V. (2018). e-Performance and reward management. In M. Thite (Ed.), *e-HRM – Digital approaches, directions and applications*. Routledge, UK.

Sangeetha, K. (2010). Effective recruitment: A framework. *IUP Journal of Business Strategy, 7*(1/2), 93–107.

Shahnawaz, M. G., & Juyal, R. C. (2006). Human resource management practices and organizational commitment in different organizations. *Journal of the Indian Academy of Applied Psychology, 32*(3), 267–274.

Shen, X., & Marks, E. (2015). Near-miss information visualisation tool in BIM for construction safety. *Journal of Construction Engineering and Management, 142*(4), 1–10.

Snell, S., & Bohlander, G. (2012). *Managing human resources* (16th ed.). Cengage Learning.

Snell, S. A., & Dean, J. W. (1992). Integrated manufacturing and human resource management: A human capital perspective. *Academy of Management Journal, 35*(3), 467–504.

Swanepoel, B., Erasmus, B., Van Wyk, M., & Schenk, H. (2000). *South African human resource management* (2nd ed.). Juta and Co. Ltd.

Tang, T. L., & Sarsfield-Baldwin, L. J. (1996). Distributive and procedural justice as related to satisfaction and commitment. *S.A.M. Advanced Management Journal, 61*(3), 25.

Tansley, C., Newell, S., & Hazel, W. (2001). Effecting HRM-style practices through an integrated human resource information system: An e-greenfield site? *Personnel Review, 30*(3), 351–370.

Teo, H. H., Wei, K. K., & Benbasat, I. (2003). Predicting intention to adopt interorganizational linkages: An institutional perspective. *MIS Quarterly, 27*(1), 19–49.

Tripathi, R. T., & Singh, P. J. (2017). A study on innovative practices in digital human resource management. *National Seminar on Digital Transformation of Business in India: Opportunities and Challenges,* 24–25 March, Dehradun, India.

Turner, P. (2017). *Talent management in healthcare – Exploring how the world's health service organisations attract, manage and develop talent.* Palgrave Macmillan Cham.

Venterink, J. (2017). *Practical future developments in e-HRM, HR SSC's and employee involvement* [Master thesis]. Submitted to University of Twente, Netherlands.

Vratskikh, I., Masa'deh, R., Al-Lozi, M., & Maqableh, M. (2016). The impact of emotional intelligence on job performance via the mediating role of job satisfaction. *International Journal of Business and Management, 11*(2), 69–91.

Warnich, S., Carrell, M. R., Elbert, N. F., & Hatfield, R. D. (2014). *Human resource management in South Africa* (5th ed.). RR Donnelley Publishing.

Welbourne, T. M., & Andrews, A. O. (1996) Predicting the performance of initial public offerings: Should human resource management be in the equation? *Academy of Management Journal, 39,* 891–919.

Werther, W. B., & Davis, K. (1996). *Human resource and personnel management.* McGraw Hill, Inc.

Whiting, H. J., Kline, T. J. B., & Sulsky, L. M. (2008). The performance appraisal congruency scale: An assessment of person-environment fit. *International Journal of Productivity and Performance Management, 57*(3), 223–236.

Williams, M. L., Brower, H. H., Ford, L. R., Williams, L. J., & Carraher, S. M. (2008). A comprehensive model and measure of compensation satisfaction. *Journal of Occupational and Organizational Psychology, 81,* 639–668.

Zhang, L. (2013). Improving performance of construction projects: A project manager's emotional intelligence approach. *Engineering, Construction and Architectural Management, 20*(2), 195–207.

Zhang, S., Teizer, J., Lee, J., Eastman, C. M., & Venugopal, M. (2013). Building information modelling (BIM) and safety: Automatic safety checking of construction models and schedules. *Automation in Construction, 29,* 183–195.

# Chapter 7

# Exploring the Conceptualised Construction Workforce Management Model Through Experts' Opinion

## Abstract

The workforce management model conceptualised for the effective management of the construction workforce was subjected to expert scrutiny to determine the suitability and applicability of the identified practices and their attributed variables to the construction industry. In achieving this, a Delphi approach was adopted using experts from construction organisations in South Africa. These experts comprised workforce management personnel and construction professionals in senior management positions. The data were analysed using appropriate statistical tools such as interquartile deviation, Kendell's coefficient of concordance, and chi square to determine consensus among these experts. After a two-round Delphi, the seven constructs proposed in the conceptualised workforce management model were adjudged to be important and worthy of adoption by construction organisations seeking to improve workforce management in the current fourth industrial revolution era.

*Keywords*: Construction workers; Delphi study; human resource management; personnel management; workforce management; Organisational performance

## Introduction

In this chapter, the result of an assessment of the suitability and applicability of the identified workforce management practices and their measurement variables in the proposed conceptual model in Chapter 6 is presented. This assessment was conducted through a Delphi involving South African construction industry experts. The chapter entails a description of the Delphi, the process involved in conducting

*Construction Workforce Management in the Fourth Industrial Revolution Era*, 159–200
Copyright © 2024 by Lerato Aghimien, Clinton Ohis Aigbavboa and Douglas Aghimien
Published under exclusive licence by Emerald Publishing Limited
doi:10.1108/978-1-83797-018-620241007

the Delphi, and the discussion of the outcomes of the Delphi conducted. In the end, the chapter presents that the seven proposed workforce management practices and their measurement variables were suitable for the effective management of the construction workforce in the current fourth industrial revolution era.

## Using a Delphi to Explore the Applicability of the Conceptualised Workforce Management Model

The proposed conceptual construction workforce management model in chapter six revealed seven practices that construction organisations seeking to get the optimum from their worker in this era of the fourth industrial revolution needs to give adequate consideration. To test the suitability and applicability of these practices, a Delphi was conducted among experts in the South African construction industry. The South African construction industry was used as a case study as it is one of the emerging construction industries with the potential for extensive growth (Construction Industry Development Board, 2019). The country also has potential for technological advancement compared to its peers within the African continent (Dall'Omo, 2017).

As part of the qualitative research approach, Delphi has been around since the early 1950s. It was first developed in the USA as a tool to help forecast the future and solve complex problems by drawing from expert opinions (Skulmoski et al., 2007). The Delphi allows anonymity, structured communication and consensus among experts (Gohdes & Crews, 2004). It is an iterative process where several rounds of feedback from experts are used to determine consensus. This feedback is based on the experts' judgement on the subject under review (Hallowell & Gambatese, 2010). To this end, the experts, after a careful selection, are asked questions in a way that they all can easily understand to avoid ambiguity. The answers given to these questions are collected over several rounds, known as iterations, and once an agreement is reached in the experts' responses, a logical conclusion is drawn, and the forecasting of future occurrences can be done (Holey et al., 2007).

The anonymity in the Delphi process creates room for a more reliable response to be given by the experts without undue pressure. One interesting way of achieving this is through using a questionnaire as a medium of communication with experts to avoid the pressure experienced in most qualitative approaches, such as interviews and focus group discussions (Aigbavboa, 2013). Also, there is a rigorous query of experts through an iterative process which provides initial feedback, analyses and presentation of analysed feedback to the experts for further evaluation (Agumba & Musonda, 2013). With this anonymity, iteration process-controlled feedback and statistical responses, the bias in the response of the experts is eliminated (Hallowell, 2008).

## Constituents of a Delphi

According to Hasson et al. (2000), the first step in adopting a Delphi is properly identifying the problem to be solved and the possibility of adopting the Delphi approach in solving the identified problem. When it is clear that Delphi can be used to solve the identified problem, it is important to carefully understand the process. The success of a Delphi relies mainly on the experts providing feedback to carefully developed questions. These experts must be carefully selected to represent a broader spectrum of opinions on the subject under discussion. It is, therefore, important to inform the selected experts early and give them appropriate information on what Delphi is all about and what is required from them. This is important as most experts might be new to the concept of Delphi; hence preparing them as regards the objective of the study and the commitment expected from them will go a long way in ensuring their continuous participation (Loo, 2002). It is important to ensure anonymity among experts; each expert must be treated as an individual entity.

The instrument for soliciting information from these experts and giving feedback to each expert is also an important component of Delphi. Open and closed-ended questionnaires have become the most favoured instrument in recent times. McKenna (1994) suggested that a questionnaire can be piloted among a small group and then administered with qualitative comments solicited from the expert panel. The first feedback from the expert panel is analysed and sent back to the experts for evaluation. This allows the experts to change their opinions based on other experts' selections. This iterative process continues until consensus is achieved. Using iterative processes through several rounds of feedback, robust information can be gathered from the experts. In terms of analysing the data, while some studies have suggested stopping the whole process when at least 80% consensus is achieved (Green et al., 1999), some have promoted stability in the data set rather than a percentage (Crisp et al., 1997). When satisfactory consensus has been achieved, a result output is generated in the form of a report outlining the findings from the Delphi process, the forecast, policies, options, and recommendations (Loo, 2002; McKenna, 1994).

## Design and Execution of the Delphi

The Delphi process adopted is depicted in Fig. 7.1. The first was to determine the Delphi questions designed to solicit expert opinion on the suitability of the derived construction workforce management practices on the conceptual model. Next was identifying the potential experts and selecting the expert panel based on certain predefined criteria. The status of the experts was then validated, and they were informed of their selection and what was required of them. Next, the first round of the questionnaire was developed and administered to the experts individually. Feedback was collected and analysed to determine the experts' rating of the assessed variables and to assess the attainment of consensus. Ideally, if consensus was achieved, then the result was reported. However, in this current study, consensus was not achieved in the first round, as such, feedback was developed for the expert panel with the result from the first round included for them to re-evaluate their initial response. This study adopted a two-round Delphi process as consensus was achieved after the second round.

### *Criteria for Expert Panel Selection*

Careful consideration was given to the selection of the expert panel, as this has been described as one of the major shortcomings of the Delphi process. The selection of the wrong set of experts might flaw the entire process. Adler and

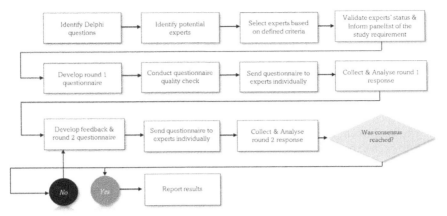

Fig. 7.1.    The Delphi Process. *Source*: Author's compilation (2023).

Ziglio (1996) have noted that knowledge and experience are essential for selecting experts. Furthermore, their willingness to participate in the entire process, which can be time-consuming, is important. Hence, Loo (2002) suggested that they must be well-informed ahead of time and given proper information regarding the commitment expected from them. Hallowell and Gambatese (2010) also suggested an unbiased approach to selecting experts. According to Linstone and Turoff (1975), selecting individuals with like minds or a group of cosy friends should be avoided. As a result of these suggestions, past studies have come up with diverse methods to ensure an unbiased selection of the appropriate experts. Specific requirements related to the field of study have been set in some studies to select the right group of experts (Chan et al., 2001; Manoliadis et al., 2006). A flexible point system that allocates points to identified experts in certain defined criteria has also been used (Hallowell & Gambatese, 2010). However, there is no agreement within the body of knowledge on the right approach to adopt in selecting experts. Most studies adopt what best suits their area of research.

Based on the foregoing, this current study identified specific requirements for experts to meet before they could be considered as part of the Delphi panel. These criteria were selected from what was obtainable in past studies, and they are related to the objectives of this current Delphi study (see Alomari et al., 2018; Chan et al., 2001; Hallowell & Gambatese, 2010; Rogers & Lopez, 2002). Each expert was expected to possess at least 50% of the identified criteria before being considered for the study. The criteria sets are:

(1)  Minimum of a bachelor's degree in the construction-related field.
(2)  At least five years of professional experience in the South African construction industry.
(3)  A current active employee of a construction organisation (either in a human resource management position or senior management position).
(4)  A registered member of their respective professional bodies.

As in the case of the criteria for selecting an expert panel, there is no guideline as regards the ideal number of experts needed for a Delphi study. However, the size mostly depends on the availability of funds and time. As such, Rowe et al. (1991) submitted that a Delphi panel size could range from 3 to 80 panellists. In construction-related studies, Ameyaw et al. (2016) observed that this number could range from three to ninety-three, with most studies sticking to between 8 and 20 panellists. It appears from these studies that the minimum number of panellists observed is 3, with a panel of between 10 and 18 experts being common (Aghimien et al., 2020; Hallowell & Gambatese, 2010; Skulmoski et al., 2007).

It is necessary to note that two major factors can influence the number of experts in a Delphi panel, namely the study characteristics such as the number of available experts, the desired geographic representation and the capability of the facilitator, and secondly, the need to have a sufficient number of experts at the end of the Delphi process since some experts might likely drop out before the end of the process (Hallowell and Gambatese, 2010). Hsu and Sandford (2007) warned that care should be taken in selecting the ideal sample size for a Delphi study, as a small sample may lead to unrealistic results since the selected experts might not represent the entire population under consideration. Also, when the sample size is too large, issues such as low response rates and excess time commitment on both the part of the researcher and the experts might be experienced.

Based on this knowledge, a list of 34 experts was drawn from different construction organisations, and they were invited through emails and telephone conversations. While all the invited experts agreed to participate in the Delphi, not all completed the first round. Only 12 experts completed the first round of the Delphi. The responses received were analysed, and the second-round questionnaire was designed based on the first results and sent back to the experts for re-evaluation. One of the experts dropped out from Delphi's second round for personal reasons, leaving 11 experts to complete the process. Based on the adopted criteria, Table 7.1 shows the criteria for the eleven experts that completed the two-round Delphi process.

## Conducting Delphi Iterations

Just like the expert selection procedure and size, no specific guidance in respect of the ideal number of rounds (iterations) for a Delphi exists in the body of literature. However, Ameyaw et al. (2016) noted that most studies have reached a consensus in the second or third round. Studies have also proposed as low as 2 and as many as 10 iterations for a Delphi process (Woudenberg, 1991). However, it has been observed that when the iterations exceed three, issues such as fatigue, cost, time, and increased attrition tend to arise (Hasson et al., 2000). When this occurs, some experts might want to withdraw from the process, leading to fewer responses and possibly inconclusive results (Chan et al., 2001; Rajendran & Gambatese, 2009).

Based on the knowledge gathered from existing literature and the attainment of consensus, testing the constructs and measurement variables of the proposed conceptual construction workforce management model was done using a

Table 7.1.   Experts' Assessment.

| S/n | Experts Select Criteria | 1 | 2 | 3 | 4 | 5 | 6 | 7 | 8 | 9 | 10 | 11 |
|-----|-------------------------|---|---|---|---|---|---|---|---|---|----|----|
| 1 | Advance degree in AEC-related field (Bachelor, Master's, PhD) | √ | √ | √ | √ | √ | √ | √ | √ | √ | √ | √ |
| 2 | Above 5 years working experience in the South Africa construction industry | √ | √ | √ | √ | √ | √ | √ | √ | √ | √ | √ |
| 3 | Current active employment in a construction organisation | √ | √ | √ | √ | √ | √ | √ | √ | √ | √ | √ |
| 4 | Professional membership | √ | – | √ | – | – | √ | √ | √ | – | √ | – |
| | Overall percentage (%) for all criteria | 100 | 75 | 100 | 75 | 75 | 100 | 100 | 100 | 75 | 100 | 75 |

two-round Delphi process. The first-round questionnaire was designed based on information gathered from the review of extant literature. After careful assessment and approval by the research promoters, the questionnaire was emailed to the selected experts for evaluation. The questionnaire was designed using open and closed-ended questions to address the objectives of the Delphi study. Based on the feedback obtained from the first round, the questionnaire for the second round was designed with the group median for each variable derived from the analysis of the first round included. Both rounds of the process took approximately two months to complete.

### *Computing the Data and Determining Consensus from the Delphi*

The constructs (workforce management practices) of the conceptualised model were assessed for their importance on a scale of 0%–100%. The measurement variables were measured on a 10-point scale ranging from 'no significance' to 'very high significance'. A Microsoft Excel spreadsheet and the Statistical Package for Social Sciences (SPSS) were used to analyse the data gathered in both rounds of the Delphi. Considering the number of experts adopted in the study, the group median ($M$) was used along with the mean ($\overline{X}$) owing to its ability to eliminate bias in smaller samples and to take into consideration outlier responses (Aigbavboa, 2013). While $M$ and $\overline{X}$ were used to determine the importance or significance attached to the identified constructs and variables, the consensus was determined using interquartile deviation (IQD), Kendall's coefficient of concordance ($W$), and Chi square ($\chi^2$).

Standard deviation (SD) and $\overline{X}$ have been used in some Delphi studies in the past as a means for determining consensus among experts (Hallowell &

Gambatese, 2010; Holey et al., 2007; Hsu & Sandford, 2007; Rayens & Hahn, 2000). However, IQD and $M$ have been suggested as the most reliable deviation approach towards attaining consensus (Aghimien et al., 2020; Aigbavboa, 2013). Aigbavboa (2013) submitted that IQD is derived using the absolute value of the difference between the 75th and 25th percentiles. While the first quartile is the 25th percentile, the second quartile is the 50th percentile, and the third is the 75th percentile. The deviation between the first and the third quartiles gives the IQD. The premise here is that when a smaller IQD is derived (i.e. ≤ 1), a higher consensus is attained (Raskin, 1994; Rayens & Hahn, 2000).

Aghimien et al. (2020) noted using Kendall's $W$ in determining consensus statistical tools. This analysis gives the degree of agreement between experts by considering the variations between the rankings of the mean of the different variables (Hon et al., 2012). A concordance coefficient of one implies 100% consensus (Yeung et al., 2007). The value of the concordance coefficient is expected to increase for each round of the Delphi process since experts are expected to confirm their responses from the previous rounds in line with the group responses. Although aiming for a perfect value of 1 for strong consensus is desirable, most Delphi studies have actually concluded consensus attainment at Kendell's $W$ of between 0.243 and 0.600 (Ameyaw et al., 2016). Kendall's $W$ calculation done using SPSS gives a $\chi^2$ value along with the degree of freedom (Df). Siegel and Castellan (1988) suggested that the $\chi^2$ should be adopted when the number of variables to be evaluated is larger than seven, as in the case of this current study, and the consensus is termed as achieved when the computed $\chi^2$ value is larger than the critical $\chi^2$ value derived from a statistical table.

In summary, the consensus was determined in this current study using IQD, Kendell's $W$ and $\chi^2$. The IQD of 60% of the assessed variable must be a score that is ≤ 1, while Kendall's $W$ must be closer to one. Furthermore, the computed $\chi^2$ value must be larger than the critical $\chi^2$ value derived from a statistical table for consensus to be achieved. Adopting three of these statistical tools in determining consensus as against the popular approach of adopting just one is premised on the need for a more robust data analysis and consensus attainment.

## Delphi Outcomes

The result presented in Table 7.2 is for the 11 experts that completed the Delphi. The table shows that most experts ($f = 8$) have bachelor's degrees. Six of these experts work within the workforce management function of their organisation, while the remaining five are construction professionals who operate at a senior management level. Similarly, six of these experts are members of their professional bodies, while five are not. An average year of experience of 12.7 years was derived for all the experts, with 6 having over 10 years of working experience within the industry. Almost all the experts ($f = 10$) are in the top management position within their respective organisations. Most of the experts were in Gauteng, while only one response came from Limpopo. Based on the result, it is evident that the experts are well equipped in terms of academic background and years of experience to contribute positively to the subject under discussion. Furthermore, they belong to the categories of people within construction organisations responsible for making

Table 7.2.    Background Information of Delphi Experts.

| Categories | Measurement Variables | Frequency | Percentage |
|---|---|---|---|
| Highest academic qualification | Bachelor of technology | 8 | 72.7 |
| | Honours | 1 | 9.1 |
| | Masters | 1 | 9.1 |
| | Doctorate | 1 | 9.1 |
| | Total | 11 | 100 |
| Category | Workforce management personnel | 6 | 54.5 |
| | Construction professional | 5 | 45.5 |
| | Total | 11 | 100 |
| Member of a professional body | Yes | 6 | 54.5 |
| | No | 5 | 45.5 |
| | Total | 11 | 100 |
| Years of experience | 5 to 10 years | 5 | 45.5 |
| | 11 to 20 years | 4 | 36.4 |
| | Above 20 years | 2 | 18.2 |
| | Total | 11 | 100 |
| | Average | 12.7 | |
| Position | Top management | 10 | 90.9 |
| | Ordinary member | 1 | 9.1 |
| | Total | 11 | 100 |

decisions; hence they have an in-depth understanding of human resource issues within their respective organisations. This makes them the ideal candidates to ascertain the applicability of the workforce-related practices gathered from the literature.

### *Main Constructs of the Construction Workforce Management Model*

The conceptual construction workforce management model proposed in Chapter 6 gave seven constructs:

(1)  recruitment and selection;
(2)  compensation and benefit;
(3)  performance management and appraisal;
(4)  training and development;
(5)  employee involvement and empowerment;
(6)  emotional intelligence; and
(7)  the external environment.

The result in Table 7.3 shows the $M$, IQD, $\overline{X}$ and SD derived from the first-round assessment of the importance of these practices to construction organisations in the current era of the fourth industrial revolution. The table also shows the $Z$-value and $p$-value derived from Mann–Whitney $U$-test (M–W) conducted. This test was done to ascertain the significant differences in the views of the experts who work within the core workforce management function and those that do not. The M–W test was adopted because it compares the $M$ of the groups to determine the significant difference between both groups. The threshold was set at the conventional $p$-value of $\leq 0.05$ for a significant difference to exist in the views of the two sets of experts (Pallant, 2011). If the derived $p$-value is $> 0.05$, it means that no significant difference exists in the views of both sets of experts.

The results in Table 7.3 reveal that there is no significant difference in the views of the experts from both groups, as the M–W test gave a $p$-value of above 0.05 for all the assessed practices. Furthermore, the Cronbach alpha ($\alpha$) test revealed that the research instrument used was highly reliable as an alpha value of 0.809, which is closer to one, was derived. While the $M$-values revealed that the experts considered all the assessed practices to be important, the IQD revealed that no consensus was achieved for five out of the seven practices as they gave an IQD of above 1. Furthermore, Kendall's $W$ gave a very low value of 0.174. The derived $\chi^2$-value of 11.475 at a Df of five and a significant $p$-value of 0.075 was derived. This $\chi^2$ is lower than the critical $\chi^2$-value of 12.592 derived from the statistical table, thus confirming a lack of consensus among the experts.

Feedback from the second round revealed that all the experts agreed with group $M$ from the first round. As a result of this agreement, an IQD of 0.00 was derived for all the practices, thus confirming consensus, as seen in Table 7.4. Furthermore, Kendall's $W$ of 0.736 was derived. The improvement of Kendall's $W$ value from 0.174 obtained in the first round further confirmed past submissions that the value of the concordance coefficient will most definitely increase with each round (Hon et al., 2012) as experts are mostly expected to either accept or reject the response obtained from previous rounds (Holey et al., 2007). The derived $\chi^2$-value of 48.564 was also greater than the critical $\chi^2$-value of 12.592 derived from the statistical table. Moreover, the M–W test revealed no significant difference in the views of both sets of experts, as a $p$-value of above 0.05 was derived for all the assessed practices. It can, therefore, be concluded that the experts for the study all considered the identified workforce management practices to have between 80% and 90% levels of importance to the overall effective management of the construction workforce in the era of the fourth industrial revolution.

## Measurement Variables of the Construction Workforce Management Model

### 1. Recruitment and Selection

A total of 21 recruitment and selection variables were identified in the conceptual model presented in Chapter 6. These variables were presented to the experts to rate in terms of their level of significance. Since the first round gives the experts the opportunity to make suggestions, one of the experts added a variable (train

Table 7.3.    Round 1 Result of the Workforce Management Practices.

| | | | | | M–W Test | |
|---|---|---|---|---|---|---|
| **Practices** | **M** | **IQD** | $\overline{X}$ | **SD** | **Z** | **p-value** |
| Training and development | 9 | 1.50 | 8.91 | 0.83 | –0.316 | 0.752 |
| Performance management and appraisal | 9 | 0.50 | 8.73 | 0.79 | –0.447 | 0.655 |
| Compensation and benefit | 9 | 1.00 | 8.64 | 1.12 | –0.311 | 0.756 |
| Recruitment and selection | 9 | 1.50 | 8.36 | 1.29 | –0.603 | 0.546 |
| Emotional intelligence | 8 | 0.50 | 8.09 | 0.70 | –0.707 | 0.480 |
| Employee involvement and empowerment | 8 | 2.00 | 7.91 | 1.64 | –0.949 | 0.343 |
| External environment | 8 | 2.00 | 7.82 | 1.54 | –1.000 | 0.317 |
| Kendall's $W$ | | | | | 0.174 | |
| $\chi^2$ | | | | | 11.475 | |
| $\chi^2$ – *Critical values from stats table (p = 0.05)* | | | | | 12.592 | |
| Df | | | | | 6 | |
| p-value | | | | | 0.075 | |
| $\alpha$ | | | | | 0.809 | |

*Note:* $\overline{X}$ = Mean, $M$ = Median, SD = Standard deviation, $\chi^2$ = Chi square, $\alpha$ = Cronbach Alpha, Df = Degree of freedom.

managers on best recruitment processes) which was believed to be absent from the list provided. The result in Table 7.5 shows that the instrument used was reliable as an $\alpha$-value of 0.801 was derived. The $M$-value for all the variables ranged from 7 to 10, while their IQD ranged from 0.00 to 2.25. Furthermore, Kendall's $W$ gave a very low value of 0.270 and a $\chi^2$-value of 53.972, which is higher than the critical $\chi^2$-value of 31.410 derived from the statistical table. The M–W test revealed that there is no significant difference in the ratings of these variables by the two different groups of experts. This is because a $p$-value above the 0.05 threshold was derived for all the assessed variables.

Following the rating of the variables from round 1, Table 7.6 shows eight variables as very significant with an $M$-value of 9. However, among these variables, the M–W test shows that the variable 'conduct seasonal recruitment' has a significant $p$-value of less than 0.05, implying that some disparity exists in how this variable was rated. The overall group $\overline{X}$ derived was 8.26, which shows that overall the variables under this construct were rated high. The IQD revealed that only this variable (i.e. conduct seasonal recruitment) had a value of 1.00, with the remaining variables having an IQD of 0.00. A Kendall's $W$ of 0.700 was derived, with a $\chi^2$-value of 146.929 at a degree of freedom (Df) of 21 and a significant $p$-value of 0.000. Since this derived $\chi^2$-value is greater than the critical $\chi^2$-value of 32.671 derived from the statistical table, Kendall's $W$ is closer to 1, and the derived IQD

Table 7.4.  Round 2 Result of the Workforce Management Practices.

|  |  |  |  |  |  | M–W Test | |
|---|---|---|---|---|---|---|---|
| **Practices** | ***M*** | **IQD** | **$\overline{X}$** | **SD** | ***R*** | ***Z*** | ***p*-value** |
| Compensation and benefit | 9 | 0.00 | 9.09 | 0.302 | 1 | −0.913 | 0.361 |
| Performance management and appraisal | 9 | 0.00 | 9.00 | 0.000 | 2 | 0.000 | 1.000 |
| Training and development | 9 | 0.00 | 8.91 | 0.302 | 3 | −0.913 | 0.361 |
| Recruitment and selection | 9 | 0.00 | 8.91 | 0.539 | 4 | −0.583 | 0.560 |
| Emotional intelligence | 8 | 0.00 | 8.18 | 0.405 | 5 | −0.136 | 0.892 |
| External environment | 8 | 0.00 | 8.09 | 0.539 | 6 | −0.466 | 0.641 |
| Employee involvement and empowerment | 8 | 0.00 | 8.00 | 0.447 | 7 | 0.000 | 1.000 |
| Kendall's *W* | | | | | | 0.736 | |
| $\chi^2$ | | | | | | 48.564 | |
| $\chi^2$ – *Critical values from stats table (p = 0.05)* | | | | | | 12.592 | |
| Df | | | | | | 6 | |
| *p*-value | | | | | | 0.000 | |

*Note:* $\overline{X}$ = Mean, *M* = Median, SD = Standard deviation, $\chi^2$ = Chi square, Df = Degree of freedom, *R* = Rank.

of all the variables are between 0 and 1, it, therefore, implies that consensus was achieved at this stage for all the 22 variables assessed.

2. *Compensation and Benefits*

Twelve variables were proposed earlier for compensation and benefits and presented to the experts to rate. The experts identified three new variables that were not on the list provided. These new variables are:

(1) ensuring employees' involvement in the selection and determination of compensation;
(2) ensuring satisfactory short-term project incentives; and
(3) understanding employees' salary expectations.

The instrument used was considered reliable as an α-value of 0.94 was derived. From Table 7.7, the *M*-value of the assessed variables ranged from 5 to 10, with their IQD ranging from 0.00 to 2.25. Kendall's *W* gave a low value of 0.342 and a $\chi^2$-value of 41.399, higher than the critical $\chi^2$-value of 19.675 derived from the statistical table. The M–W test further revealed no significant difference in the ratings of these variables by the two different groups of experts. This is because a *p*-value above 0.05 was derived for all the assessed variables.

Table 7.5.    Round 1 Result of the Recruitment and Selection Variables.

| Recruitment and Selection | M | IQD | $\overline{X}$ | SD | M–W Test Z | p-value |
|---|---|---|---|---|---|---|
| Analyse long-term resource requirements of the organisation | 9 | 2.25 | 8.25 | 1.54 | –0.082 | 0.935 |
| Advertise vacancies using electronic platforms | 9 | 2.25 | 8.00 | 1.76 | –0.330 | 0.742 |
| Determine an appropriate reward system that will attract talents | 8 | 1.25 | 8.08 | 1.24 | –0.998 | 0.318 |
| Create realistic job previews/description | 8 | 2.00 | 7.91 | 1.04 | –0.857 | 0.391 |
| Use electronic platforms to screen and evaluate selected candidates carefully | 9 | 0.25 | 8.58 | 1.38 | –0.268 | 0.788 |
| Employ an internal recruitment system | 8 | 2.25 | 7.17 | 1.70 | –0.327 | 0.744 |
| Employ an external recruitment system | 8 | 0.00 | 7.92 | 0.79 | –1.051 | 0.293 |
| Recruit and select impartially in the absence of favouritism | 9 | 1.00 | 8.64 | 1.36 | –0.300 | 0.764 |
| Use unbiased interview panels | 9 | 0.25 | 8.67 | 1.30 | –0.538 | 0.591 |
| Adopt competency and experience-based recruitment | 9 | 1.25 | 8.17 | 1.27 | –1.006 | 0.315 |
| Profile behaviour of selected candidates | 8 | 1.25 | 7.58 | 1.56 | –0.740 | 0.459 |
| Use of preliminary online measures to match candidates with vacant positions | 8 | 2.00 | 8.00 | 1.28 | –0.906 | 0.365 |
| Allow collaborative decisions on conditions of employment | 7 | 2.25 | 7.25 | 1.66 | –0.164 | 0.870 |

Table 7.5. (*Continued*)

| Recruitment and Selection | M | IQD | $\overline{X}$ | SD | M–W Test Z | M–W Test p-value |
|---|---|---|---|---|---|---|
| Conduct reference and background checks | 9 | 2.00 | 8.83 | 1.11 | −1.500 | 0.134 |
| Provide applicants with information about the organisation for an easy decision on offer acceptance | 7 | 2.00 | 7.75 | 1.22 | −0.431 | 0.667 |
| Include the line manager in the recruitment and selection process | 8 | 1.00 | 8.33 | 1.44 | −0.168 | 0.867 |
| Conduct induction to instil a strong sense of vision and values | 8 | 1.25 | 8.58 | 1.00 | −0.259 | 0.796 |
| Conduct seasonal recruitment | 9 | 1.50 | 6.25 | 1.60 | −0.982 | 0.326 |
| Base appointments on merit | 8 | 1.00 | 8.58 | 0.79 | −0.903 | 0.367 |
| Promote internship and learnership programmes | 8 | 0.50 | 7.67 | 1.97 | −0.686 | 0.492 |
| Use head-hunting process | 8 | 1.25 | 6.92 | 1.88 | −0.837 | 0.403 |
| Train managers on best recruitment processes | 8 | 0.00 | 8.00 | – | – | – |
| Kendall's $W$ | | | | 0.270 | | |
| $\chi^2$ | | | | 53.972 | | |
| $\chi^2$ – *Critical values from stats table (p = 0.05)* | | | | 31.410 | | |
| Df | | | | 20 | | |
| p-value | | | | 0.000 | | |
| $\alpha$ | | | | 0.801 | | |

*Note:* $\overline{X}$ = Mean, $M$ = Median, SD = Standard deviation, $\chi^2$ = Chi square, $\alpha$ = Cronbach Alpha, Df = Degree of freedom.

Table 7.6. Round 2 Results of the Recruitment and Selection Variables.

| Recruitment and Selection | M | IQD | $\overline{X}$ | SD | R | M–W Test Z | M–W Test p-value |
|---|---|---|---|---|---|---|---|
| Use unbiased interview panels | 9 | 0.00 | 9.00 | 0.000 | 1 | 0.000 | 1.000 |
| Adopt competency and experience-based recruitment | 9 | 0.00 | 9.00 | 0.447 | 2 | –1.354 | 0.176 |
| Use electronic platforms to screen and evaluate selected candidates carefully | 9 | 0.00 | 8.91 | 0.302 | 3 | –1.095 | 0.273 |
| Advertise vacancies using electronic platforms | 9 | 0.00 | 8.91 | 0.302 | 3 | –1.095 | 0.273 |
| Analyse the long-term labour needs of the organisation | 9 | 0.00 | 8.91 | 0.302 | 3 | –1.095 | 0.273 |
| Conduct reference and background checks | 9 | 0.00 | 8.82 | 0.405 | 6 | –1.361 | 0.174 |
| Recruit and select impartially in the absence of favouritism | 9 | 0.00 | 8.82 | 0.405 | 6 | –1.361 | 0.174 |
| Conduct seasonal recruitment | 9 | 1.00 | 8.45 | 1.214 | 8 | –2.121 | 0.034* |
| Profile behaviour of selected candidates | 8 | 0.00 | 8.27 | 0.647 | 9 | 0.000 | 1.000 |
| Conduct induction to instil a strong sense of vision and values | 8 | 0.00 | 8.18 | 0.603 | 10 | –0.913 | 0.361 |
| Train managers on best recruitment processes | 8 | 0.00 | 8.09 | 0.302 | 11 | –0.913 | 0.361 |
| Base appointments on merit | 8 | 0.00 | 8.09 | 0.302 | 11 | –0.913 | 0.361 |
| Use of preliminary online measures to match candidates with vacant positions | 8 | 0.00 | 8.09 | 0.302 | 11 | –0.913 | 0.361 |

Table 7.6.   (*Continued*)

| Recruitment and Selection | M | IQD | $\overline{X}$ | SD | R | M–W Test | |
|---|---|---|---|---|---|---|---|
| | | | | | | Z | p-value |
| Employ an internal recruitment system | 8 | 0.00 | 8.09 | 0.701 | 14 | −1.354 | 0.176 |
| Use head-hunting process | 8 | 0.00 | 8.00 | 0.000 | 15 | 0.000 | 1.000 |
| Promote internship programmes and learnership programmes | 8 | 0.00 | 8.00 | 0.000 | 15 | 0.000 | 1.000 |
| Employ an external recruitment system | 8 | 0.00 | 8.00 | 0.000 | 15 | 0.000 | 1.000 |
| Determine an appropriate reward system that will attract talents | 8 | 0.00 | 8.00 | 0.000 | 15 | 0.000 | 1.000 |
| Include line managers in the recruitment and selection process | 8 | 0.00 | 8.00 | 0.447 | 19 | −1.354 | 0.176 |
| Create realistic job previews | 8 | 0.00 | 8.00 | 0.447 | 19 | −1.354 | 0.176 |
| Provide applicants with information on the organisation for an easy decision on the offer of acceptance | 7 | 0.00 | 7.18 | 0.603 | 21 | −0.913 | 0.361 |
| Allow collaborative decisions on conditions of employment | 7 | 0.00 | 7.00 | 0.471 | 22 | −1.369 | 0.171 |
| Kendall's $W$ | | | | | | 0.700 | |
| $\chi^2$ | | | | | | 146.929 | |
| $\chi^2$ – *Critical values from stats table (p = 0.05)* | | | | | | 32.671 | |
| Df | | | | | | 21 | |
| p-value | | | | | | 0.000 | |

*Note:* $\overline{X}$ = Mean, $M$ = Median, SD = Standard deviation, $\chi^2$ = Chi square, Df = Degree of freedom, $R$ = Rank, * = sig@ $p < 0.05$.

Table 7.7. Round 1 Result of the Compensation and Benefits Variables.

| Compensation and Benefits | *M* | IQD | $\overline{X}$ | SD | M–W Test Z | M–W Test *p*-value |
|---|---|---|---|---|---|---|
| Design compensation and benefits in accordance with labour law | 9 | 2.25 | 8.17 | 2.25 | –1.840 | 0.066 |
| Ensure equity in the salary scale | 8 | 2.00 | 8.58 | 1.08 | –1.369 | 0.171 |
| Ensure employees' satisfaction with direct wages/salary | 9 | 1.25 | 8.33 | 1.44 | 0.000 | 1.000 |
| Ensure employees' satisfaction with the pay structure within the organisation | 9 | 1.25 | 8.82 | 0.98 | –1.143 | 0.253 |
| Ensure employees' satisfaction with their pay raise | 9 | 1.25 | 8.50 | 1.45 | –0.496 | 0.620 |
| Ensure employees' satisfaction with variable pay procedures (bonuses, commissions, incentives) | 8 | 1.00 | 8.33 | 1.30 | –0.691 | 0.490 |
| Ensure employees' satisfaction with the policies and procedures of pay administration | 8 | 2.00 | 7.67 | 1.61 | 0.000 | 1.000 |
| Ensure employees' satisfaction with benefits received | 8 | 2.25 | 7.92 | 1.44 | –0.165 | 0.869 |
| Ensure employees' satisfaction with the procedure for benefits determination | 8 | 2.25 | 7.75 | 1.60 | –0.487 | 0.626 |
| Ensure employees' satisfaction with the policies and procedures of benefits administration | 8 | 2.25 | 7.67 | 1.50 | –0.326 | 0.744 |

Table 7.7.   (*Continued*)

| Compensation and Benefits | M | IQD | $\overline{X}$ | SD | M–W Test Z | M–W Test p-value |
|---|---|---|---|---|---|---|
| Show appreciation and recognition for good performance | 10 | 1.00 | 9.42 | 0.90 | −0.274 | 0.784 |
| Use of information technology tools in the compensation process | 9 | 1.25 | 8.83 | 1.11 | −0.604 | 0.546 |
| Involve employees in the selection and determination of compensation | 5 | 0.00 | 5.00 | – | – | – |
| Give satisfactory short-term project incentives | 7 | 0.00 | 7.00 | – | – | – |
| Understand employees' salary expectations | 9 | 0.00 | 9.00 | – | – | – |
| Kendall's *W* | | | | 0.342 | | |
| $\chi^2$ | | | | 41.399 | | |
| $\chi^2$ – *Critical values from stats table (p = 0.05)* | | | | 19.675 | | |
| Df | | | | 11 | | |
| *p*-value | | | | 0.000 | | |
| $\alpha$ | | | | 0.914 | | |

*Note:* $\overline{X}$ = Mean, *M* = Median, SD = Standard deviation, $\chi^2$ = Chi square, $\alpha$ = Cronbach Alpha, Df = Degree of freedom.

In the second round, the experts presented 15 variables (12 existing and three from the first round) to rate. Table 7.8 shows that the experts consider the first seven variables to have very high significance as they all have an *M*-value of 9 and 10. Interestingly, the least rated variable, suggested by one of the experts in the first round, was considered to be on the average with a median of 5 (i.e. ensure employees' involvement in selection and determination of compensation). This implies that this variable is most likely not applicable to the construction industry; thus, it can be dropped from further assessment. The overall group $\overline{X}$ derived was 8.06, which shows that overall the variables under this construct were rated high. The IQD derived shows very strong consensus among the experts as the IQD values were between 0.00 and 0.50. Furthermore, Kendall's *W* gave a high value of 0.825, closer to one. In confirmation of the strong consensus among

Table 7.8.   Round 2 Result of the Compensation and Benefits Variables.

| Compensation and Benefits | M | IQD | $\overline{X}$ | SD | R | M–W Test | |
|---|---|---|---|---|---|---|---|
| | | | | | | Z | p-value |
| Show appreciation and recognition for good performance | 10 | 0.00 | 10.00 | 0.000 | 1 | 0.000 | 1.000 |
| Use of information technology tools in the compensation process | 9 | 0.00 | 9.09 | 0.302 | 2 | –0.913 | 0.361 |
| Ensure employees' satisfaction with direct wages/salary | 9 | 0.00 | 9.00 | 0.000 | 3 | 0.000 | 1.000 |
| Ensure employees' satisfaction with their pay raise | 9 | 0.00 | 8.91 | 0.302 | 4 | –0.913 | 0.361 |
| Ensure employees' satisfaction with the pay structure within the organisation | 9 | 0.00 | 8.91 | 0.302 | 4 | –1.095 | 0.273 |
| Design compensation and benefits in accordance with labour law | 9 | 0.00 | 8.55 | 0.688 | 6 | –0.512 | 0.609 |
| Understand employee salary expectations | 9 | 0.50 | 8.45 | 1.036 | 7 | –0.232 | 0.816 |
| Ensure equity in the salary scale | 8 | 0.50 | 8.18 | 0.603 | 8 | –0.913 | 0.361 |
| Ensure employees' satisfaction with variable pay procedures (bonuses, commissions, incentives) | 8 | 0.00 | 8.00 | 0.000 | 9 | 0.000 | 1.000 |
| Ensure employees' satisfaction with benefits received | 8 | 0.00 | 7.45 | 0.522 | 10 | –0.316 | 0.752 |
| Ensure employees' satisfaction with the policies and procedures of benefits administration | 8 | 0.00 | 7.36 | 0.505 | 11 | –0.218 | 0.827 |

Table 7.8.    (*Continued*)

| Compensation and Benefits | M | IQD | $\overline{X}$ | SD | R | M–W Test Z | p-value |
|---|---|---|---|---|---|---|---|
| Ensure employees' satisfaction with the procedure for benefits determination | 8 | 0.00 | 7.36 | 0.505 | 11 | −0.218 | 0.827 |
| Ensure employees' satisfaction with the policies and procedures of pay administration | 8 | 0.00 | 7.36 | 0.505 | 11 | −0.218 | 0.827 |
| Satisfactory with short-term project incentives | 7 | 0.00 | 7.00 | 0.447 | 14 | −1.354 | 0.176 |
| Involve employees in the selection and determination of compensation | 5 | 0.50 | 5.27 | 1.849 | 15 | −0.742 | 0.458 |
| Kendall's *W* | | | | | | 0.825 | |
| $\chi^2$ | | | | | | 127.082 | |
| $\chi^2$ – *Critical values from stats table (p = 0.05)* | | | | | | 23.685 | |
| Df | | | | | | 14 | |
| p-value | | | | | | 0.000 | |

*Note:* $\overline{X}$ = Mean, *M* = Median, SD = Standard deviation, $\chi^2$ = Chi square, Df = Degree of freedom, *R* = Rank.

the experts, the derived $\chi^2$-value of 127.082 was higher than the critical $\chi^2$-value of 23.685 derived from the statistical table.

3. *Performance Management and Appraisal*

A total of 13 performance management and appraisal variables from the proposed model were assessed by the experts. In the first round, one more variable was suggested by the experts. The result in Table 7.9 shows that the instrument used was reliable as an $\alpha$-value of 0.931 was derived. The *M*-values of all the variables ranged from 7 to 10, while their IQD ranged from 0.00 to 1.25. Furthermore, Kendall's *W* gave a very low value of 0.169 and a $\chi^2$-value of 22.400, higher than the critical $\chi^2$-value of 21.026 derived from the statistical table. The M–W test revealed no significant difference in the rating of these variables by the two different groups of experts. This is because a *p*-value above the 0.05 threshold was derived for all the assessed variables.

Table 7.9. Round 1 Result of the Performance Management and Appraisal Variables.

| Performance Management and Appraisal | M | IQD | $\overline{X}$ | SD | M–W Test | |
|---|---|---|---|---|---|---|
| | | | | | Z | p-value |
| Set achievable organisational objectives for employees | 9 | 1.00 | 8.83 | 0.72 | −0.874 | 0.382 |
| Constant review of setting organisational objectives | 9 | 0.50 | 9.09 | 0.70 | −0.303 | 0.762 |
| Clearly communicate set objectives to the employee | 10 | 1.00 | 9.42 | 0.67 | −0.267 | 0.789 |
| Evaluate employees' progress using digital assessment tools | 9 | 1.25 | 8.83 | 0.94 | −0.506 | 0.613 |
| Ensure individual goals align with organisational goals | 9 | 1.25 | 9.17 | 0.83 | −1.450 | 0.147 |
| Develop an action plan to correct deviations in performance | 9 | 1.25 | 8.58 | 1.08 | −0.829 | 0.407 |
| Provide coaching and mentoring | 9 | 1.00 | 8.58 | 1.08 | 0.000 | 1.000 |
| Constantly review individual and group performance | 9 | 1.25 | 8.50 | 1.24 | −0.248 | 0.804 |
| Provide quality performance feedback | 9 | 1.25 | 8.83 | 0.94 | −0.506 | 0.613 |
| Ensure a bias-free performance rating | 9 | 1.50 | 8.50 | 1.51 | −0.419 | 0.675 |
| Practise fairness in the evaluation process | 9 | 0.25 | 9.08 | 0.67 | −0.451 | 0.652 |
| Ensure accurate performance appraisal using appropriate digital tools | 9 | 1.25 | 9.08 | 0.79 | −0.426 | 0.670 |

Table 7.9.   (*Continued*)

|  |  |  |  |  | M–W Test | |
| Performance Management and Appraisal | *M* | IQD | $\overline{X}$ | SD | *Z* | *p*-value |
| --- | --- | --- | --- | --- | --- | --- |
| Ensure fair performance appraisal | 9 | 1.25 | 9.00 | 0.95 | −0.339 | 0.734 |
| Ensure consistency in the method of performance management | 7 | 0.00 | 7.00 | – | – | – |
| Kendall's *W* | | | | 0.169 | | |
| $\chi^2$ | | | | 22.400 | | |
| $\chi^2$ – *Critical values from stats table (p = 0.05)* | | | | 21.026 | | |
| Df | | | | 12 | | |
| *p*-value | | | | 0.034 | | |
| *A* | | | | 0.931 | | |

*Note:* $\overline{X}$ = Mean, *M* = Median, SD = Standard deviation, $\chi^2$ = Chi square, $\alpha$ = Cronbach Alpha, Df = Degree of freedom.

The result in Table 7.10 shows that 13 of the 14 assessed variables were very significant, with a *M*-value of 10 and 9. The overall group $\overline{X}$ derived was 8.90, which shows that overall the variables under this construct were rated high. The IQD derived at this stage shows a strong consensus among the experts as the value ranged between 0.00 and 0.5. Furthermore, Kendall's *W* gave a high value of 0.798, closer to one. In confirmation of the strong consensus among the experts, the derived $\chi^2$-value of 103.755 was higher than the critical $\chi^2$-value of 22.362 derived from the statistical table. The M–W test also revealed no significant difference in the views of the two groups of experts, as a *p*-value of above 0.05 was derived for all assessed variables.

### 4. *Training and Development*

For training and development, 20 variables were assessed by the experts. Table 7.11 reveals that the instrument used was reliable as an $\alpha$-value of 0.884 was derived. The *M*-values of all the variables ranged from 8 to 10, while their IQD ranged from 0.50 to 2.25. Kendall's *W* gave a very low value of 0.170 and a $\chi^2$-value of 35.464, which is higher than the critical $\chi^2$-value of 30.144 derived from the statistical table. The M–W test revealed no significant difference in the rating of these variables by the two groups of experts. This is because a *p*-value above 0.05 was derived for all the assessed variables.

Table 7.10. Round 2 Results of the Performance Management and Appraisal Variables.

| Performance Management and Appraisal | M | IQD | $\overline{X}$ | SD | R | M–W Test | |
|---|---|---|---|---|---|---|---|
| | | | | | | Z | p-value |
| Clearly communicate set objectives to the employee | 10 | 0.00 | 9.91 | 0.302 | 1 | −1.095 | 0.273 |
| Review individual and group performance continuously | 9 | 0.00 | 9.09 | 0.302 | 2 | −0.913 | 0.361 |
| Ensure accurate performance appraisal using appropriate digital tools | 9 | 0.00 | 9.00 | 0.000 | 3 | 0.000 | 1.000 |
| Practise fairness in the evaluation process | 9 | 0.00 | 9.00 | 0.000 | 3 | 0.000 | 1.000 |
| Constant review of setting organisational objectives | 9 | 0.00 | 9.00 | 0.000 | 3 | 0.000 | 1.000 |
| Develop an action plan to correct deviations in performance | 9 | 0.00 | 9.00 | 0.000 | 3 | 0.000 | 1.000 |
| Set achievable organisational objectives for employees | 9 | 0.00 | 9.00 | 0.000 | 3 | 0.000 | 1.000 |
| Ensure fair performance appraisal | 9 | 0.00 | 8.91 | 0.302 | 8 | 0.000 | 1.000 |
| Ensure a bias-free performance rating | 9 | 0.00 | 8.91 | 0.302 | 8 | −1.095 | 0.273 |
| Provide quality performance feedback | 9 | 0.00 | 8.91 | 0.302 | 8 | −1.095 | 0.273 |
| Provide coaching and mentoring | 9 | 0.00 | 8.91 | 0.302 | 8 | −1.095 | 0.273 |
| Ensure individual goals align with organisational goals | 9 | 0.00 | 8.91 | 0.302 | 8 | −1.095 | 0.273 |
| Evaluate employees' progress using digital assessment tools | 9 | 0.00 | 8.91 | 0.302 | 8 | −1.095 | 0.273 |

Table 7.10.   (*Continued*)

| Performance Management and Appraisal | M | IQD | $\overline{X}$ | SD | R | M–W Test Z | p-value |
|---|---|---|---|---|---|---|---|
| Ensure consistency in the method of performance management | 7 | 0.50 | 7.18 | 0.405 | 14 | −1.633 | 0.102 |
| Kendall's W | | | | | | 0.798 | |
| $\chi^2$ | | | | | | 103.755 | |
| $\chi^2$ – *Critical values from stats table (p = 0.05)* | | | | | | 22.362 | |
| Df | | | | | | 13 | |
| p-value | | | | | | 0.000 | |

*Note:* $\overline{X}$ = Mean, M = Median, SD = Standard deviation, $\chi^2$ = Chi square, Df = Degree of freedom, R = Rank.

Table 7.11.   Round 1 Result of the Training and Development Variables.

| Training and Development | M | IQD | $\overline{X}$ | SD | M–W test Z | p-value |
|---|---|---|---|---|---|---|
| Conduct training need assessment | 9 | 1.5 | 8.50 | 1.168 | −0.494 | 0.621 |
| Use formal training process extensively | 9 | 1.5 | 8.25 | 1.545 | −1.083 | 0.279 |
| Top management commitment to training and development | 10 | 1.0 | 9.42 | 0.996 | −0.096 | 0.924 |
| Invest in digital technologies and training needs | 9 | 2.5 | 8.83 | 1.267 | −0.843 | 0.399 |
| Create avenues for employees to discuss their training and development requirement | 9 | 2.0 | 8.82 | 1.401 | −0.385 | 0.700 |
| Promote skills development | 8 | 2.5 | 8.25 | 1.357 | −0.656 | 0.512 |

(*Continued*)

Table 7.11. *(Continued)*

| Training and Development | M | IQD | $\overline{X}$ | SD | M–W test Z | p-value |
|---|---|---|---|---|---|---|
| Promote career development | 9 | 2.0 | 8.58 | 1.311 | −0.416 | 0.677 |
| Ensure newly acquired skills are applied on the job | 8 | 2.0 | 8.08 | 1.165 | −0.662 | 0.508 |
| Ensure newly acquired skills are shared with other employees | 8 | 0.5 | 8.17 | 0.835 | −2.152 | 0.031 |
| Use an off-the-job training method | 8 | 2.0 | 7.67 | 1.303 | −0.744 | 0.457 |
| Use on-the-job training method | 9 | 1.0 | 8.67 | 0.888 | −1.357 | 0.175 |
| Use of emerging technologies in training | 9 | 1.0 | 8.50 | 0.674 | −1.734 | 0.083 |
| Use of apprenticeships | 7 | 1.5 | 7.25 | 1.545 | −0.250 | 0.803 |
| Use of induction and orientation | 9 | 1.0 | 8.25 | 2.137 | −0.601 | 0.548 |
| Use of job rotation | 8 | 1.5 | 7.00 | 3.015 | −0.328 | 0.743 |
| Promote acting capacity | 8 | 2.0 | 7.58 | 2.021 | −0.331 | 0.741 |
| Promote leadership development | 9 | 1.0 | 8.08 | 2.193 | −1.006 | 0.315 |
| Ensure future competence development | 9 | 1.0 | 8.58 | 0.900 | −0.509 | 0.611 |
| Use coaching/supervisor training | 8 | 1.0 | 8.33 | 0.651 | −0.178 | 0.859 |
| Use understudy and mentoring | 8 | 1.5 | 8.25 | 0.965 | −0.251 | 0.802 |
| Kendall's $W$ | | | | 0.170 | | |
| $\chi^2$ | | | | 35.464 | | |
| $\chi^2$ – *Critical values from stats table (p = 0.05)* | | | | 30.144 | | |
| Df | | | | 19 | | |
| p-value | | | | 0.012 | | |
| $\alpha$ | | | | 0.884 | | |

*Note:* $\overline{X}$ = Mean, $M$ = Median, SD = Standard deviation, $\chi^2$ = Chi square, $\alpha$ = Cronbach Alpha, Df = Degree of freedom.

The round two analysis results in Table 7.12 reveal that the experts considered 11 of the identified variables to have very high significance. The overall group $\overline{X}$ derived was 8.50, which shows that overall the variables under this construct were rated high. The IQD derived at this stage shows a strong consensus among the experts as the value ranged between 0.00 and 1.00. Furthermore, Kendall's $W$ gave a high value of 0.922, which is very close to one. In confirmation of the strong consensus among the experts, the derived $\chi^2$-value of 192.662 was higher than the critical $\chi^2$-value of 30.144 derived from the statistical table. The M–W test also revealed no significant difference in the views of the two groups of experts, as a $p$-value of above 0.05 was derived for all assessed variables.

## 5. *Employee Involvement and Empowerment*

In assessing the variables for employee involvement and empowerment, 13 variables were presented to the experts to rate in terms of their significance level. The result in Table 7.13 shows that the instrument used was reliable as an $\alpha$-value of 0.903 was derived. The $M$-values of all the variables ranged between 8 and 9, while their IQD ranged from 0.25 to 2.00. Kendall's $W$ gave a very low value of 0.188 and a $\chi^2$-value of 27.014, higher than the critical $\chi^2$-value of 21.026 derived from the statistical table. The M–W test revealed no significant difference in the rating of these variables by the two different groups of experts. This is because a $p$-value above the 0.05 threshold was derived for all the assessed variables.

For the second round, Table 7.14 shows that all the assessed variables have high $M$-values of between 8 and 9. The overall group $\overline{X}$ derived was 8.53, which shows that overall the variables under this construct were rated high. The IQD derived at this stage shows a strong consensus among the experts as the value ranged between 0.00 and 0.75. Furthermore, Kendall's $W$ gave a value of 0.585. To confirm the attainment of consensus at this second round, $\chi^2$-value revealed a value of 70.229, which is higher than the critical $\chi^2$-value of 21.062 derived from the statistical table. The M–W test also revealed no significant difference in the view of the two groups of experts, as a $p$-value of above 0.05 was derived for all assessed variables.

## 6. *Emotional Intelligence*

The 20 variables derived from Goleman's emotional intelligence theory were presented to the experts for assessment. The result in Table 7.15 reveals that all the variables were considered significant as they had $M$-values of between 8 and 9. The IQD of the variables ranged from 1.00 to 2.25, while Kendall's $W$ gave a very low value of 0.125. The derived $\chi^2$-value was 28.479, lower than the critical $\chi^2$-value of 31.144 derived from the statistical table. The M–W test revealed no significant difference in the rating of these variables by the two different groups of experts. This is because a $p$-value above a 0.05 threshold was derived for all the assessed variables. Furthermore, an $\alpha$-value of 0.948 was derived, thus implying that the instrument used was highly reliable.

The result from the round two analysis in Table 7.16 reveals that all the variables assessed were considered to have high significance with an $M$-value of

Table 7.12.  Round 2 Result of the Training and Development Variables.

| Training and Development | M | IQD | $\overline{X}$ | SD | R | M–W test Z | p-value |
|---|---|---|---|---|---|---|---|
| Top management commitment to training and development | 10 | 0.00 | 9.91 | 0.302 | 1 | –0.913 | 0.361 |
| Ensure future competence development | 9 | 0.00 | 9.00 | 0.000 | 2 | 0.000 | 1.000 |
| Promote leadership development | 9 | 0.00 | 9.00 | 0.000 | 2 | 0.000 | 1.000 |
| Use of induction and orientation | 9 | 0.00 | 9.00 | 0.000 | 2 | 0.000 | 1.000 |
| Use of emerging technologies in training | 9 | 0.00 | 9.00 | 0.000 | 2 | 0.000 | 1.000 |
| Invest in digital technologies and training needs | 9 | 0.00 | 9.00 | 0.000 | 2 | 0.000 | 1.000 |
| Use on-the-job training method | 9 | 0.00 | 8.91 | 0.302 | 7 | –0.913 | 0.361 |
| Create avenues for employees to discuss their training and development requirement | 9 | 0.00 | 8.91 | 0.302 | 7 | –0.913 | 0.361 |
| Use formal training process extensively | 9 | 0.00 | 8.91 | 0.302 | 7 | –1.095 | 0.273 |
| Conduct training need assessment | 9 | 0.00 | 8.91 | 0.302 | 7 | –0.913 | 0.361 |
| Promote career development | 9 | 0.50 | 8.82 | 0.405 | 11 | –0.913 | 0.361 |
| Use of job rotation | 8 | 0.00 | 8.09 | 0.302 | 12 | –1.095 | 0.273 |
| Use of understudy and mentoring | 8 | 0.00 | 7.91 | 0.302 | 13 | –0.913 | 0.361 |
| Use of coaching/ supervisor training | 8 | 0.00 | 7.91 | 0.302 | 13 | –0.913 | 0.361 |
| Promote acting capacity | 8 | 0.00 | 7.91 | 0.302 | 13 | –0.913 | 0.361 |
| Use an off-the-job training method | 8 | 0.00 | 7.91 | 0.302 | 13 | –1.095 | 0.273 |

Table 7.12.   (*Continued*)

| Training and Development | M | IQD | $\overline{X}$ | SD | R | M–W test Z | p-value |
|---|---|---|---|---|---|---|---|
| Ensure newly acquired skills are shared with other employees | 8 | 0.00 | 7.91 | 0.302 | 13 | –0.913 | 0.361 |
| Promote skills development | 8 | 0.00 | 7.91 | 0.302 | 13 | –1.095 | 0.273 |
| Ensure newly acquired skills are applied on the job | 8 | 0.50 | 7.82 | 0.405 | 19 | –0.136 | 0.892 |
| Use of apprenticeships | 7 | 1.00 | 7.27 | 0.467 | 20 | –0.825 | 0.409 |
| Kendall's *W* | | | | | | 0.922 | |
| $x^2$ | | | | | | 192.662 | |
| $x^2$ – *Critical values from stats table (p = 0.05)* | | | | | | 30.144 | |
| Df | | | | | | 19 | |
| p-value | | | | | | 0.000 | |

Note: $\overline{X}$ = Mean, $M$ = Median, SD = Standard deviation, $x^2$ = Chi square, Df = Degree of freedom, $R$ = Rank.

Table 7.13.   Round 1 Result of the Employee's Involvement and Empowerment Variables.

| Involve and Empower Employees | M | IQD | $\overline{X}$ | SD | M–W test Z | p-value |
|---|---|---|---|---|---|---|
| Promote leadership | 9 | 1.00 | 8.25 | 1.29 | –0.254 | 0.800 |
| Create systems that promote empowerment and involvement | 8 | 1.25 | 8.08 | 1.31 | –0.499 | 0.618 |
| Make resources available for continuous training | 8 | 1.25 | 7.83 | 1.27 | –0.335 | 0.737 |

(*Continued*)

Table 7.13. (*Continued*)

| Involve and Empower Employees | M | IQD | $\overline{X}$ | SD | M–W test Z | M–W test p-value |
|---|---|---|---|---|---|---|
| Ensure enthusiastic participation in the attainment of the company's goals | 8 | 2.00 | 7.58 | 2.27 | –0.579 | 0.563 |
| Use self-service digital platforms to promote participation | 8 | 1.25 | 8.08 | 1.38 | –0.417 | 0.676 |
| Promote teamwork | 9 | 1.00 | 7.92 | 2.31 | –0.169 | 0.866 |
| Align individual strength with empowerment goals | 8 | 2.00 | 8.17 | 1.03 | –0.084 | 0.933 |
| Ensure continuous measurement of performance | 9 | 1.00 | 8.50 | 0.80 | –0.518 | 0.604 |
| Promote reward and recognition | 9 | 0.25 | 9.00 | 0.85 | –1.441 | 0.150 |
| Allow collaborative setting of organisational goals and objectives | 8 | 2.00 | 7.67 | 1.56 | –0.410 | 0.682 |
| Ensure the right staff at the right place of service | 9 | 0.25 | 8.75 | 0.75 | –1.051 | 0.293 |
| Ensure employee involvement in quality control circles | 8 | 1.25 | 8.17 | 0.94 | –1.855 | 0.064 |
| Brief teams, communicate and give feedback using digital tools | 9 | 1.00 | 8.42 | 0.90 | –2.289 | 0.022 |
| Kendall's W | | | | 0.188 | | |
| $\chi^2$ | | | | 27.014 | | |
| $\chi^2$ – Critical values from stats table (p = 0.05) | | | | 21.026 | | |
| Df | | | | 12 | | |
| p-value | | | | 0.008 | | |
| $\alpha$ | | | | 0.903 | | |

*Note:* $\overline{X}$ = Mean, M = Median, SD = Standard deviation, $\chi^2$ = Chi square, $\alpha$ = Cronbach Alpha, Df = Degree of freedom.

Table 7.14. Round 2 Result of the Employee's Involvement and Empowerment Variables.

| Employee Involvement and Empowerment | M | IQD | $\overline{X}$ | SD | R | M–W Test Z | M–W Test p-value |
|---|---|---|---|---|---|---|---|
| Ensure the right staff at the right place of service | 9 | 0.00 | 9.00 | 0.000 | 1 | 0.000 | 1.000 |
| Promote reward and recognition | 9 | 0.00 | 9.00 | 0.000 | 1 | 0.000 | 1.000 |
| Ensure continuous performance measurement | 9 | 0.00 | 9.00 | 0.000 | 1 | 0.000 | 1.000 |
| Promote teamwork | 9 | 0.00 | 9.00 | 0.000 | 1 | 0.000 | 1.000 |
| Brief teams, communicate and give feedback using digital tools | 9 | 0.00 | 8.91 | 0.302 | 5 | −0.913 | 0.361 |
| Promote leadership | 9 | 0.00 | 8.91 | 0.302 | 5 | −0.913 | 0.361 |
| Create systems to promote empowerment and involvement | 8 | 0.50 | 8.30 | 0.675 | 7 | −0.149 | 0.881 |
| Align individual strength with empowerment goals | 8 | 0.00 | 8.27 | 0.647 | 8 | −0.271 | 0.787 |
| Ensure enthusiastic participation in the attainment of the company's goals | 8 | 0.75 | 8.18 | 0.603 | 9 | −1.095 | 0.273 |
| Ensure employee involvement in quality control circles | 8 | 0.00 | 8.09 | 0.701 | 10 | −1.354 | 0.176 |
| Use self-service digital platforms to promote participation | 8 | | 8.09 | 0.701 | 10 | −1.354 | 0.176 |
| Make resources available for continuous training | 8 | 0.00 | 8.09 | 0.701 | 10 | −1.354 | 0.176 |
| Set the goals and objectives of the organisation collaboratively | 8 | 0.50 | 8.00 | 0.447 | 13 | −1.354 | 0.176 |

| | |
|---|---|
| Kendall's $W$ | 0.585 |
| $\chi^2$ | 70.229 |
| $\chi^2$ – *Critical values from stats table (p = 0.05)* | 21.026 |
| Df | 12 |
| p-value | 0.000 |

*Note:* $\overline{X}$ = Mean, $M$ = Median, SD = Standard deviation, $\chi^2$ = Chi square, Df = Degree of freedom, $R$ = Rank.

Table 7.15.  Round 1 Result of the Emotional Intelligence Variables.

| Emotional Intelligence | M | IQD | $\overline{X}$ | SD | M–W test Z | M–W test p-value |
|---|---|---|---|---|---|---|
| Promote emotional self-awareness | 9 | 2.00 | 8.17 | 1.193 | −0.084 | 0.933 |
| Promote accurate self-awareness | 9 | 2.00 | 8.00 | 1.414 | −0.254 | 0.800 |
| Promote self-confidence | 8 | 2.00 | 7.92 | 1.379 | 0.000 | 1.000 |
| Promote self-control | 8 | 1.25 | 8.17 | 1.030 | −1.087 | 0.277 |
| Promote trustworthiness | 9 | 1.25 | 8.00 | 2.730 | −0.330 | 0.742 |
| Promote conscientiousness (care and diligence in carrying out tasks) | 9 | 1.00 | 8.67 | 0.985 | −1.032 | 0.302 |
| Ensure adaptability | 8 | 2.00 | 8.00 | 1.044 | −1.012 | 0.312 |
| Promote achievement drive | 8 | 1.00 | 8.08 | 1.379 | −0.762 | 0.446 |
| Create an environment that promotes initiative | 9 | 1.25 | 8.08 | 1.564 | −0.084 | 0.933 |
| Empathy | 8 | 2.00 | 7.83 | 1.467 | −1.012 | 0.312 |
| Promote service orientation | 9 | 2.00 | 8.00 | 1.128 | −0.436 | 0.663 |
| Ensure organisational awareness among employee | 9 | 2.00 | 8.25 | 1.055 | −0.254 | 0.799 |
| Promote employee-to-employee mentoring (developing others) | 8 | 2.00 | 8.17 | 1.030 | −0.084 | 0.933 |
| Influence | 8 | 2.25 | 7.50 | 2.195 | −0.162 | 0.871 |
| Promote effective communication | 9 | 2.00 | 8.83 | 1.193 | −1.092 | 0.275 |
| Practise conflict management | 8 | 2.00 | 8.00 | 1.128 | 0.000 | 1.000 |
| Promote leadership among employees | 9 | 1.25 | 8.08 | 2.151 | −0.584 | 0.559 |
| Be a change catalyst | 8 | 2.25 | 7.50 | 2.236 | −1.223 | 0.222 |
| Promote building bonds | 8 | 2.25 | 7.33 | 2.188 | −0.407 | 0.684 |
| Promote teamwork | 8 | 1.00 | 7.92 | 2.021 | −0.508 | 0.612 |

Table 7.15. (*Continued*)

| Emotional Intelligence | M | IQD | $\overline{X}$ | SD | M–W test | |
|---|---|---|---|---|---|---|
| | | | | | Z | p-value |
| Kendall's *W* | | | | 0.125 | | |
| $\chi^2$ | | | | 28.479 | | |
| $\chi^2$ – *Critical values from stats table (p = 0.05)* | | | | 30.144 | | |
| Df | | | | 19 | | |
| p-value | | | | 0.075 | | |
| A | | | | 0.948 | | |

*Note:* $\overline{X}$ = Mean, M = Median, SD = Standard deviation, $\chi^2$ = Chi square, $\alpha$ = Cronbach Alpha, Df = Degree of freedom.

Table 7.16. Round 2 Results of the Emotional Intelligence Variables.

| Emotional Intelligence | M | IQD | $\overline{X}$ | SD | R | M–W test | |
|---|---|---|---|---|---|---|---|
| | | | | | | Z | p-value |
| Promote effective communication | 9 | 0.00 | 9.00 | 0.000 | 1 | 0.000 | 1.000 |
| Ensure organisational awareness among employee | 9 | 0.00 | 9.00 | 0.000 | 1 | 0.000 | 1.000 |
| Promote conscientiousness (care and diligence in carrying out tasks) | 9 | 0.00 | 9.00 | 0.000 | 1 | 0.000 | 1.000 |
| Promote trustworthiness | 9 | 0.00 | 9.00 | 0.000 | 1 | 0.000 | 1.000 |
| Promote service orientation | 9 | 0.00 | 8.91 | 0.302 | 5 | −1.095 | 0.273 |
| Create an environment that promotes initiative | 9 | 0.00 | 8.91 | 0.302 | 5 | −1.095 | 0.273 |
| Promote accurate self-awareness | 9 | 0.00 | 8.91 | 0.302 | 5 | −1.095 | 0.273 |
| Promote emotional self-awareness | 9 | 0.00 | 8.91 | 0.302 | 5 | −1.095 | 0.273 |

(*Continued*)

Table 7.16.    (*Continued*)

| Emotional Intelligence | M | IQD | $\overline{X}$ | SD | R | M–W test Z | M–W test p-value |
|---|---|---|---|---|---|---|---|
| Promote leadership among employees | 9 | 0.50 | 8.82 | 0.405 | 9 | –0.136 | 0.892 |
| Empathy | 8 | 0.75 | 8.09 | 0.302 | 10 | –0.913 | 0.361 |
| Practice conflict management | 8 | 0.00 | 8.00 | 0.000 | 11 | 0.000 | 1.000 |
| Promote self-control | 8 | 0.00 | 8.00 | 0.000 | 11 | 0.000 | 1.000 |
| Promote achievement drive | 8 | 0.00 | 8.00 | 0.447 | 11 | –1.354 | 0.176 |
| Ensure adaptability | 8 | 0.00 | 8.00 | 0.447 | 11 | –1.354 | 0.176 |
| Promote teamwork | 8 | 0.00 | 7.91 | 0.302 | 15 | –1.095 | 0.273 |
| Promote employee-to-employee mentoring (developing others) | 8 | 0.00 | 7.91 | 0.302 | 15 | –0.913 | 0.361 |
| Promote self-confidence | 8 | 0.00 | 7.91 | 0.302 | 15 | –1.095 | 0.273 |
| Be a change catalyst | 8 | 0.00 | 7.82 | 0.405 | 18 | –0.136 | 0.892 |
| Influence | 8 | 0.00 | 7.82 | 0.405 | 18 | –0.136 | 0.892 |
| Promote building bonds | 8 | 0.50 | 7.73 | 0.467 | 20 | –0.825 | 0.409 |
| Kendall's W | | | | | | | 0.868 |
| $\chi^2$ | | | | | | | 181.317 |
| $\chi^2$ – *Critical values from stats table (p = 0.05)* | | | | | | | 30.144 |
| Df | | | | | | | 19 |
| p-value | | | | | | | 0.000 |

*Note:* $\overline{X}$ = Mean, M = Median, SD = Standard deviation, $\chi^2$ = Chi square, Df = Degree of freedom, R = Rank.

between 8 and 9 derived. The overall group $\overline{X}$ derived was 8.38, which shows that the overall variables under this construct were rated high. The IQD derived shows a strong consensus between the experts as the value ranged between 0.00 and 0.75. Furthermore, Kendall's W gave a high value of 0.868, which is very close to one. In confirmation of the strong consensus among the experts, the derived $\chi^2$-value of 181.317 was higher than the critical $\chi^2$-value of 30.144 derived from the statistical table. The M–W test also revealed no significant difference in the views of the two groups of experts, as a p-value of above 0.05 was derived for all assessed variables.

## 7. External Environment

The external environment, which is viewed from the pressure exacted on workforce management by some external environmental factors, was assessed using fourteen variables, as seen in Table 7.17. The $\alpha$-value of 0.952 derived shows that the instrument used was reliable. The $M$-values for all the variables range between 7 and 9, while their IQD ranged from 0.50 to 3.25. Kendall's $W$ gave a very low value of 0.165 and a $\chi^2$-value of 25.758, higher than the critical $\chi^2$-value of 22.362 derived from the statistical table. The M–W test revealed no significant difference in the rating of these variables by the two groups of experts. This is because a $p$-value above the 0.05 threshold was derived for all the assessed variables.

The result from the round two analysis in Table 7.18 reveals that all the variables assessed were considered to have high significance with an $M$-value of between 7 and 9 derived. The overall group $\overline{X}$ derived was 8.25, which shows that overall the variables under this construct were rated high. The IQD derived shows a strong consensus between the experts as the value ranged between 0.00 and 0.50. Kendall's $W$ gave a high value of 0.893, close to one. In confirmation of the strong consensus among the experts, the derived $\chi^2$-value of 127.684 was higher than the critical $\chi^2$-value of 22.362 derived from the statistical table. The M–W test also revealed no significant difference in the view of the two groups of experts, as a $p$-value of above 0.05 was derived for all assessed variables.

### *Overall View of the Workforce Management Practices*

Based on the group $\overline{X}$ for each of the workforce management practices derived in the second round, Fig. 7.2 was computed. The figure gives a view of the significance attached to each of the practices by the respondents. In general, based on the Likert Scale adopted, it is evident that all the practices and their attributed variables were considered to be very significant as they all had a group $\overline{X}$ of above 8.0. A critical evaluation shows that the variables associated with performance management and appraisal were considered the most significant with an overall group $\overline{X}$ of 8.90. In the current fourth industrial revolution era, where technology continues to advance and revolutionalise the way construction projects are being delivered, it is necessary for construction organisations to continuously evaluate the performance of their workforce and provide measures for improvement. Also, involving and empowering employees, training and developing them to match the required skills, as well as ensuring that they are emotionally intelligent, were rated high by the experts. The practice with the lowest group $\overline{X}$ is compensation and benefits. However, the group $\overline{X}$ of 8.06 derived for this practice and its attributed variables indicates that construction organisations seeking to get the best out of their employees cannot afford to overlook this practice in managing their workforce. It is important to note that the experts in the study considered the two gaps introduced in this study (i.e. emotional intelligence and external environment) were considered as important to the successful management of the construction workforce in the era of the fourth industrial revolution.

Table 7.17.   Round 1 Results of the External Environment Variables.

| External Environment | M | IQD | $\overline{X}$ | SD | M–W test Z | M–W test p-value |
|---|---|---|---|---|---|---|
| Government policies and legislation | 9 | 2.75 | 8.25 | 2.26 | –0.335 | 0.737 |
| Clients' demand for personnel and technologies | 9 | 1.25 | 8.25 | 1.14 | –0.335 | 0.737 |
| Suppliers and subcontractors demand personnel and technologies | 8 | 1.25 | 7.50 | 1.68 | –0.247 | 0.805 |
| Nature of the labour market | 8 | 3.25 | 7.67 | 1.92 | –0.325 | 0.745 |
| Culture and values in the construction industry | 9 | 2.00 | 8.17 | 1.19 | –0.419 | 0.675 |
| Evolving nature of the construction industry | 9 | 2.25 | 8.00 | 1.65 | –0.246 | 0.806 |
| Construction industry's regulations | 9 | 1.50 | 8.25 | 1.76 | –0.412 | 0.680 |
| Use of technologies to provide safety and security for workers | 8 | 2.00 | 8.08 | 1.31 | –0.247 | 0.805 |
| Scope of the market of the organisation (Specific boundaries of the organisation's activities) | 8 | 1.50 | 7.50 | 1.73 | –0.749 | 0.454 |
| Industry's regulation on the use of digital technologies | 7 | 3.25 | 7.17 | 1.85 | –0.410 | 0.682 |
| Regulations on the extent of partnership | 7 | 3.25 | 7.00 | 1.86 | –0.082 | 0.934 |
| Political climate | 8 | 0.50 | 7.75 | 1.48 | –0.772 | 0.440 |
| Socio-economic climate | 9 | 1.25 | 8.00 | 1.86 | –0.247 | 0.805 |
| Competitive pressure | 9 | 1.25 | 8.33 | 1.23 | –0.577 | 0.564 |

Table 7.17.   (*Continued*)

| External Environment | M | IQD | $\overline{X}$ | SD | M–W test Z | p-value |
|---|---|---|---|---|---|---|
| Kendall's *W* | | | | 0.165 | | |
| $\chi^2$ | | | | 25.758 | | |
| $\chi^2$ – *Critical values from stats table (p = 0.05)* | | | | 22.362 | | |
| Df | | | | 13 | | |
| p-value | | | | 0.018 | | |
| $\alpha$ | | | | 0.952 | | |

*Note:* $\overline{X}$ = Mean, $M$ = Median, SD = Standard deviation, $\chi^2$ = Chi square, $\alpha$ = Cronbach Alpha, Df = Degree of freedom.

Table 7.18.   Round 2 Results of the External Environment Variables.

| External Environment | M | IQD | $\overline{X}$ | SD | R | M–W test Z | p-value |
|---|---|---|---|---|---|---|---|
| Construction industry's regulations | 9 | 0.00 | 9.00 | 0.000 | 1 | 0.000 | 1.000 |
| Culture and values in the construction industry | 9 | 0.00 | 9.00 | 0.000 | 1 | 0.000 | 1.000 |
| Clients' demand for personnel and technologies | 9 | 0.00 | 9.00 | 0.000 | 1 | 0.000 | 1.000 |
| Government policies and legislation | 9 | 0.00 | 9.00 | 0.000 | 1 | 0.000 | 1.000 |
| Socio-economic climate | 9 | 0.00 | 8.91 | 0.302 | 5 | –0.913 | 0.361 |
| Evolving nature of the construction industry | 9 | 0.00 | 8.82 | 0.603 | 6 | –1.095 | 0.273 |
| Competitive pressure | 9 | 0.50 | 8.64 | 0.809 | 7 | –0.136 | 0.892 |
| Scope of the market of the organisation (Specific boundaries of the organisation's activities) | 8 | 0.00 | 8.00 | 0.000 | 8 | 0.000 | 1.000 |
| Political climate | 8 | 0.00 | 7.91 | 0.302 | 9 | –0.913 | 0.361 |
| Use of technologies to provide safety and security for workers | 8 | 0.00 | 7.91 | 0.302 | 9 | –0.913 | 0.361 |

(*Continued*)

Table 7.18.    (*Continued*)

|                                   |       |       |                |       |       | M–W test |         |
| --------------------------------- | ----- | ----- | -------------- | ----- | ----- | -------- | ------- |
| **External Environment**          | **M** | **IQD** | $\overline{X}$ | **SD** | **R** | **Z**    | **p-value** |
| Nature of the labour market       | 8     | 0.00  | 7.82           | 0.405 | 11    | –0.136   | 0.892   |
| Suppliers and subcontractors demand personnel and technologies | 8 | 0.00 | 7.73 | 0.647 | 12 | –1.625 | 0.104 |
| Regulations on the extent of partnership | 7 | 0.00 | 6.91 | 0.302 | 13 | –0.913 | 0.361 |
| Industry's regulation on the use of digital technologies | 7 | 0.00 | 6.91 | 0.302 | 13 | –0.913 | 0.361 |
| Kendall's *W*                     |       |       |                |       |       | 0.893    |         |
| $\chi^2$                          |       |       |                |       |       | 127.684  |         |
| $\chi^2$ – *Critical values from stats table (p = 0.05)* |  |  |  |  |  | 22.362 |  |
| Df                                |       |       |                |       |       | 13       |         |
| *p*-value                         |       |       |                |       |       | 0.000    |         |

*Note:* $\overline{X}$ = Mean, *M* = Median, SD = Standard deviation, $\chi^2$ = Chi square, Df = Degree of freedom, *R* = Rank.

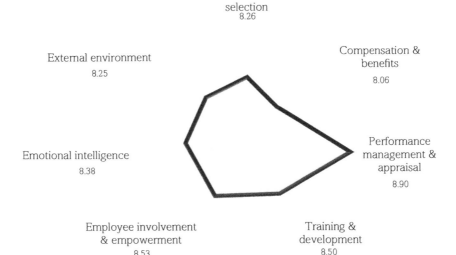

Fig. 7.2.   Overall Significance of the Construction Workforce Management Practices. *Source*: Author's compilation (2023).

## Discussing the Delphi Outcomes

The findings from Delphi revealed that the workforce management practices proposed in the conceptual model in Chapter 6 were considered important for the effective management of workers in construction organisations. It is imperative to note that since the Delphi was conducted among experts in South Africa, the submissions might be peculiar to the country and not be entirely applicable to other countries' construction industries. It is advised that before adopting the conceptualised construction workforce management model in this study, a careful assessment of the applicability of these proposed practices and their attributed variables in the country where the model is to be applied.

For recruitment and selection, the result from the second round of the Delphi revealed that all the assessed variables have a high significance. However, the highest rated variables are the use of unbiased interview panels, adopting competency and experience-based recruitment, screening and evaluating selected candidates carefully using electronic platforms, advertising vacancies through electronic platforms, analysing long-term labour needs of the organisation, conducting reference and background checks, impartial recruitment and selection process, and conducting seasonal recruitment. The interview panel plays a crucial role in determining the successful candidate for a job, and as such, having a panel that is unbiased is important for a transparent and fair selection process. This finding is in tandem with the views of Edgar and Geare (2005), who submitted that an impartial recruitment and selection process, a recruitment and selection process void of favouritism, the use of interview panels, and appointments based on merits are some essential recruitment and selection factors that need to be considered by construction organisations. The findings also align with the submissions of Naidu and Chand (2014), who noted the need to use a competence and experience-based recruitment approach. This is essential for construction organisations where diverse competencies are needed for successful project delivery, and experience also plays an essential factor in project construction delivery. To have a good assessment of the competence and experience of the selected candidates, organisations must be ready to conduct careful screening and evaluation of the candidates. This is also in line with the submission of past studies that have explored the best approaches to recruiting and selecting employees (Nel and Werner, 2017). Using different electronic platforms to advertise job positions has also been promoted in past studies (Brandão et al., 2019). With the evolution of technology and easy internet access, organisations can use online social media platforms such as LinkedIn to attract candidates for professional positions.

For compensation and benefits, the findings revealed that the most significant variables to be considered are appreciation and recognition for good performance, use of information technology tools in the compensation process, ensuring employees' satisfaction with direct wages/salary, ensuring employees' satisfaction with their pay raise, ensuring employees' satisfaction with pay structures within the organisation, designing compensation and benefit in accordance with labour laws and understanding employees' salary expectations. However, ensuring employees' involvement in selecting and determining compensation was rated the least.

This variable was suggested by one of the experts from the first round. However, the result from the second resound shows that this variable is insignificant. Furthermore, the whole idea of the interview process is to understand the capability of the employee to carry out the job and, in most cases, to negotiate the amount for their services. This implies that employees are already included in the compensation determination right from the onset. Having this as a separate variable becomes unnecessary. However, construction organisations need to consider appreciation and recognition for good performance. This finding further confirmed Naidu and Chand's (2014) assertions that this factor is crucial compensation and benefit factor that should not be overlooked in the quest for effective workforce management.

Regarding performance management and appraisal, the findings revealed that the most significant variable is clearly communicating set objectives to the employees. This is understandable as with a clear set purpose that the employee can work towards, it becomes easier for them to focus on specific objectives. This submission further corroborates the submission of Nel and Werner (2017), who noted the issue of communicating objectives to employees clearly as an essential driver towards good performance management. Some other essential practices are the continuous review of individual and group performance, ensuring accurate performance appraisal using appropriate digital tools, fairness in the evaluation process, continuous review of the set organisational objectives, developing an action plan to correct the deviation in performance and continuously setting achievable organisational objectives for employees. These variables have also been considered crucial for effective performance management in past studies (Nel & Werner, 2017; Whiting et al., 2008)

In terms of training development, the findings revealed that while the assessed variables were considered significant, top management commitment to training and development was the most significant. The importance of this variable has been reiterated in past studies (Edgar & Geare, 2005; Ohabunwa, 1999). Other crucial training and development factors identified from the Delphi include ensuring future competence development, promoting leadership development, use of induction and orientation, use of emerging technologies in training, and investing in the organisation's digital technologies and training needs. Coyle-Shapiro et al. (2016) earlier noted the need to develop competence among workers, while Ojambati et al. (2012), as well as Bradley and Karl (2011), advocated the need to promote leadership among workers as a form of development. The findings are also in line with past studies that have advocated the use of induction and orientation as a means to training new employees and acquainting them with their job functions (Aboramadan et al., 2020; Bradley & Karl, 2011; Naidu & Chand, 2014).

Ensuring the right staff at the right place of service, promoting reward and recognition, ensuring continuous performance measurement, promoting teamwork, team briefing teams and communicating feedback using digital tools, and promoting leadership are the most significant variables in the employee involvement and empowerment practice. These findings are in line with past studies. For instance, Naidu and Chand (2014) noted the importance of ensuring that the right staff is doing the right job to create some sort of empowerment. Similarly, Holt et al. (2000) and Nesan (1997) highlighted the importance of performance measurement regularly and the need to promote leadership and teamwork, which will allow employees to participate actively in organisation activities.

Apostolou (2000) also suggested that a proper communication and feedback system is essential in ensuring employees' involvement.

For the gaps in the literature, the findings revealed that all the 20 variables identified from Goleman's mixed model for emotional intelligence were significant. However, nine variables had very high significance levels. These nine variables cut across the four major dimensions of the model, which are self-awareness (promote accurate self-awareness, promote emotional self-awareness), self-management (promote conscientiousness, promote trustworthiness, and create an environment that promotes initiative), social skills (organisational awareness among employee, and promote service orientation) and relationship management (promote effective communication and promote leadership among employees).

For the external environment, the result revealed very high significance for seven of the variables. These are construction industry's regulations, culture and values in the construction industry, clients' demand for personnel and technologies, government policies and legislations, the socio-economic climate in the country, the evolving nature of the construction industry, and competitive pressure. Since the construction industry plays a crucial role in how organisations conduct their business, it is not surprising to see that the industry's regulations, as well as the culture and values of the industry, are key external environmental variables that can influence workforce management. A similar observation was made by Awa et al. (2017). Similarly, the important role of construction clients and government policies in shaping organisations' decisions to adopt one concept or the other has been noted in past studies (Hsu et al., 2006; Teo et al., 2003).

## Summary

This chapter, through a Delphi of experts' opinion explored the suitability and applicability of the conceptualised construction workforce management model presented in Chapter 6. The Delphi revealed that all seven constructs and their attributed variables proposed in this study are suitable for adoption and are applicable to happenings within construction organisations in this current era of the fourth industrial revolution. It is worthy of note that the findings presented are peculiar to the South African construction industry, as the experts for Delphi were drawn from construction organisations within the country. Therefore, the submissions cannot be generalised to other countries. As such, it is advisable for construction organisations, industry practitioners and researchers seeking to adopt the conceptual model to first test its suitability and applicability in the country where the model is to be applied.

## References

Aboramadan, M., Albashiti, B., Alharazin, H., & Dahleez, K. A. (2020). Human resources management practices and organisational commitment in higher education: The mediating role of work engagement. *International Journal of Educational Management, 34*(1), 154–174.

Adler, M., & Ziglio, E. (1996). *Gazing into the oracle: The Delphi method and its application to social policy and public health.* Kingsley Publishers.

Aghimien, D. O., Aigbavboa, C. O., & Oke, A. E. (2020). Critical success factors for digital partnering in construction organisations – A Delphi Study. *Engineering, Construction and Architectural Management*, *27*(10), 3171–3188.

Agumba, J., & Musonda, I. (2013). Experience of using Delphi method in construction health and safety research. In *Seventh International Conference on Construction in the 21st Century CITC-VII*, December 19–21, Bangkok, Thailand.

Aigbavboa, C. (2013). *An integrated beneficiary centred satisfaction model for publicly funded housing schemes in South Africa*. A PhD thesis submitted to the Postgraduate School of Engineering Management, University of Johannesburg, Johannesburg, South Africa.

Alomari, K. A., Gambatese, J. A., & Tymvios, N. (2018). Risk perception comparison among construction safety professionals: Delphi perspective. *Journal of Construction Engineering & Management*, *144*(12), 1–12.

Ameyaw, E. E., Hu, Y., Shan, M., Chan, A. P. C., & Le, Y. (2016). Application of Delphi method in construction engineering and management research: A quantitative perspective. *Journal of Civil Engineering and Management*, *22*(8), 991–1000.

Apostolou, A. (2000). *Employee involvement*. Report produced for the EC funded project. https://www.urenio.org/tools/en/employee_involvement.pdf

Awa, H. O., Ojiabo, O. O., & Orokor, L. E. (2017). Integrated technology-organisation-environment (T-O-E) taxonomies for technology adoption. *Journal of Enterprise Information Management*, *30*(6), 893–921.

Bradley, T. B., & Karl, H. (2011). Training and development. *Encyclopedia of Business* (2nd ed.). https://www.encyclopedia.com/social-sciences-and-law/economics-business-and-labor/businesses-and-occupations/training-and-development

Brandão, C., Silva, R., & dos Santos, J. V. (2019). Online recruitment in Portugal: Theories and candidate profiles. *Journal of Business Research*, *94*, 273–279.

Chan, A. P. C., Yung, E. H. K., Lam, P. T. I., Tam, C. M., & Cheung, S. O. (2001). Application of Delphi method in selection of procurement systems for construction projects. *Construction Management and Economics*, *19*(7), 699–718.

Construction Industry Development Board. (2019). *CIDB SME Business Condition Survey: Quarter 3*. Construction Industry Development Board, October 2019. www.cidb.org.za

Coyle-Shapiro, J. A.-M., Diehl, M.-R., & Chang, C. (2016). The employee–organisation relationship and organisational citizenship behaviour. In P. M. Podsakoff, S. B. Mackenzie, & N. P. Podsakoff (Eds.), *The Oxford handbook of organizational citizenship behaviour*. Oxford University Press.

Crisp, J., Pelletier, D., Duffield, C., Adams, A., & Nagy, S. (1997). The Delphi method? *Nursing Research*, *46*(11), 6–8.

Dall'Omo, S. (2017). *Driving African development through smarter technology*. African Digitalisation Maturity Report, 1–45.

Edgar, F., & Geare, A. (2005). HRM practice and employee attitudes: Different measures – Different results. *Personnel Review*, *34*(5), 534–549.

Gohdes, S. L. W., & Crews, B. T. (2004). The Delphi technique: A research strategy for career and technical education. *Journal of Career and Technical Education*, *20*(2), 55–67.

Green, B., Jones, M., Hughes, D., & Williams, A. (1999). Applying the Delphi technique in a study of GP's information requirement. *Health and Social Care in the Community*, *17*(3), 198–205.

Hallowell, M. (2008). *A formal model of construction safety and health risk management* [Ph.D. dissertation]. Oregon State University, Corvallis, Ore, USA.

Hallowell, M. R., & Gambatese, J. (2010). Qualitative research: Application of the Delphi method to CEM research. *Journal of Construction Engineering and Management*, *136* (1), 99–107.

Hasson, F., Keeney, S., & McKenna, H. (2000). Research guidelines for the Delphi survey technique. *Journal of Advanced Nursing*, *32*(4), 1008–1015.

Holey, E. A., Feeley, J. L., Dixon, J., & Whittaker, V. J. (2007). An exploration of the use of simple statistics to measure consensus and stability in Delphi studies. *BMC Medical Research Methodology, 7*(52), 1–10.

Holt, G. D., Love, P. E. D., & Nesan, L. J. (2000). Employee empowerment in construction: An implementation model for process improvement. *Team Performance Management: An International Journal, 6*(3/4), 47–51.

Hon, C. K. H., Chan, A. P. C., & Yam, M. C. H. (2012). Empirical study to investigate the difficulties of implementing safety practices in the repair and maintenance sector in Hong Kong. *Journal of Construction Engineering and Management, 138*(7), 877–884.

Hsu, C., & Sandford, B. A. (2007). The Delphi technique: Making sense of consensus. *Practical Assessment Research and Evaluation, 12*(10), 1–8.

Hsu, P. F., Kraemer, K. L., & Dunkle, D. (2006). Determinants of e-business use in US firms. *International Journal of Electronic Commerce, 10*, 9–45.

Linstone, H. A., & Turoff, M. (1975). *The Delphi method: Techniques and applications.* Addison Wesley.

Loo, R. (2002). The Delphi method: A powerful tool for strategic management, policing. *An International Journal of Police Strategies and Management, 25*(4), 762–769.

Manoliadis, O. G., Tsolas, I., & Nakou, A. (2006). Sustainable construction and drivers of change in Greece: A Delphi study. *Construction Management and Economics, 24*(2), 113–120.

McKenna, H. (1994). The Delphi technique: A worthwhile research approach for nursing? *Journal of Advanced Nursing, 19*(6), 1221–1225.

Naidu, S., & Chand, A. (2014). A comparative analysis of best human resource management practices in the hotel sector of Samoa and Tonga. *Personnel Review, 43*(5), 798–815.

Nel, P. S., & Werner, A. (2017). *Human resource management* (10th ed.). Oxford Press, South Africa.

Nesan, L. J. (1997). *A generic model for effective implementation of empowerment in construction contractor organisations* [PhD thesis]. Built Environment Research Unit, University of Wolverhampton, Wolverhampton.

Ohabunwa, S. (1999). *Nigeria business environment in the new millennium* [Paper presentation]. HRDB UNILAG on Renovating our corporate management practices for the New Millemium, Lagos, Nigeria, 19 May.

Ojambati, T. S., Akinbile, B. F., & Abiola-Falemu, J. O. (2012). Personnel training and development: A vital tool for construction workers performance. *Journal of Emerging Trends in Engineering and Applied Sciences, 3*(6), 996–1004.

Pallant, J. (2011). *SPSS Survival Manual* (4th ed.). Allen & Unwin.

Rajendran, S., & Gambatese, J. A. (2009). Development and initial validation of sustainable construction safety and health rating system. *Journal of Construction Engineering and Management, 135*(10), 1067–1075.

Raskin, M. S. (1994). The Delphi study in field instruction revisited: Expert consensus on issues and research priorities. *Journal of Social Work Education, 30*, 75–89.

Rayens, M. K., & Hahn, E. J. (2000). Building consensus using the policy Delphi method. *Policy Politics Nursing Practice, 1*(2), 308–315.

Rogers, M. R., & Lopez, E. C. (2002). Identifying critical cross-cultural school psychology competencies. *The Journal of Social Psychology, 40*(2), 115–141.

Rowe, G., Wright, G., & Bolger, F. (1991). Delphi – A re-evaluation of research and theory. *Technological Forecasting and Social Change, 39*, 238–251.

Siegel, S., & Castellan, N. J. (1988). *Nonparametric statistics for the behavioral sciences* (2nd ed.). McGraw-Hill.

Skulmoski, J. G., Hartman, T. F., & Krahn, J. (2007). The Delphi method for graduate research. *Journal of Information Technology Education, 6*, 1–21.

Teo, H. H., Wei, K. K., & Benbasat, I. (2003). Predicting intention to adopt interorganizational linkages: An institutional perspective. *MIS Quarterly, 27*(1), 19–49.

Whiting, H. J., Kline, T. J. B., & Sulsky, L. M. (2008). The performance appraisal congruency scale: An assessment of person-environment fit. *International Journal of Productivity and Performance Management, 57*(3), 223–236.

Woudenberg, F. (1991). An evaluation of Delphi. *Technological Forecasting and Social Change, 40*, 131–150.

Yeung, J. F. Y., Chan, A. P. C., Chan, D. W. M., & Li, L. K. (2007). Development of a partnering performance index (PPI) for construction projects in Hong Kong: A Delphi study. *Construction Management and Economics, 25*(12), 1219–1237.

# Chapter 8

# Conclusion

## Abstract

This chapter gives the conclusion of the book. The chapter draws from the discussion from previous chapters to make logical conclusions and recommendations. The chapter concludes that construction industries are failing to imbibe workforce management practices, resulting in high employee turnover, dissatisfaction among existing workers and ultimately, low productivity of workers and organisations. It was also noted that the fourth industrial revolution offers emerging technologies that, when adopted within construction organisations, can help improve how organisations deliver their projects and manage their workers. Therefore, implementing a construction workforce management model that recognises the impact of digital tools is crucial for organisations seeking to get the optimum productivity out of their workers. Thus, this book's conceptualised construction workforce management model can be a valuable tool for construction organisations. Also, more credibility is given to the model's structure by exploring the conceptualised model through experts' opinions.

*Keywords*: Construction; employee management; human resources; workforce management; digitalisation

## Introduction

The general objective of this book was to provide a conceptualised construction workforce management model that will assist construction organisations in effectively managing their workforce in the current era of the fourth industrial revolution. By exploring existing workforce management theories, models, and practices, the study conceptualised a construction workforce management model for construction organisations. The conceptualised model was further examined through experts' opinions to determine the suitability and applicability of the proposed workforce management practices and their attributed measurement variables. Consequently, this last chapter concludes the book by highlighting the

Construction Workforce Management in the Fourth Industrial Revolution Era, 201–206

Copyright © 2024 by Lerato Aghimien, Clinton Ohis Aigbavboa and Douglas Aghimien

Published under exclusive licence by Emerald Publishing Limited

doi:10.1108/978-1-83797-018-620241008

significant conclusions drawn from the different areas covered in the study. The chapter also outlines the theoretical and practical contributions of the conceptualised construction workforce management model.

## Conclusion

The construction industry is essential to socio-economic growth and a considerable employer of labour due to its reliance on people to deliver its products successfully. Managing these people on which the industry depends becomes crucial to the continuous survival of the industry. Exploring extant literature revealed that workforce management has received less attention within construction organisations. Several factors are accountable for this lack of attention given to workforce management in construction. These factors include the nature of construction projects and the construction industry, the temporary nature of construction teams, over-reliance on transient workers, skills shortage, and an unsafe working environment, among others. Furthermore, the traditional management of workers in a typical organisation might be ineffective in a construction organisation as construction activities are project-based and require careful consideration of the working environment.

The fourth industrial revolution brings emerging technologies that are changing every business environment. The construction industry is not excluded from this change as digital technologies are being adopted to improve project delivery. This adoption of digital technologies impacts the delivery of projects within construction organisations and the management of workers. For instance, digital technologies such as big data analytics and cloud computing can help workforce management departments analyse construction workers' personalities and behavioural patterns, especially during recruitment and selection, training and development, performance evaluation and compensation. In the same vein, three-dimensional printing, robotics and UAVs offer a safer method of delivering construction projects which impacts the occupational health and safety function of workforce management. In addition, cyber-physical systems, AI, augmented, virtual and mixed realities are all helpful learning tools for construction workers. However, the construction industry has been lagging in adopting these digital tools compared to other sectors. This lag can result from the constant fear of job losses among construction workers, which has led to resistance to change noticed within the industry. More so, the complexity of technologies, the need for training and the associated financial implications, among other factors, have led to construction organisations' slow use of beneficial digital technologies.

This slow adoption of beneficial digital technologies, coupled with the inadequate attention given to workforce management in construction organisations, necessitated the development of a conceptual workforce management practices model for construction organisations. To achieve this, the review of existing theories, models and practices revealed that while several approaches have been adopted over time, five practices are common. These five practices are pertinent to achieving strategic 'soft' workforce management rooted in a classical approach of maximising the potential of the workers within an organisation and embracing employees' empowerment and development through trust. These 5 practices measured by 84 different variables are:

(1)  recruitment and selection;
(2)  compensation and benefits;
(3)  performance management and appraisal;
(4)  training and development; and
(5)  employee involvement and empowerment.

More specifically, when recruiting and selecting employees, among other factors, care must be given to selecting interview panels to eliminate biases. Also, competency and experience-based recruitment can be adopted as construction heavily relies on workers' experience. Electronic platforms that could aid the advertising, screening and evaluation of candidates must be prioritised. Organisations need to carefully consider 15 proposed variables in terms of compensations and benefits as these can influence workers' motivation and satisfaction. Showing appreciation and recognition of good performance use of technology in the compensation process to build credibility, among other factors, is crucial. When managing and appraising performance, construction organisations need to carefully consider 14 factors, including clear communication of set objectives to workers and using digital tools to frequently review individual and group performance to ensure areas of improvement are identified and addressed timely.

Furthermore, construction organisations need to manage training and development variables properly. This entails support from top management for the training and developing workers, ensuring future competence development, investing in digital technologies and training needs, and even ensuring newly acquired skills are shared with other employees and applied on the job. For employee involvement and empowerment, care must be given to 13 factors, including such as promoting reward and recognition, ensuring continuous performance measurement, aligning individual strength with empowerment goals, ensuring the right staff at the right place of service, ensuring the availability of resources for constant training, and collaboratively setting the goals and objectives of the organisation.

Reviewing these existing theories, models, and practices within construction revealed that construction activities require significant human contact and interaction. As such, essential aspects of human psychology, such as emotional intelligence, are worthy of attention if workers are to interact effectively and deliver projects successfully. This concept of emotional intelligence has received less attention in existing theories, models and practices reviewed. Also, following the notion that the construction industry is unique and the traditional workforce management approaches cannot be adopted holistically for the industry, the impact of the environment becomes a crucial element for a tailor-made workforce management model for the industry. This is coupled with the fact that the current fourth industrial revolution era has provided emerging digital tools that are positively disrupting business environments. Again, this concept of the external environment has received less attention in existing theories, models and practices reviewed. As such, these two concepts were explored to give a holistic workforce management practice model for construction organisations. These two concepts were measured using 33 variables. For emotional intelligence, variables relating to self-awareness, self-management, social awareness, and relationship management were drawn from Goleman's mixed model. Also, the external environment was viewed from the perspective of handling pressure exacted by the environment that forces organisations to adopt innovative ideas and practices. These pressures are normative, coercive, and mimetic. Factors relating to the industry's regulation, culture and values, clients' demand for the use of personnel and technologies, and the industry's regulation on the use of digital technologies, among other factors, are crucial to the successful management of construction workforce in the era of the fourth industrial revolution.

Based on the above, the study achieved its set objective of delivering a conceptualised construction workforce management model. The conceptualised model was further explored within the construction industry using a Delphi of experts' opinions, and the practices, as well as their measurement variables, were adjudged to be suitable and applicable to the construction industry.

## Contribution to Knowledge

### *Theoretical Contribution*

The issue of effective workforce management has gained attention in the past as people have been regarded as one of the significant resources driving the production of most industries. Even with the advent of the fourth industrial revolution, human input is still significantly needed for the overall production success of most organisations. Similarly, the construction industry has been characterised as labour-intensive, and the need to effectively manage these workers cannot be over-emphasised. Therefore, past studies have concentrated on the various practices that can help improve workforce management within diverse industries, including construction. However, despite the different existing studies on workforce management, there is a lack of studies on a workforce management practice model for the construction industry in the fourth industrial revolution era.

Therefore, this book serves as an excellent theoretical background for future studies exploring workforce management practices in the construction industry. The conceptualised model presents the theory that the attainment of increased employee and organisational performance, job satisfaction, better quality and innovative construction, harmony in the work environment, and organisational citizenship, among other successful outcomes within the construction industry, is dependent on the effective management of recruitment and selection, compensation and benefits, performance management and appraisal, training and development, employee involvement and empowerment, emotional intelligence, and the external environment. This theory promotes the need for 'soft' workforce management in the construction industry, where practices promoting proactiveness, participation, and improved skills are adopted to give better quality and flexibility within construction organisations.

Furthermore, the book revealed a dearth of literature in studies concentrating on the potential impact of emerging digital technologies on construction workforce management. Most studies exploring this relationship have emanated from other sectors with less attention from construction. By showcasing these possible impacts and envisaged challenges, this book offers a platform for future empirical works to investigate this relationship in the context of construction.

### *Practical Contribution*

This book makes practical contributions as it showcases the significant areas on which construction organisations need to focus in their quest for increased organisational performance, job satisfaction, better quality and innovative construction, harmony in the work environment, and organisational citizenship, among other possible outcomes. The submissions in the book will serve as guidelines for organisations when improving their workforce through proper workforce management practices as the study showcases the major areas on which they need to concentrate. Construction organisations will do well by promoting fair and effective recruitment and selection processes, better compensation and benefits, improved performance management and appraisal, improved training and development, and more employee involvement and empowerment. It is also necessary to put measures in place to promote workers' emotional intelligence while simultaneously channelling the pressure from their external environment to promote and improve the management of their employees.

The book's submissions are beneficial not only to construction organisations alone but also to construction industry regulatory bodies. These regulatory bodies can use the findings to assess their members' compliance with improving their respective workforce. It is evident from the submission of the book that environmental issues relating to industry regulations can help shape how workers are managed in construction organisations. Therefore, construction industry regulatory bodies can assist in improving workforce management within construction organisations by ensuring that favourable regulations (including those that support emerging technologies) are developed. Furthermore, unemployment is one of the major challenges faced by many countries worldwide, with several initiatives being put in place to address this excruciating issue. If construction organisations can adopt the submissions of this study, there will be a better-trained and developed skilled workforce, and this will lead to less employee turnover and, by extension, a reduction in the number of unemployed individuals.

## Recommendations

The review of existing literature shows that despite being a significant factor in the success of construction projects, the construction workforce is not given proper attention within the construction industry. Therefore, if the construction industry continues to deliver its projects successfully and plays its role in socio-economic development, careful attention must be given to managing the industry's workforce. There is a need for construction organisations to invest in workforce management practices for better outcomes. Policies that will promote the seven workforce management practices highlighted in this book should be adopted within construction organisations.

Also, the fourth industrial revolution offers emerging technologies that provide solutions to the age-long problems of the construction industry. Adopting these technologies will solve these problems and positively impact the management of workers in the industry. More so, contrary to the popular opinion that the advents in technologies will lead to job losses, it has been observed that these technologies will only make human operations better and, in the process, open up new markets for more job opportunities. As such, it is recommended that construction organisations carefully assess the digital technologies available to them and adopt them in a manner that benefits both the organisation's project delivery and the management of the organisation's workforce.

Notably, the conceptualised construction workforce management model in this book provides a broad view of the practices and their measurement variables needed for the effective management of construction workers. Therefore, it is necessary for practitioners and researchers to further test the suitability and applicability of the conceptualised model in the context of the country where the model is to be applied.

# Index